KARL MARX'S THEORY

VOLUME V — WAR & REVOLUTION

Copyright © Center for Socialist History 2005
All rights reserved

Library of Congress Cataloging-in-Publications Data
is available frm the publisher.

MONTHLY REVIEW PRESS
122 West 27th Street
New York, NY 10001
www.monthlyreview.org

CENTER FOR SOCIALIST HISTORY
PO Box 626
Alameda CA 94501
www.socialisthistory.org

ISBN 1456303503
EAN-13 9781456303501

KARL MARX'S THEORY OF REVOLUTION

VOLUME 5 — WAR & REVOLUTION

Hal Draper & E Haberkern

FOREWORD

This is the fifth in a projected six volume exposition of Marx and Engels' political views which they never reduced to a coherent, all-encompassing, work on the lines of *Capital*; although Marx had intended a final volume on the State which, unfortunately, he never got around to starting.

The first three volumes, plus an addendum on *The "Dictatorship of the Proletariat" from Marx to Lenin*, were the work of Hal Draper. The fourth volume, *Critique of Other Socialisms* was, with the exception of one appendix, in the form of a complete final draft on Hal Draper's death in 1990. At the request of Monthly Review Press I completed that manuscript. The sixth, and last, volume will be ready shortly under the title *The Road to Power*.

The main question which needs to be addressed in this author's forward is the relation of Hal Draper's notes to the final product. There was no complete draft of any chapter. Some sections — the chapter on the Crimean War and Special Note D on the (mis)treatment of Engels' so-called "last testament" practically wrote themselves because the notes were so complete. In addition, Draper outlined his views on the Crimean War and on the Franco-Prussian war in a chapter of his *The Myth of Lenin's "Revolutionary Defeatism."*

At the other extreme are the chapter of KMTR V on Bonaparte vs. Bismarck from 1859 to 1866 entitled *Pulling the Plug*, the special note on Rosdolsky, and the two notes on Marx and the American Civil War which are mine.

In between are the chapters on 1848 and 1870. Hal Draper wrote a long review in the socialist periodical *Labor Action* in 1958 which stated his basic view on Engels' articles in the *Neue Rheinische Zeitung* on "Non-Historic Peoples" and my reading of the sources reinforced that view but Draper's notes on this question, while extensive, are not in the form of a draft which states explicitly the thesis outlined in chapters one and two of this work. In the case of 1870, where I explain "Marx and Engels' position on the Franco-Prussian War" by pointing out that there wasn't one since they disagreed, Draper's remarks in *Myth* state clearly that Marx and Engels arrived at a position after a period of thinking and rethinking and that Engels, but not Marx, considered critical support of "the German national movement" at one point. I think Draper would agree with my resolution of this problem but I cannot claim that he explicitly stated it. (EH)

THE COVER DESIGN

The cover design is based on a photograph of the *volksmarine division* of 1918. Originally a division of mutinous sailors (in Germany, as in Russia, the navy depended heavily on skilled, and unionized, workers who were overwhelmingly Social Democrats); this rebellious division gathered around itself militant workers throughout Berlin. Its dissolution by the Scheideman-Ebert government led to the uprising misnamed the Spartacist uprising.

I like the fact that this demonstration is led by a gent in a bowler hat. A sure sign of a skilled worker. Note also the marcher at the right who appears to be leaving the demonstration. Probably stopping off at the local to try and think it all through.

These are the people Engels was thinking of and addressing in the period covered by the last chapter of this book and the final special note.

ACKNOWLEDGMENTS

I would like to take this opportunity to thank several people for their help with this project. Marty Lipow read the manuscript and his comments were very helpful. Professor John-Paul Himka, the translator of Roman Rosdolsky's *Engels and the "Nonhistoric" Peoples: The National Question in the Revolution of 1848*, kindly provided me with a copy of Rosdolsky's doctoral thesis which I found very helpful. I expect Professor Himka would disagree with at least some of my conclusions but he sent me a copy of this very interesting manuscript without asking how I intended to use it—a display of disinterested scholarship that is, unfortunately, rare these days. Professor David Smith of the University of Kansas and Andreja Zivkovic and Dragan Plavsic of *Revolutionary History* reviewed a first draft of this work. Their remarks were very helpful even if I didn't always take their advice.

As is the usual custom I take full responsibility for all the errors of omission and commission which appear in this volume.

A NOTE ON STYLE

I have followed the convention of the earlier volumes of this work and used the degree mark "o" to mark off words, phrases, and even whole paragraphs of Marx and Engels' translated writings which were in English in the original. The distinction between footnotes, relevant but digressive material which is placed at the bottom of the page, and reference notes, citings of sources and similar material which are listed at the end of the book, has been maintained. I have also left intact Draper's translations which were done before the relevant volume of the English *Collected Works* appeared but have referenced those volumes after the quote. Most of the time the differences in translation are minor. Where I think a difference is significant I have pointed that out.

There is also a question of spelling. In order to avoid confusion, I have adopted the spelling used by the English translation of the collected works in cases where there exists more than one possible transliteration of foreign names and words—Jellachich and Tsar, for example, instead of Jellačič or Czar.

Finally, I have consistently used the pronoun 'I' to refer to the author. The alternative would be to follow the pronoun with initials in parentheses or to use the pronoun 'we.' The first is clumsy and the second pretentious. I have already explained how responsibility for authorship should be assigned and Hal Draper's notes and drafts are in the collection of the library of the University of California at Davis along with his other papers and his library.

E Haberkern

TABLE OF CONTENTS

INTRODUCTION.. 9
    The "Revolution" of August 14, 1914 (9), Lenin, Potresov and Kautsky (10), Three Epochs (12), "No Other Question Could Have Been Posed" (14), Two Barking Dogs (15), What Engels Did and Didn't Say (17)

CHAPTER 1. WAR AND THE DEMOCRACY IN 1848............................ 19
    War and Revolution 1793-1848 (19), The Main Enemy (21), A Nation That Oppresses Others Cannot Itself Be Free (23), War With Russia (25), "Sea-Girt Schleswig-Holstein" (28), Hungarians and Poles (31), The Old Poland and the New (33), Revolutionary Cattle Dealers (39), The Workers Have No Country (46)

CHAPTER 2. "NON-HISTORIC" PEOPLES.................................. 51
    Twenty Vendées (52), Hegel on "Residual Fragments of Peoples" (55), The "Non-Historic" Czechs (56), "Counterrevolutionary Peoples" (59), Bakunin's 'Völkisch' Nationalism (64), Democratic Pan-Slavism (70)

CHAPTER 3. THE SIXTH POWER... 79
    Marx's "Russophobia" (80), First Impressions (83), The Revolutionary Side (84), The Peace Party in England (86), The Russian Menace (87), Two Ex-Revolutionaries (91), The "Sixth Power" (95)

CHAPTER 4: PULLING THE PLUG.. 99
    The Demagogy of "National Revolution" (101), Po and Rhine (103), Lassalle's Appeasement Policy (105), Germany's Unification in "A Prussian Barracks" (108), Bismarck's Coup (109), "The Prussian Military Question and the German Workers' Party" (111), Engels on Universal Conscription (113), A Bourgeois Bluff (114), The "Workers' Party" and Universal Suffrage (115), "Bourgeois Freedoms" (116), Engels as "Military Expert" in 1866 (118)

CHAPTER 5. "THE DESPOTS OF *ALL* COUNTRIES ARE OUR ENEMIES"....... 121
    The 1870 Split in the German Social Democracy (121), Marx and Engels' 'Defensism' (124), Marx's 'Pro-Prussianism' (129), The "Neutrality Spirit" (133), The Trouble With Wilhelm Liebknecht (135), Engels' Attack on Liebknecht (138), Marx's Reply to Engels (142), The Letter to the Brunswick Committee (147), What Changed at Sedan (151), Postscript (152), "How to Fight the Prussians" (153), Treason (155)

CHAPTER 6. BURYING THE 'TSARIST MENACE'........................... 159
    The Danger of War (159), The Tsarist Threat (161), Engels' 1891 "Prowar" Aberration (164), The Tsar Learns to Sing the Marseillaise (167), The Dispute With Bebel (169), The French Reaction (175), A New Stage of Capitalism? (176), Internment (178)

CHAPTER 7. BURNING DOWN THE EMPEROR'S PALACE.................... 179
    Can Europe Disarm? (179), "... and the German Army Is Ours" (185), The Fight Over *The Class Struggles in France* (186)

SPECIAL NOTE A: ROSDOLSKY VS. ROSDOLSKY............................ 189
    Marx and Engels on 1846 (191), Two Diversions (202), The Neue Rheinische Zeitung and the Jews (204), Rosdolsky: 1929 and 1948 (209)

SPECIAL NOTE B. "CONSTITUTIONAL" OR "REVOLUTIONARY" WAR?........ 215
    Lincoln and Slavery (215), The Abolitionists in Charge (216), Marx on the Secession Crisis (216), Lincoln's Fear of Revolution (218), Marx as commentator on the American Civil War (220), Why? (222)

SPECIAL NOTE C: THE LINCOLN MYTH................................... 225

SPECIAL NOTE D: ENGELS' "LAST TESTAMENT" A TRAGI-COMEDY IN FIVE ACTS.... 231
    Enter Wilhelm Liebknecht Stage Right—Stumbling (233), Enter Bernstein—Twirling a Long Black Mustache (235), D. Riazonov Discovers Engels' Original Draft (237), The Communists vs. the Socialist Labor Party—Comic Relief (238)

LIST OF ABBREVIATIONS.. 245

BIBLIOGRAPHY... 247

NOTES... 253

INDEX... 277

INTRODUCTION

The subject of this volume is Marx and Engels' views on the *relation* between war and revolution. Its thesis is that, over the course of decades, their views on this question changed—evolved is a better word—although, in this case as in others, they wrote no definitive statement of their views. Instead, we have a considerable corpus of *ad hoc* responses to the events of the hour, many of them politically explosive, from which we have to reconstruct, not a line, but an approach. To complicate things further, many of these crises, while they were the news of the day at the time, have since faded from memory.

1. The "Revolution" of August 14, 1914

On August 4, 1914, the Reichstag delegation of the German Social-Democratic Party joined the bourgeois parties and supported the government request for emergency war credits. It wrote a political as well as a financial blank check made out to German militarism. This political earthquake destroyed the Second International and the after shocks are still being felt.

Like most earthquakes this one was unexpected, although it had been preceded by the usual tremors. Everyone had expected the socialists to follow the example of Liebknecht and Bebel in 1870 and at least abstain on the vote. The socialists expected that themselves. Almost up to the day of the vote the Party press had continued to expose the provocative, bellicose, maneuvers of the Austrian and Prussian diplomats. And it was the German Party that had dominated the prewar conferences of the International where the movement had almost unanimously denounced the war preparations of the governments and the slavish support the bourgeois parties gave those governments as they rushed towards Armageddon.

The causes and consequences of this unexpected betrayal have been the topic of thousands of books, articles and doctoral theses. I am concerned with a narrower question. In order to cover themselves politically, the pro-war socialists looked for precedents in Marx and Engels. And they found more than enough for their purposes. They found evidence "proving" Marx and Engels to be rabid Russophobes who welcomed a war against Tsarist Russia by practically anybody.

Everyone, of course, was aware that hostility to Tsarism had been a prominent part of Marx and Engels' politics. But no one had previously claimed that this hostility led to a support for the war policy of Tsarism's great power rivals. Yet, after the swing of the German party majority into the prowar camp, even socialist opponents of the war, people like Lenin and Rosa Luxemburg, accepted this rewrite of history. These antiwar socialists could only argue that the policy Marx and Engels had pursued was outdated. What else could they have done under the circumstances? As we shall see, Marx and Engels wrote no systematic study of "the war question." Their views were expressed in specific discussions of specific crises whose historical circumstances were, by 1914, often obscure if not completely forgotten. And Marx and Engels' views evolved over decades as the state structure of Europe altered in response to war, national revolutions and the economic triumph of capitalism. The pressure to avoid a detailed historical account—and the lengthy research involved in constructing such an account—was overwhelming. Both Luxemburg and Lenin, not to mention lesser figures, simply decided to accept the main charge against Marx and Engels and move on. In doing so for obvious and compelling reasons they, nevertheless, put their *imprimatur* on the fabricated history of the prowar socialists.

Luxemburg, in the deservedly famous antiwar *Junius Pamphlet,* contrasted the Tsarist Russia of 1848 with the revolutionary post–1906 Russia, thus implying that Engels had died without changing his views on the Russian threat.[1] But, as we will see, Engels had long abandoned the 1848 position and done so publicly in pamphlets and articles once well known not only to German socialists but to the international movement.

But it was Lenin's antiwar polemics that were most responsible for leading practically all future historians astray.

2. Lenin, Potresov and Kautsky

In 1915, Lenin drafted an article titled "Under a False Flag" which was not published until 1917.[2] In it he outlined his own position which he claimed was also that of Marx and Engels. He was to repeat this argument in several articles and resolutions which were published during the war but this draft presented his schema in greater detail.

Lenin's article was provoked by the anti-Kautsky polemic of the prowar socialist, Alexander N. Potresov, writing in the magazine *Nashe Dyelo*. Potresov attacked Kautsky for not choosing sides in the war.

One recent biographer describes Kautsky's dilemma in 1914.[3] At the start of the war he had hoped to persuade the SPD delegation in the

Introduction

Reichstag to follow the example of Bebel and Liebknecht during the Franco-Prussian war and abstain in the vote for war credits. When it became clear that this would not be possible, he tried to get the party delegation to denounce the imperialist ambitions of all sides which had brought on the war and limit support to the government to what was required solely by the need to defend the country from attack. When this maneuver also failed, Kautsky was faced with the choice between concealing his antiwar sentiments and splitting the party in the midst of war.[4] He rejected the second alternative and confined his public pronouncements to justifying "defensive wars" by citing the record of Marx and Engels while rejecting the annexionist plans of all the belligerents.[5]

For Potresov that was not good enough. It was no good arguing that Marx and Engels were for the right of each nation to self defense. That was just a device for avoiding any stand on the war. That was not what Marx and Engels had done. Their writings provided, he claimed, precedents for his prowar politics.

Potresov chose for his main precedent Louis Bonaparte's Italian campaign of 1859. It was a particularly useful precedent because all sides were repugnant not only to socialists but to many halfway decent liberals. In this incident, which was pretty obscure even by 1915, Bonaparte, in secret alliance with the Russians, attacked Austria's Italian possessions. The announced aim of the campaign was to liberate Italy. And Garibaldi's troops *were* involved in the fighting—basically as auxiliaries of the French. The real aim was to cement a Franco-Russian alliance against Austria and keep the German states in turmoil. And, in the end, the Italian revolutionaries were swindled by Bonaparte.

In this crisis, Potresov claimed that Marx and Engels, when forced to decide "which Power in the Concert of Europe was the main evil: the reactionary Danubian monarchy or other outstanding representatives of this Concert," refused "to step aside and say that the two are equally bad."[6] Marx and Engels, in Potresov's version of history, urged intervention by Prussia in defense of Austria and in the name of Germany's national interest. Lassalle, the other "great teacher" of the movement, used the same "lesser evil" methodology. Only he came to the opposite conclusion and supported Bonaparte. No matter. The important thing is the "Marxist" method not the conclusion. And Potresov wanted to use this "Marxist" method to decide which of two very reactionary sides in World War I was the main evil. Presumably, in 1915, Potresov was more concerned with coming to the correct (that is, pro-Entente) conclusion.

Lenin accepted Potresov's argument while rejecting the conclusion. He agreed that Marx and Engels threw their support to one side or another "notwithstanding the highly reactionary character of the governments of *both* belligerent sides."[7] Lenin, in fact, went further than Potresov or Kautsky. He insisted that "*no other* question could have been posed at the time."[8] He corrected Potresov's phrasing of the question "the success of which side is more desirable" to "the success of which bourgeoisie was more desirable."[9] Both men claimed to be quoting, or at least paraphrasing, Marx but neither bothered to point to a reference. Everybody agreed, without need of evidence, that Marx was prowar in 1859, and so were Engels and Lassalle.

3. Three Epochs

Lenin, apparently, felt all this was beyond dispute. His solution to this problem was to argue that Marx and Engels were dealing with a political and international configuration that was long past by 1914. They were dealing with a world dominated by the conflict between the bourgeois revolution and feudal absolutism. The world of 1914 was dominated by the competition of developed capitalist powers fighting over the division of the world's markets and sources of raw materials.[10]

> The first epoch from the Great French Revolution to the Franco-Prussian war is one of the rise of the bourgeoisie, ... The second epoch is that of the full domination and decline of the bourgeoisie, one of transition from its progressive character toward reactionary and even ultra-reactionary finance capital. ... The Third epoch, which has just set in, places the bourgeoisie in the same "position" as that in which the feudal lords found themselves during the first epoch.[11]

Introduction

Lenin repeated these themes throughout World War I and afterwards. It was his final word on Marx and Engels' position; and, given this *imprimatur*, it has been accepted as a definitive, if perhaps oversimplified statement, of their views.

There is nothing wrong with Lenin's schema in itself. Its virtue is that it provides a theoretical underpinning for the change in the attitudes of socialists towards war that followed 1871. But the difficulty is that Lenin claims he is expounding Marx and Engels' views on war. And there is no evidence that this is so. If Lenin (or Kautsky or Potresov) thought they had such evidence they didn't bother to exhibit it.

As an outline of Marx and Engels' views on war and its relation to revolution, there are several problems with Lenin's schema. Despite his repeated insistence, neither Marx nor Engels anywhere used the criterion "the success of which bourgeoisie is most desirable." From the time of their earliest writings on the subject, both men saw the dynastic imperialism of the absolute monarchies as the main cause of war in Europe. This relic of the medieval, pre-bourgeois past, naturally, led to wars between the dynasties themselves over the division of the continent into spheres of influence. More important, however, was the military threat the dynasties, especially the Russian one, posed for any renewed revolutionary activity after 1815. It was the conflict between the old world of feudalism and the new world of the bourgeois revolution that was the real source of war. Not only did neither Marx nor Engels ever use the phrase "the success of which bourgeoisie is more desirable," the concept cannot be found in their writings, public or private. When conflict between the bourgeoisie and the old order broke out in either domestic or international politics, they tended to urge the bourgeoisie forward. At the same time, because of their experience in 1848, they expected the liberal bourgeoisie would shrink from any serious confrontation. On a number of occasions, they tended to accuse liberals of what we today would call "appeasement" in the face of Tsarist, Bonapartist, or Hapsburg provocations.

Lenin, himself, in the very articles quoted here, recognizes that what characterized his "first epoch" was just this conflict between the old order and the new. His insistence on the formula "the success of which *bourgeoisie*" can only be explained by his eagerness to enlist Marx and Engels on *his* side in the contemporary dispute over World War I which, in his view and that of most other opponents of the war, was a conflict between states where the bourgeoisie was effectively master.

4. "No Other Question Could Have Been Posed"

Equally unfounded is Lenin's assertion that, for Marx and Engels, "no other question could have been posed." It is true that Lenin does not explicitly attribute this formula to Marx and Engels but the drift of his argument implies, indeed requires, such an attribution. It is Lenin's apologia for Marx and Engels' reputed prewar politics. But Marx and Engels never asked themselves this question. As early as the Crimean crisis of 1853, they expected the conflict between the old regime and the new to lead to revolution; a continuing revolution in which the working class would soon come to power. Given this perspective, it would have made no sense, in most cases, to support one government against the other. Marx and Engels' hopes and expectations were not fulfilled as we know. The process of modernization and bourgeoisification eroded the position of the old ruling classes in Europe to the point where medieval relics like absolute monarchy became hollow shells. But this happened without a revolutionary confrontation. There were plenty of pre-revolutionary crises, but a compromise was always found short of a final conflict.

In this sense, Lenin was right. His schema better reflected what had happened. Marx and Engels, however, were writing in the midst of events. Maybe they should have realized that their expectations for revolution were premature and adopted a policy of supporting the "lesser evil" as Potresov maintained. But it is hard to imagine men of their temperament (or Lenin's temperament) taking such a contemplative and disinterested view of political events. It would have required them to remain politically passive in one crisis after another because, as we now know and as Lenin knew, none of these crises would actually lead to revolution. But this is something they could not have known. They would have been acting like a trade unionist who, after soberly evaluating the "objective" situation, concludes that the strike cannot win and goes back to work. And, in doing so, helps to defeat the strike.

If Marx and Engels, and other socialists, had taken this passive attitude the socialist movement of the late nineteenth and early twentieth century would never have come into being. Without defeats and partial victories no final victory is possible. Or, as Luxemburg put it, "every revolution is bound to be defeated except the last."[12]

A second problem with this schema is that even the vaguer formulation used by Potresov and Kautsky—"the success of which side is more desirable"—has nothing to do with Marx and Engels. If we were to make explicit the criterion they used in analyzing the wars in question—something they did not do—it would have to be "how can revolutionaries best exploit this conflict." In the cases examined by Potresov and Kautsky, the record shows that Marx and Engels did not advocate support for either side *even when they thought the victory of one side would facilitate revolution*. Potresov clearly wishes Marx and Engels had preceded him in advocating a prowar position. Kautsky would have liked them to have reluctantly abstained from political opposition as he did throughout most of World War I. Unfortunately, for people looking for such precedents, Marx and Engels in the instances cited energetically denounced both sides and used what means were available to them to rally the organized working class against support for either side.

5. Two Barking Dogs

There is a Sherlock Holmes story in which a key piece of evidence, overlooked, of course, by the bumbling Dr. Watson, is something that is missing. A dog didn't bark when it should have. In the case we are investigating, practically all participants played the role of Watson. Only, they had less excuse. It wasn't that the dog didn't bark; it was that there were two dogs, both barking loudly, and no one noticed them. Neither Kautsky, nor Potresov, nor Lenin, nor, as far as I have been able to determine, any other socialist during Word War I, cited the two wars after 1848 in which Marx and Engels unambiguously took a prowar stand in support of a bourgeois government.

During the American Civil War, Marx actively campaigned for the Union. His support was unconditional and unqualified. He did not ask himself which side's victory would be "most desirable." He came down solidly on the side that was fighting slavery. His activity was not only literary. A significant section of the British bourgeoisie, led by Gladstone's liberals, favored an alliance with the Confederacy. Marx, together with his friends in the movement, mostly ex-Chartists, carried on a counter campaign, organizing rallies and meetings in support of the Union. Given the economic crisis created in the textile industry by the Union blockade of cotton exports from the slave-holding South, England's main supplier, this campaign by Marx and the former Chartist leaders required a confrontation with conservative trade unionists in what was a relatively well-organized trade. But Marx's support of the Union, while unqualified, was not uncritical. The *conduct* of the war by the Lincoln administration was pilloried in Marx and Engels' correspondence and their public comments, while more restrained, were also harsh.[13]

Even more surprising is the failure of any of the participants in the 1914 debates to make much of Engels' extensive writings on the Franco-Prussian war in *The Pall Mall Gazette*. From the fall of the Second Empire in September of 1870 up to the insurrection of the Paris Commune in March of the following year, Engels wrote as an outspoken partisan of the bourgeois Third Republic. And Marx used all his influence in the IWMA to swing that organization into the pro-Republican camp. Here again, from the beginning, neither Marx nor Engels held any illusions about the bourgeoisie. They predicted its betrayal of the working classes before the insurrection in Paris even broke out. And this skeptical assessment of the bourgeoisie as a class, and of its political leaders, radically shaped the policy they advocated. But their support for this Republican government, which was soon to ally itself with the Prussians to crush the Commune, was unqualified as long as it fought against the Prussians and for the Republic. What "support" for one side in a war meant for Marx is illustrated by these cases; it was of no use for socialists who, like Potresov, were arguing for a policy of social peace in World War I. It should be obvious why this was so. Any comparison of Kaiser Wilhelm, Emperor Franz Joseph, Tsar Nicholas, or even the politicians of the Third Republic to Abraham Lincoln, let alone the American abolitionists, would have been ridiculous. The comparison itself would have highlighted the demagogy behind the claim of any of the former to be fighting for "freedom." What is more to the point, Marx's support for the union side *militarily* in that conflict took the form of *political* opposition to the Lincoln administration's handling of the war. And the same distinction was made in his support of the Third Republic.

6. What Engels Did and Didn't Say

Finally, however valuable the schemas put forward by Lenin might be in themselves, they were unknown to Marx and Engels. The following chapters will show them evolving from belligerent champions of war against Russia by 'the Democracy' in 1848 to prophets denouncing the war preparations of capitalist governments by 1870. Engels, by the 1880s, clearly dreaded the prospect of war. It is also true that the Franco-Prussian war was a political watershed for them.

In his last years, Engels developed the consistent antiwar politics that were the source of the resolutions of the Second International. It was his influence that guaranteed a hearing for the antiwar left even as the leadership moved to right. Most importantly, it was Engels who explicitly rejected anti-Tsarism as the basis of a revolutionary socialist position in the impending world war. But he never explicitly reexamined the theoretical basis of the politics he and Marx had held since the 1840s.

Engels continued to write on numerous occasions as if the main threat to the working class and even "European civilization" came from Tsarism.* Even in these instances, however, he explicitly repudiated any support to the governments—especially the Prussian government—opposed to Tsarism. At the same time, moreover, sometimes in the same article or letter, he recognized how weak Tsarist Russia had become. He recognized that it was the junior partner in its dealings with Germany and France. He wrote with eager anticipation of the anti-Tsarist revolution that he believed imminent. On a number of occasions, again in juxtaposition with passages repeating the old "line" about the Tsarist threat, he offhandedly describes imperialist drives leading to war that emanated from capitalist competition not dynastic ambition.**

---

* For an interesting treatment of the continuing debates over this question by Balkan socialists see the anthology of translated material *The Balkan Socialist Tradition* by Andreja Živkovič and Dragan Plavšič.

** There is one, and only one, exception to this. It is discussed in Chapter 6. In a *private letter* to August Bebel, Engels flirted with the possibility of supporting the German government in a real case of defense of the country. The complicated
(continued...)

Perhaps, Engels, by the 1890s, should have realized more clearly what was going on. Perhaps, he should have anticipated Lenin and written *Imperialism, The Highest Stage of Capitalism*. But he didn't. What he did do was to imprint on the newly born Second International his own passionately held conviction that there was only one way to respond to the drive to war. Socialists had to make clear not only that they would not support any of the governments in a crisis but that they would use such a crisis to overthrow those governments.

** (...continued)
story behind this letter is discussed in some detail in Chapter 6, but the dénoument can be simply stated here. In the article he *published* on the question Engels explicitly rejected support for any of the governments.

CHAPTER 1. WAR AND THE DEMOCRACY IN 1848

What strikes the modern reader who turns to the speeches, pamphlets and articles of Marx and Engels of the period surrounding the revolution of 1848 is their bellicose, "prowar" tone. In the twentieth century, the rivalry of the great powers led to brutal and exhausting world wars which ground up the smaller countries and ended in the collapse of one or more of the major contestants. Winners were often difficult to distinguish from losers. Revolutionaries, revolted by the slaughter, were antiwar almost by instinct. The only alternatives they saw were opposition to war on principle—from either a revolutionary or a pacifist standpoint—or capitulation to chauvinism.

1. War and Revolution 1793-1848

This was not the case with Marx and Engels. They began by using the words war and revolution almost interchangeably. Like most of their contemporaries, when they thought of revolution the image that preoccupied them was the revolutionary war of the French Republic in 1793-4. War and revolution were then merged. In that war—or so Marx, Engels, and most of their contemporaries, thought—the nation defended itself by mobilizing the population. And that was only possible because the people were convinced that the France they were defending was their democratic, revolutionary France; not the old France. The alliance of all the great powers against France, in turn, was provoked by the hostility of the old world to the revolution and democracy.

Modern scholarship has tended to question this oversimplified picture.[1] In the beginning it was the pro-monarchists and the Gironde who formed the war party in France and those members of the Convention most sympathetic to the popular movement opposed the provocations of the French government. Robespierre was the most outspoken opponent of the war while moderates like Lafayette hoped to drown the revolutionary movement in a flood of patriotic sentiment. On this question, as on others, the politics of the French Revolution were more modern than is generally realized. Marx and Engels, however, did not know what we know now.

In any case, in 1793 the war *had turned into* a war between defenders of the old order and the new. What is more important for us, from 1815 on, from the signing of the treaties drawn up at the Congress of Vienna until 1848 and beyond, the diplomatic policy of the European powers aimed at subordinating dynastic conflicts and national interests to the common need to defend traditional, and not so traditional, privileges against the republican and egalitarian demons wakened by the French Revolution. They saw in every moderate liberal measure and every tentative attempt by oppressed nations to ameliorate their position the specters of Jacobinism and Napoleon. This policy, of course, made revolutionaries out of very mild reformers.

In the aftermath of Napoleon's defeat liberalism in Germany especially was humiliated. After backing a war of liberation against the French Emperor spurred in part by promises of reform liberals were rewarded with a strengthened bureaucratic absolutism. Austria and Prussia, backed by Russia, placed the Germans under a kind of house arrest. The press was strictly censored, the Universities subjected to police control, and the radical students' associations outlawed. All this for the sole purpose of preserving the division of the country into some thirty-odd mini-states ruled by petty princes whose cruelty was moderated only by their sloth and incompetence

Poland, however, was the lynch-pin of the whole system. This country, whose dynasty was at least as legitimate as that of the Russian Romanovs, the Austrian Hapsburgs and the Prussian Hohenzollerns, had been partitioned between the latter three for over seventy years. The *Holy Alliance* between Russia, Prussia and Austria was cemented by the parties' common need to keep Poland down and, especially, to keep it from becoming a point of contention between them. That could wreck the whole system. As Engels put it "The tearing asunder of Poland by the three powers is the tie which links them together; the robbery they jointly committed forces them to support one another."[2] In 1830 and 1846 Polish insurrections, bloodily suppressed, provoked European wide outrage. They did not lead to a European war only because liberal and democratic opposition in Europe was weak or compromised.

In 1848, as in 1830, a revolution in France was simultaneously a revolt against the European-wide order policed by the Holy Alliance and backed by England. The spread of that revolution into Central and Eastern Europe *had* to lead to war between the revolutionary governments and the Holy Alliance. The war did not come because the revolution won out nowhere. Only in Hungary did the republican party carry out its program to the point of open rupture with the Alliance. Hungary was crushed.

In Marx and Engels' day, then, the more consistent the revolutionary the more "prowar." But something else, something more important, followed from the reliance on the 1793-4 analogy. The war being advocated was not a war in support of any of the existing states. It was a war against all of them by the loose coalition of opposition classes and tendencies that was called "the Democracy."

2. The Main Enemy

This is the background which explains the contradictory combination (so it seems to us) that characterized the foreign policy of the newspaper edited by Marx in Cologne, the *Neue Rheinische Zeitung (NRZ)*. On the one hand, there were the patriotic calls for a war against Russia in the interest of a united Germany and, on the other, a steady stream of articles which could be summarized under the head—"the main enemy is at home."

In Engels' case this identification of patriotism and hostility to the existing authorities predated his association with Marx or his interest in socialism. Writing as a "Young German,"[3] in 1841 he took for his target the apologists for German backwardness. Perhaps the best example of Engels *Young German* period, this article, titled "The 'War of Liberation' Against Napoleon," was an attack on the hysterical Francophobia of the "Franzözenfresser"*—the defenders of Christian-German reaction. No, says Engels, the French are a model for us Germans; they represent "civilization." The enemy is the alliance of England and Russia. Later, the post-Marx Engels would be more specific. He would identify "civilization" with the bourgeoisification of Germany (and other backward countries) and explain why England and Russia, for different reasons feared the spread of the bourgeois order in Europe.** In this early article Engels is expressing the "left"

---

* Literally, "French-eaters." A better contemporary translation would be "French-bashers" on the analogy of "Japan-basher."

** A caveat. Neither Marx nor Engels ever stopped using terms like "civilization," "European civilization" or "Western civilization" interchangeably

(continued...)

nationalism that was common to all the young radicals who felt ashamed of the backwardness of their country. His was the defensive nationalism of the citizen of a fragmented country.

Writing in this context Engels gives his own twist to the German nationalist glorification of the "War of Liberation" against Napoleon. Like most Rhinelanders—not just radicals—Engels tended to look on the French occupation favorably because of its "civilizing"[4] effect. The subsequent occupation of the Rhineland by backward, feudal-absolutist, bureaucratic, Prussia reversed the gains that had been made under Napoleon. As a Young German Engels was torn between admiration for the rebellion against Napoleon and skepticism as to its results:

> ... the greatest result of the struggle was not the shaking off of foreign rule [which would have crashed anyway] ..., it was the deed itself ... That we became conscious of the loss of our national sanctuaries, that we armed ourselves without waiting for the most gracious permission of the sovereigns, that we actually *compelled* those in power to take their place at our head, in short, that for a moment we acted as the source of state power, as a sovereign nation, that was the greatest gain of those years..."[5]

Engels was to comment later, on a number of occasions, on the *half-heartedness* of this imitation of 1793. In fact, his estimation of the national movement of the Germans, as of the French and other nationalities, varied over time depending on political circumstances. What was to remain

---

** (...continued)
and meaning thereby bourgeois civilization.
Marx and Engels' attitude towards the process of bourgeoisification and modernization is complex enough as it is. *KMTR II* discussed in some detail Marx and Engels' estimation of the bourgeoisie as a revolutionary class, their insistence on its progressive character *vis à vis* pre-bourgeois social strata in European society and the political conclusions they drew from these assumptions. The task is not made easier by Marx and Engels' imprecise use of language. In this early passage, of course, it is the idea, not just the language, that is imprecise.

constant was his emphasis on rebellion against the existing authorities as the real measure of a nation's greatness and viability.

3. A Nation That Oppresses Others Cannot Itself Be Free

<< Index will generate here >>In 1848, the *NRZ* emphasized throughout that the main obstacle to German unification and self-determination was not foreign militarism but the slavish political traditions of the Germans themselves. Their collaboration in the oppression of other peoples was what kept them chained to their own rulers. One chain could not be broken without breaking the other.

Within a month of the paper's first appearance,[6] Engels recounted in detail the role of Germans as mercenaries, especially in the pay of England, from North America to Greece and Italy, but, he concluded:

> The blame for the infamies committed with the aid of Germany in other countries falls not only on the governments but to a large extent also on the German people. But for the delusions of the Germans, their slavish spirit ... the German name would not be so detested, cursed and despised, ... Now that the Germans are throwing off their own yoke, their whole foreign policy must change too. Otherwise the fetters with which we have chained other nations will shackle our own new freedom, which is as yet hardly more than a presentiment. Germany will liberate herself to the extent to which she sets free neighboring nations.[7]

Engels proceeded to argue that things were getting better. Chauvinist propaganda, "the turgid phrases proclaiming that German honor or German power is at stake" are no longer effective. The article concluded by turning the argument around. If freedom at home is incompatible with oppression abroad a revolutionary foreign policy also requires a revolutionary domestic one.

> ... we must achieve a really popular government, and the old edifice must be razed to the ground. Only then can an

international policy of democracy take the place of the sanguinary, cowardly policy of the old, revived system. How can a democratic foreign policy be carried through while democracy at home is stifled.[8]

What did the *NRZ* mean by a "democratic foreign policy"? The clearest editorial statement of what was meant came very early on, little more than a month after the paper began publishing. The occasion was the uprising in Prague.[9]

The right in Germany attempted to portray this rising, which was brutally crushed by Austrian troops under Prince Alfred zu Windischgrätz, commander of the Imperial forces, as an anti-German nationalist uprising. There were even hints and rumors that the Russians were behind the whole thing. Leading the campaign were German speaking inhabitants of Bohemia organized in groups like the *League to Preserve German Interests in the East*. The *NRZ* devoted some space to reports from the scene by German supporters of the uprising. According to these reports the rising was supported by both German and Czech democrats fighting for "the preservation of Bohemia's independence and the equal rights of both nationalities";[10] the opposition came from the defenders of the old order and the defenders of German minority rights were simply stalking horses for the right with no significant support. How accurate were these reports? Contemporary sources as well as modern historians tend to endorse this description of the Czech national movement *at this stage of the revolution*.[11] The uprising was, apparently, based on the largely Czech-speaking lower class with the energetic leadership of students.

Both Czech nationalists and German chauvinists reacted to this class threat by backing off from the uprising.[12]

In short, modern historians generally *tend* to support Engels view of the situation. But that is not really the relevant question if what we want to know is: What was the foreign policy of the *NRZ*? If the paper did exaggerate for polemical purposes the degree to which the uprising was a social rather than a national revolution that is significant in itself. Political propaganda in this kind of situation is not simply an impartial commentary on events. It is an attempt to intervene, to strengthen one side or the other. The *NRZ* editorial on the report from Prague concluded that "German reaction is seeking to rouse a narrow-minded nationalism just as in Posen and in Italy, partly *in order to suppress the revolution in the interior of Germany* and partly to *train the soldiery for civil war.*"[13]

Looking at the events in Prague from the perspective of the German revolution, the *NRZ* boasted that:

> Despite the patriotic shouting and beating of the drums of almost the entire German Press, the *Neue Rheinische Zeitung* from the very first moment has sided with the Poles in Posen, the Italians in Italy, and the Czechs in Bohemia.[14]

The old regime "shaking in its foundations in the interior of Germany" sought to save itself by "calling forth a narrow-minded *national hatred.* Were the Germans to "crusade against the freedom of Poland, Bohemia and Italy" under the leadership of the very governments they were fighting at home? No, the editorial claimed:

> Only a *war against Russia* would be a war of *revolutionary Germany*, a war by which she could cleanse herself of her past sins, could take courage, defeat her own autocrats, spread civilization by the sacrifice of her own sons as becomes a people that is shaking off the chains of long, indolent slavery and make herself free within her own borders by bringing liberation to those outside.

A modern editor would undoubtedly send the article back for revision or insert a transitional paragraph or two herself. In 1848, it wasn't necessary. *Everyone* understood the connection between revolution at home and a war against the Holy Alliance.

4. War With Russia

There were three incidents which forced the Frankfurt Assembly to face up to the prospect of war with Russia. In each case, the Assembly backed off. And, in each case, the result was a weakening of the Assembly itself within Germany.

The incident that caused the most trouble, naturally, concerned the Poles. The problem was: what to do with the large chunk of Poland that had been seized by the Kingdom of Prussia? The proposal debated by the Frankfurt Assembly, the proposal that eventually passed, Engels rightly called a new partition of Poland. Poland was to be reduced to a strip of land on the fringe of the Russian occupied area. A new Duchy of Posen(present day Poznán) was to become part of the German Confederation.

This decision was presented as a defense of the national rights of the alleged half-million German speaking inhabitants of Posen. Included in this total were some 80,000 allegedly German-speaking Jews. Although they probably spoke Yiddish rather than German and would have been deprived of civic rights in the German states because of their religion, in the debates of the Assembly they became representatives of German culture.

Engels' reports on the debates are an extended and detailed comment on his 1847 thesis that Germany could only be free if she renounced all claims to Poland.

> So long, therefore, as we help to subjugate Poland, so long as we keep part of Poland fettered to Germany, we shall remain fettered to Russia and to the Russian policy, and shall be unable to eradicate patriarchal feudal absolutism in Germany. The creation of a democratic Poland is a primary condition for the creation of a democratic Germany.[15]

There was, of course, plenty of rhetoric in favor of Polish freedom in the debates of the Assembly. The cause of Polish freedom was also dear to middle class public opinion. Engels reports on touching demonstrations of this concern such as the rallies and speeches praising Polish freedom fighters as they passed through railway stations. Practical steps to end the occupation of part of Poland by Prussian troops, however, would certainly turn the area into a staging ground for a Polish insurrection in Russian and Austrian occupied Poland.

> ... but to start a war with Russia, to endanger the European balance of power and, to cap it all, hand over some scraps of the annexed territory—only one who does not know the Germans could expect that.
>
> And what would a war with Russia have meant? A war with Russia would have meant a complete, open and effective break with the whole of our disgraceful past, the real liberation and unification of Germany, and the establishment of democracy on the ruins of feudalism and on the wreckage of the short-lived bourgeois dream of power. War with Russia would have been the only possible way of vindicating our honor and our own interests with regard to our Slav neighbors, and especially the Poles. ... We shrank from it and the inevitable happened—the reactionary soldiery, beaten in Berlin, raised their head again in Posen; under the pretext of saving Germany's honor and national integrity they raised the banner of counterrevolution and crushed our allies, the revolutionary Poles.[16]

Engels in these reports ridicules the claims put forward on behalf of the German-speaking minority in Poland. Had the German revolution from the beginning come out for Polish independence and backed the demand up by force of arms, the matter of border disputes would have been a minor issue. "... both parties would have had to make some concessions to one another, some Germans becoming Polish and some Poles German, and this would have created no difficulties."[17]

Even at the relatively late date when Engels was writing he still believed that the Assembly could have mended matters. They could have excluded Posen from the German Confederation and dealt with the reconstituted Poland as an equal in negotiations over the fate of the German-speaking minority.[18] The Frankfurt Assembly was not even up to that. It annexed Posen to Germany which meant it left it in control of Prussian troops. These were the same mercenaries who were later to be used to disperse the Assembly itself. Bohemia, Poland and Italy became the training ground for the counterrevolution in Germany.

5. "Sea-Girt Schleswig-Holstein"

The second incident that drove the Frankfurt Assembly towards a conflict with Russia is more confusing from our vantage point. The two provinces of Schleswig and Holstein had for some time been a source of dispute between Prussia and the Danish monarchy. Both had a German majority—Holstein's was larger than Schleswig's and the latter had a significant Danish population—but the ruler of both was the Danish monarch and the landed aristocracy was pro-Danish. It was typical of the ramshackle German state system of the time that one of these provinces, Holstein, was a member of the German Confederation while the other was not. Not only was the German speaking population represented in the Danish legislative assembly, its delegates were permitted to use their own language. This was not the most outrageous case of national oppression in Europe.

Nevertheless, in 1848, the German population of the two Duchies, swept up in the revolutionary agitation of the day demanded independence from their Danish lords and the liberation of the plucky Schleswig-Holsteiners became a rallying point for the Democracy. Its cause was taken up by the Frankfurt Assembly and *meerumschlungen Schleswig-Holstein*— "Sea-girt Schleswig-Holstein"—became a part of the national legend. Few seem to have found it silly to apply this high-sounding Homeric epithet to what was, after all, a small piece of territory.

That the Frankfurt Assembly was swept up in the general agitation was understandable. That body was capable of endless debates over trivialities especially if they served to distract its attention, and that of the public, from more pressing issues. But the *NRZ* also made an issue of the Schleswig-Holstein campaign. Why would what appears in hindsight to have been a relatively insignificant issue have attracted Marx and Engels attention? Indeed, their apparently unwarranted concern has often been used as proof of their latent German nationalism. In World War I, their position on Schleswig-Holstein in 1848 became one more precedent for the pro-war socialists.

From the beginning, Marx and Engels made it clear that they were aware of the relative unimportance of the cause of the Schleswig-Holsteiners *taken by itself*. In fact, and I have not seen this point made elsewhere, they supported the Danes initially.* Engels had written an article only a month before the outbreak of the revolution in Germany on "Three New Constitutions"[19] in which he ridiculed the claims of the German inhabitants of two Duchies, compared the Danish Constitution favorably to that of Prussia's, and pointed to the extremely favorable status the German minority in the Danish kingdom enjoyed. He claimed that they had as many delegates in the Danish legislature as the Danes by law even though they were far less numerous.

> In short the Danes make every possible concession to the Germans, and the Germans persist in their absurd national obstinacy. The Germans have never been national-minded where the interests of nationality and the interests of progress have coincided; they were always so where nationality has turned against progress.

The "interests of progress" in this case were represented by the relatively liberal Danish constitution. But the bourgeois liberals whose political pressure had won constitutional reform were also champions of Danish nationalism and cultural independence from Germany. It was a typical combination in 1848. Prussia as the stronghold of constitutional conservatism was only too willing to use the cause of the oppressed, and politically backward, German population of the territory as a weapon against the Danish liberals. This political lineup explains Engels' hostility to the agitation of the Germans of Schleswig-Holstein in 1847. It was consistent with his, and Marx's, general hostility to national movements that "turned against progress."

What changed? Well, for one thing, there was a revolution in Germany. And that brought to the fore an aspect of international diplomacy that Engels had previously ignored. This was not simply a

---

* Franz Mehring, in his biography of Marx, has a passage which explains the politics of the war with Denmark very well. He does not mention, however, Engels initial support for the Danes. It is a good example of Mehring's consistent downplaying or belittling of Marx and Engels anti-Prussianism.

contest between tiny Denmark and the might of Prussia. Behind Denmark stood England and Russia. For them, and especially for Russia, a successful revolution against their client in the heated atmosphere of June 1848 could be a disaster. What had been a minor squabble between the powers earlier in the year was now a serious matter. Worse, Russia and England's formerly trustworthy ally, the King of Prussia, was apparently being taken captive by the revolution. As Count Nesselrode, the Russian Foreign Minister complained in his private correspondence:

> ... my patience is at an end. ... Yesterday, Saturday, a courier brought me the news of Wrangel's refusal to sign the armistice straight from Copenhagen. ... Our forbearance has really been abused. We have often repeated to Prussia that she is allowing things to reach a point where we will not be able to maintain a defensive posture towards her as we would wish because of her blind submission to the whims of the German demagogues.[20]

Marx and Engels' appreciation of the situation was similar to that of von Nesselrode. What he saw as a danger they, of course, saw as an opportunity.

It should also be understood, as part of the background, that Prussia in 1848 was not the military power that the German Empire was to become after 1870. The course of the war, in which the Prussians were humiliated, makes that clear.

In the first *NRZ* article on the crisis—"Defeat of the German Troops at Sundewitt"[21]—Engels ridiculed the Prussian army. The article is full of contempt for the Germans and quite complimentary to the Danes. It also makes explicit what really lay behind the *NRZ* prowar stand in the affair of *meerumschlungen Schleswig-Holstein*.

> If this [the lackadaisical conduct of the war by the Prussians] is not a case of open treason, then it is a manifestation of such immense incompetence that in any case the management of the whole affair must be placed

in other hands. Will the National Assembly in Frankfurt at last feel compelled to do what it should have long since, that is take over foreign policy itself?

Engels expressed some scepticism in this article concerning the Assembly but at this early period both Marx and Engels still expected that the German bourgeoisie would be forced in their own interest to act out the role of their *Girondin* predecessors of fifty years before. They still believed that the bourgeois leadership of the Assembly would, in its own self-interest, embroil the country in a war with the monarchies that only a revolutionary government could win.

The *NRZ* addressed its demands and its criticism to the Frankfurt Assembly, not to the German governments, because the Assembly was the first, hesitant, step to a united, republican Germany. Marx and Engels did not invent the issue of war with the Alliance any more than they invented the other issues which agitated the country. What distinguished the *NRZ* was that the "Marx party" whipped up public opinion where the Frankfurt Assembly, even its left wing, tried to calm the people down.

In the end, when Prussia signed a humiliating peace rather than be forced into a war with England and Russia, the Assembly simply capitulated. It was one of the events that helped persuade Marx and Engels that the German bourgeoisie was not capable of imitating its French predecessors.

6. Hungarians and Poles

The last incident that raised the specter of 1793 was the Russian invasion of Hungary in April 1849. Up till this point the Hungarian insurrection had appeared on the verge of victory. And not only victory in Hungary. After being driven out of its main strongholds by numerically superior forces the Hungarian revolutionary forces aided by international allies, especially Poles, had waged a successful guerilla war that demoralized the armies of the Empire. At one point they appeared to be in a position to take Vienna. Even after the defeat of the revolution elsewhere it took a Russian invasion in April of 1849 to finally break the Hungarian resistance. *We* know that this was the last act of the 1848 revolution. From the vantage point of Engels and the *NRZ* it looked like the opening of a new round. In the second to last issue of the paper, just before it was shut down, Engels outlined what was at stake:

> ... the Magyar war very soon lost the national character it had in the beginning, and assumed a clearly European character, precisely as a result of what would seem to be a purely national act, as a result of the declaration of independence. Only when Hungary proclaimed her separation from Austria, and thereby the dissolution of the Austrian monarchy, did the alliance with the Poles for the liberation of both countries, and the alliance with the Germans for the revolutionisation of Eastern Germany acquire a definite character and a solid basis. If Hungary were independent, Poland restored, German Austria turned into the revolutionary focus of Germany, with Lombardy and Italy winning independence—these plans, if carried out, would destroy the entire East-European system of states: Austria would disappear, Prussia would disintegrate and Russia would be forced back to the borders of Asia.[22]

Engels predicted that the German insurrectionary forces in the Baden-Palatinate, which he was shortly to join, and the troops of a renewed French revolutionary movement would meet with the Polish and Hungarian armies before the walls of Berlin. It was not to be. The German and French revolutionary movements were spent and the Hungarians and their Polish allies were crushed by Austrian and Russian troops.

But Hungarians and Poles were united by something else than their mutual antagonism to the international relations of post-1815 Europe. For some time before the outbreak of revolution Marx and Engels had come to the conclusion that in Poland the only successful national uprising had to be based on a democratic social revolution and that, in a country like Poland, the only possible democracy was an agrarian democracy. In Poland, then, a successful uprising could only be an uprising which was also a civil war.

Already the first partition led quite naturally to an alliance of the other classes, i.e. the nobles, the townspeople and to some extent the peasants, both against the oppressors of Poland and against the big Polish aristocracy. The Constitution of 1791 shows that already then the Poles clearly understood that their independence in foreign affairs was inseparable from the overthrow of the aristocracy and from agrarian reform within the country.[23]

When the Hungarian revolution, somewhat unexpectedly, broke out in late 1848, the *NRZ* found its hypothesis derived from the Polish case confirmed in this corner of Eastern Europe. Polish and Hungarian revolutionary democrats, leaders of independence movements on whose success or failure the success or failure of the revolution itself depended, also faced an enemy at home.

7. The Old Poland and the New

The Marxologists almost universally allege that Marx and Engels ignored the reactionary tendencies in the national movement of these two countries. Some go so far as to accuse them of deviating from Marxism in this respect.* The allegations are unfounded and, as is often the case, ignore the explicit statements of Marx and Engels themselves. In the Polish case, one of the explicit statements is found in the *Communist Manifesto*. While terse, like much else in the *Manifesto*, the statement ought to at least tempt the researcher to look a little further.

It so happens that the question of Polish independence and its relation to the class struggle *in Poland* was on everyone's mind while Marx was writing the *Manifesto*. This was just before the outbreak of the revolution in 1848. The question had been put on the agenda by the Austrian Foreign Minister Prince von Metternich who, in his own way, was one of the leading revolutionaries of the day. It was Metternich who, in

---

* A detailed discussion of the references by other writers to Marx and Engels on "the National Question in 1848" would be digressive in this chapter. These views are taken up in Special Note A.

1846, faced with an insurrection of the Polish gentry and the urban classes, demagogically, and successfully, appealed to the class and religious hostility of the mostly Ukrainian peasantry in Galicia towards their Polish lords. His skillful playing of this card isolated the radical, democratic insurrection in Cracow. Even in 1848, the politics of this defeated insurrection continued to preoccupy the left. The relatively minor *contemporary* disturbances in Poland raised no comparable political questions concerning the internal politics of *Poland*.

As early as 1830, when a Polish uprising also coincided with a revolution in France and jeopardized the international order constructed in 1815, the class question forced itself on the nationalist movement. In that year, the landowning classes who led the insurrection promised an end to feudal obligations; in particular, the hated obligation to provide free labor at the landowners' demand. But, hard pressed to meet the needs of the population under war time conditions, they reinstituted the system "temporarily" until the foreign armies were defeated. After this temporary sacrifice to ensure the defeat of the common enemy, the reforms would certainly be reintroduced. The peasants found the argument unconvincing and the insurrection was defeated.

In 1846, this precedent weighed on the minds of all parties. The Polish emigration was split on several lines but the main division was between the partisans of the old Poland—the patrimony of the powerful families who hoped to restore the old kingdom intact including its rule over non-Polish minorities and its exploitation of Polish peasants—and the partisans of a new, democratic Poland. The latter were organized in the Polish Democratic Association which was loosely allied with other Democratic Associations including that of Brussels in which Marx was active. One of their most prominent representatives was Joachim Lelewel who was also a member of the Brussels Democratic Association. Lelewel, a personal and political friend of Marx in 1846, had been a former Deputy in the Polish Diet in 1828 and a member of the Provisional Government during the insurrection of 1830.

In 1846 there were three centers of revolutionary activity in Poland. Perhaps, it would be better to say two centers of revolutionary activity and one of counterrevolutionary activity. The more conservative wing of the emigration hoped to use the conflicts between the occupying powers to maneuver their way back to power. Their hopes centered on organizing an insurrection against the Russians based in Prussian occupied Posen (present day Poznan.) However, when the representative of the insurrectionaries, Ludwik Mieroslawski arrived in Posen he was arrested.[24] The Prussian monarchy was willing to flirt with the Poles to gain a little diplomatic leverage but anything serious was out of the question.

The real insurrection took place in Cracow which had been granted the status of free city under the terms of the Congress of Vienna. It was organized by the democratic wing of the emigration and held the city against overwhelming odds for ten days. Its program was one of agrarian reform, which meant the abolition of all feudal obligations without compensation, separation of church and state, which meant the emancipation of the Jews, and a democratic constitution, which meant the abolition of the old Poland. It enjoyed enormous popular support in the town and the surrounding countryside and it required some effort on the part of the Austrian and Russian forces to retake the city. Cracow was subsequently incorporated into the Austrian occupied sector of Poland.[25]

The third front was opened, not by the revolutionaries but by Metternich, in Galicia. In November of 1846, a new Conservative Party with an advanced program of agrarian reforms was formed with Metternich's support. And when the Polish gentry revolted against the empire, they were met by a counter-revolt of the peasantry. There were charges made and countered that Metternich paid and organized peasant agitators to spread rumors that the plans of the government for reform were being frustrated by the Polish gentry and to organize the subsequent pogroms against the gentry. The facts behind these charges and countercharges are still a matter of controversy.[26] What is not in dispute is that what followed was a *jacquerie* of particularly brutal character against the Polish landlords. The agrarian revolution which might have provided a broader base for the Cracow insurrection was diverted into a counterrevolutionary movement in support of the Hapsburg dynasty. The peasantry, with their traditional trust in the "little Father" whose good will was always frustrated by bad advisers and greedy landlords, fought for the phantom reforms of the government rather than the real ones of the Cracow revolutionaries.

Marx and Engels did not need to be reminded of the importance of an agrarian revolution by these events. Marx had made the abolition of feudal obligations or what remained of them a central issue when he was still the liberal editor of the *Rheinische Zeitung*. This was before he became a socialist. Nor was this a peculiar "Marxist" position. Most radicals and liberals shared his views on this issue at least in the abstract. What the events in Cracow and Galicia did was to force supporters of "the Democracy" to take a stand *on the issues which divided the Polish émigrés* who were their friends.

Marx and Engels addressed two meetings of "the Democracy" memorializing Polish insurrections in the year preceding the *Manifesto*. The first was in London on November 29, 1847; the occasion was the seventeenth anniversary of the 1830 uprising. On this occasion, neither Marx nor Engels had much to say about Poland! They mainly took the opportunity to emphasize the international and social character of the coming revolution. Engels' only reference to Poland emphasized the responsibility of Germans to oppose the German occupation of Poland and went on to stress the international character of the movement. It was Marx who "internationalized" the issue of Polish independence and emphasized its relation to the "social question."

> The old Poland is lost in any case and we would be the last to wish for its restoration. But it is not only the old Poland that is lost. The old Germany, the old France, the old England, the whole of the old society is lost. But the loss of the old society is no loss for those who have nothing to lose in the old society, and this is the case of the great majority in all countries at the present time.[27]

And that is all there is about Poland in Marx's speech.

The second meeting took place on February 22, 1848 to commemorate the 1846 insurrection. The *Manifesto* was probably published in the same week. On this occasion both Marx and Engels addressed the social character of the insurrection directly and in considerable detail considering that these were both short speeches.

Marx emphasized that the standard denunciations of the Cracow revolutionary government as "communist" by the establishment press was hysteria designed to conceal the fact that the property abolished by the insurrectionaries was feudal property such as no longer existed in France. What they aimed at in their brief reign was to establish the property relations that already existed in France, Belgium, Switzerland and North America. Had the French proprietor been told this, Marx says, he would have replied "They are quite right." However, on being told that the insurrectionaries were revolutionaries and communists who were abolishing property rights the French property owner replied "What, ... these scoundrels must be trampled down!" Marx praises the Cracow revolutionaries because they saw that only a democratic Poland could be independent and only a Poland which had abolished feudal rights could be democratic.

> Replace the Russian autocrat by Polish aristocrats and you will have given despotism naturalisation papers. ... If the Polish lord no longer has a Russian lord over him, the Polish peasant will still have a lord over him, but a free lord in place of a slave lord. This political change will have altered nothing in his social position.[28]

Please note that this passage comes pretty close to saying that it doesn't matter whether the Polish peasant is exploited by a foreign lord or a domestic one. In terms of the later debates over this question it would appear that Marx is anticipating the position of Rosa Luxemburg. But that would be overstating the case. That is not the point Marx is trying to make. What we have here is a sharp attack on the "pure and simple" nationalists in the Polish emigration. It is also an anticipatory repudiation of the paranoid anti-Russian position often attributed to Marx.

The adherents of the pro-aristocratic wing of the Polish independence movement in the audience would not have found much to cheer in Engels' speech either. After a salute to the fallen heroes and a lament for suffering Poland, Engels, ever the optimist, goes on to announce that the defeat of the Cracow insurrection is also a victory that the meeting should celebrate! A victory over whom? It is the "... victory of young democratic Poland over the old aristocratic Poland."

> Yes, the latest struggle of Poland against its foreign oppressors has been preceded by a hidden struggle, concealed but decisive within Poland itself, a struggle of oppressed Poles against Polish oppressors, a struggle of democracy against the Polish aristocracy.[29]

As he warms to the subject, Engels claims that the Cracow revolution was "even more hostile to Poland itself than to the foreign oppressor." What was this old Poland? Engels spells it out in a passage pillorying the aristocratic revolutionaries of 1830.

> What did the Polish aristocracy want in 1830? To safeguard its own acquired rights with regard to the Emperor. It limited the insurrection to the little country which the Congress of Vienna was pleased to call the Kingdom of Poland; it restrained the uprising in the other Polish provinces; it left intact the degrading serfdom of the peasants and the infamous condition of the Jews. If the aristocracy, in the course of the insurrection, had to make concessions to the people, it only made them when it was too late, when the insurrection had failed.[30]

Yet, this was an insurrection which Engels supported! He makes that clear by holding up as an example Lelewel (who was in the audience.) This was the one man, according to Engels, who, in 1830, fought for the emancipation of the Jews and peasants and for restoring all of Poland thus "turning the war of Polish independence into a European war."

These two speeches have to be read in their entirety to get a real feel for the way the Polish independence movement was linked in Marx and Engels' mind to the struggle to free Europe from the Holy Alliance and how both were seen as dependent on a democratic and social revolution internationally.

In the *Manifesto*, whose analysis of the relationship of the various national movements to the social revolution we will look at later, the Polish question is reduced to the following sentence:

> In Poland they [the Communists] support the party that insists on an agrarian revolution as the prime condition for national emancipation, that party which fomented the insurrection in Cracow in 1846.[31]

Today, this is an obscure reference. It probably was already obscure in 1888 when Engels and Samuel Moore translated the *Manifesto* into what has become the standard English version. In that translation (quoted above) the original German phrase *Unter den Polen* appears as "in Poland." Literally, it means "among the Poles." At the time the *Manifesto* was written, this paragraph was practically a declaration of war on the right wing of the Polish *emigration*. In Engels' 1888 translation this point is lost.

8. Revolutionary Cattle Dealers

The revolt of the Hungarians, like that of the Czechs and Poles, divided left from right in Germany. Throughout 1849 coverage of this rebellion of the Hungarian people against the Austrian Empire dominated the columns of the *NRZ*. Prior to the outbreak of the 1848 revolution, however, there are only scattered references to Hungary by Engels and none by Marx.[32] Certainly, the country had not played a role in the politics of the European left comparable to that played by Poland.

In early 1847, Engels did write two articles for the *Deutscher-Brüsseler-Zeitung*, by this time the semi-official voice of the Democratic Association, in which he mentioned, very briefly, revolutionary developments in Hungary. In the first of these, "The Movements of 1847,"[33] an overview of the political and social movements that were pushing Europe toward revolution, Hungary is mentioned in a passage summarizing the revolutionary effects of bourgeoisification in previously backward areas:

> Even in quite barbarous lands the bourgeoisie is advancing. ... In Hungary, the feudal magnates are more and more changing into wholesale corn and wool

merchants and cattle dealers, and consequently now appear in the Diet as bourgeois.

In a second article in the same paper, "The Beginning of the End in Austria,"[34] Engels describes the Habsburg Empire as a patchwork of "A dozen nations whose customs, character, and institutions were flagrantly opposed to one another." They have clung together "on the strength of their common dislike of civilization." The geographical position of these "patriarchal" peoples in the middle of Europe, isolated from one another and from the more civilised peoples to the north and south by impassable mountains and lack of accesses to the sea or great rivers, made possible the rule of the House of Austria, "the representative of barbarism, of reactionary stability in Europe." Engels concludes:

> Hence the House of Austria was invincible as long as the barbarous character of its subjects remained untouched. Hence it was threatened by only one danger—the penetration of bourgeois civilization.

Engels then lists the disruptive effects of this inevitable penetration. His sole mention of Hungary is to the Diet which "is preparing revolutionary proposals and is sure of a majority for them." What these "revolutionary proposals" are is not made explicit but the rest of the article would indicate that Engels is referring to proposals to eliminate the remaining feudal obligations, in particular *corvée* labor. The Hungarian landowners-turned-bourgeoisie who, according to Engels' earlier article, dominated the Diet were presumably the driving force behind these "revolutionary proposals." However, when Engels uses the word "revolutionary" in this article he is referring to the objective consequences of these measures and not a conscious or organized subversive political movement. In the next sentence he states that "Austria, which needs Hungarian Hussars in Milan, Moderna and Parma, Austria itself puts forward revolutionary proposals to the Diet although it knows very well that these are its own death warrant." The Hungarian landlords in this article are a revolutionary force willy-nilly, like the Hapsburg monarchy itself.

The next mention of Hungary by either Marx or Engels is in January of 1849. This is a major analytical article in which Engels announces that the Hungarian revolution is as important for 1849 as the Paris revolt was for 1848.

> For the first time in the revolutionary movements of 1848, for the first time since 1793, a nation surrounded by superior counterrevolutionary forces dares to counter the cowardly counterrevolutionary fury by revolutionary passion, the *terreur blanche* by the *terreur rouge*. For the first time after a long period we meet with a truly revolutionary figure, a man who in the name of his people dares to accept the challenge of a desperate struggle, who for his nation is Danton and Carnot in one person—*Lajos Kossuth*.[35]

Did the feudal magnates turned bourgeois corn dealers and wool merchants suddenly become Jacobins? Engels did not think so. There was no doubt that the Hungarian rebellion *began* as a defense of the traditional rights of the Magyar* nobility against the centralizing tendency of the

---

* A word on the use of the terms 'Hungary' and 'Magyar' in 1848. Generally speaking, 'Magyar' refers to an ethnic group speaking a non-Indo-European language akin neither to that of the Germans or Slavs who surrounded them. 'Hungary' refers both to a geographical area and to the traditional kingdom of the Magyars. The distinction is important because the Magyar ethnic group was a privileged minority within the kingdom of Hungary. They were the largest minority in a country of minorities. The political significance in 1848 was that the revolutionaries claimed to be fighting for a state in which all citizens were equal. The 'Hungarians' were the citizens of this 'Hungarian' state regardless of ethnic group.
But the legacy of centuries of Magyar privilege could not be overcome in a few months. A particularly thorny issue was the insistence of the revolutionary government on Magyar as the official language. Nevertheless, the claim that the revolutionaries were fighting for a modern national state based on equality before the law was not just propaganda. The militant support of the Jewish minority for the revolutionary government despite the widespread and virulent antisemitism

(continued...)

Hapsburgs. Like Poland, Hungary had been for centuries a kind of feudal democracy. The king was elected and responsible to a Diet of the Magyar nobility. But "nobility" in Hungary as in Poland was a relative term. Engels undoubtedly went too far in describing "the greater part of the Hungarian nobility" as "mere proletarians [sic] whose aristocratic privileges are confined to the fact that they cannot be subjected to corporal punishment."[36] Nevertheless, both contemporary and modern observers have also emphasized that "noble" status in Hungary as in Poland was enjoyed by a large percentage of the rural population many of whom would look to us, as they did to their contemporaries, very much like free-holding peasants, and not always very well off peasants at that. There was an egalitarian, "democratic" feel about this constitutional set up which appeared quite modern although it was in reality based on a feudal social form that predated the modernizing absolute monarchy of the Hapsburgs.

The Hapsburgs became Kings of Hungary not by conquest or marriage but by election. The Diet, for diplomatic reasons, offered the crown to the Hapsburgs in the 17th century and with one exception, the "enlightened" Joseph II, Hapsburg emperors went through the motions of accepting the crown of St. Stephen after election by the Diet. For the Hapsburgs this was a legal fiction. The Hungarians looked at it differently.

To complicate matters, there was a large Slavic peasant population and a significant German and German-Jewish bourgeoisie in Hungary. There were also German and Wallachian (modern Roumanian) peasants. To these large minorities the traditional "liberties" of the ethnic Hungarians were a source of resentment and envy. For a modern observer it is hard to overlook the resemblance of the Hungarian "nation" to a semi-independent military caste like the Cossacks in the Russian Empire. The latter also enjoyed certain "liberties," that is to say privileges, *vis-à-vis* the absolute monarchy. The social structure of the Cossack "nation" was also relatively egalitarian compared to the Empire as a whole. In the Hapsburg

---

* (...continued)
of Magyars and non-Magyars alike was noted by all. The question of the response of the Slavic, German and Romanian minorities to the revolution is more controversial and will be dealt with later.
Engels most often used the term Hungarian and Hungarian revolution.

War and the Democracy in 1848

Empire similar privileges were also enjoyed by the Croats who were to become the most bitter opponents of Hungarian independence.

All this broke down in 1848. The conflict between the centralizing tendencies of the Hapsburg monarchy and the claims of the Hungarian Diet, especially over the always awkward question of taxation, had long been a source of tension even in peaceful times. With demands for constitutional liberties and representative government—even for democracy!—threatening the existence of the Hapsburg monarchy and the old regime throughout Europe, the "liberties" of the Hungarians were a dangerous example despite their originally feudal content. As in France in 1789-91, the liberal-minded, "improving," nobility—the noble corn dealers Engels had referred to earlier—were forced to take extreme measures to defend their traditional privileges. In Hungary in 1848 they also had to defend their national independence. As in France in 1789, the resistance to the absolute monarchy initiated from above in response to a crisis provoked a revolution from below.

Democratic opinion in Germany was overwhelmingly in support of the Hungarian rising. Even the Frankfurt Assembly, which had hesitated when it came to opposing Prussian occupation of Poland, supported the Hungarians against Austria. There were, of course, those who feared the defeat of the Austrians by a popular uprising. One of the journalistic adherents of this point of view was the main rival of the *NRZ*, the *Kölnische Zeitung*. At the height of the rebellion the paper ridiculed the democratic supporters of Hungarian independence

> The so-called democratic press in Germany has sided with the Magyars in the Austro-Hungarian conflict. ... Certainly strange enough! The German democrats siding with that aristocratic caste, for which, in spite of the nineteenth century, its own nation has never ceased to be *misera contribuens plebs* [a pitiful tax-burdened plebian mass]; the German democrats siding with the most arrogant oppressors of the people![37]

Engels polemic against this editorial, "The *Kölnische Zeitung* on the Magyar Struggle," begins by arguing that even if the *Kölnische Zeitung* were right, even if this were an uprising of an "aristocratic caste," the fact would be irrelevant. The Austrian troops and their Croatian allies were not fighting for an end to feudalism. They were not aiming at the suppression of the "aristocratic caste." Engels then compares the Hungarian revolt to the 1830 uprising in Poland, an uprising whose defeat Engels himself had argued little more than a year before was a direct result of the domination of that revolt by an "aristocratic caste."

> In 1830, when the Poles rose against Russia, was it then a question whether merely an "aristocratic caste" was at their head? At that time it was in the first place a question of driving out the foreigners. The whole of Europe sympathized with the "aristocratic caste," which certainly started the movement, for the Polish Republic of the nobility was at any rate a huge advance compared with Russian despotism.[38]

Engels goes on to point out that the suffrage in France after the revolution of 1830 was restricted to some 250,000 voters and the rule of the French bourgeoisie was also based on the exploitation of the *misera contribuens plebs*. He does not argue that the bourgeois constitutional monarchy of Louis Philippe was a step forward as compared to the Bourbon restoration. He simply assumes that his audience, including the *Kölnische Zeitung*, takes that for granted.

But Engels does not leave it there. He is not content to defend national independence and representative institutions as progressive *vis à vis* absolutism and desirable ends to be fought for in their own right. In defending these basic democratic rights the Hungarian revolution has had to go farther:

> The great Schwanbeck, [Eugen Alexis Schwanbeck, the Vienna correspondent of the *Kölnische Zeitung*] of course, is even less obliged to know that Hungary is the only country in which since the March revolution feudal burdens on the peasants have legally and in fact totally ceased to exist. The great Schwanbeck declares the

> Magyars to be an "aristocratic caste," "most arrogant oppressors of the people," ... Schwanbeck does not know, or does not want to know, that the Magyar *magnates,* the Esterházys etc., deserted at the very beginning of the war and came to Olmütz [Austrian headquarters] to pay homage, and that it is precisely the "aristocratic" officers of the Magyar army who from the beginning of the struggle until now have every day carried out a fresh betrayal of their national cause! Otherwise, how is it that today the majority of the Chamber of Deputies is still with Kossuth in Debreczin, whereas only eleven magnates are to be found there?[39]

In another article, "Croats and Slovaks in Hungary," Engels, discussing the fate of the "loyal" Slavic troops on the Imperial side, reports that the victorious Austrian authorities were restoring traditional Hungarian privileges despite their previous promises to the Slavs.

> It is obvious that the aristocrat Windischgrätz knows full well that he can only achieve his goal of maintaining the power of the nobility in Hungary by maintaining the *Magyar* nobility in power. ...having finished the business of subduing Hungary and restoring the rule of the aristocracy there, he will manage to deal with the Slavs...[40]

There is a great deal of material like this in Engels' articles during 1849 dealing with disaffection within the ranks of the Imperial forces, which is largely ignored by most commentators. The whole issue of the disruptive effect of the social program of the Hungarian revolution within the *non-Hungarian* population is best dealt with in another section. Here, it is Engels' stress on the disruptive effect of this program *within* Hungary that is relevant. In practically his last article on the subject he referred to the Polish example and emphasized that in Hungary too social revolution and national liberation are inextricably linked.

> The Magyar war of 1849 has strong points of resemblance with the Polish war of 1830-31. But the great difference is that the factors which were against the Poles at the time now act in favor of the Magyars. Lelewel, as we know, unsuccessfully urged ... that the mass of the population be bound to the revolution by emancipating the peasants and the Jews. ... *The Magyars started at the point* which the Poles only achieved when it was *too late*. The Hungarians' first measure was to carry out a social revolution in their country, to abolish feudalism...[41]

Again, as in the case of the insurrections in Cracow in 1846 and Prague in 1848, it was only the advanced minority that advocated this complete program of democratic revolution. And in this instance Engels appears to have been ignorant of the real political line-up. Kossuth was *not* the democrat portrayed in the columns of the *NRZ*. Alexander Petöfi and the radical students and workers in Budapest occupied that particular point on the political spectrum. Kossuth was the man in the middle. He was the man whose job it was to *mediate* between the radicals in the clubs and the more conservative delegates in the Assembly.[42] But if the *NRZ* was mistaken in its estimation of Kossuth, it was certainly consistent in its political judgement based on the facts available to its editors. Conservative public opinion in Germany and Hungary made Kossuth the representative of the Hungarian Democracy and the editors of the *NRZ* responded by embracing him.

9. The Workers Have No Country

The emphasis placed by Marx and Engels on the national liberation movements of Germans, Poles and Magyars in the 1848 revolution has been especially confusing for both friends and foes, honest critics and dishonest ones. Why should internationalists care so passionately about these national struggles? Didn't the *Communist Manifesto* itself state flat out that "the workers have no country"?

Well, actually, it didn't. At least it didn't in the original German edition. Part of the confusion stems from a mistranslation in the standard English version. The *Manifesto* actually said that the workers had no

Vaterland. The resonance of that term in 1848 was not quite what it is today but it was close enough. It was not simply a narrow chauvinism that Marx and Engels rejected, however. In the *Manifesto* the question of nationalism, like other questions, is introduced by way of the refutation of a charge made against the communists by their opponents. The accusation in this instance is that the communists want to do away with the *Vaterland* and nationalities. The answer of the *Manifesto* is that the workers' have no *Vaterland* because they do not have political power anywhere. The communists could not take from them what they did not have. In 1848 this was a pretty obvious statement of fact. The passage goes on to state that the proletariat in all the leading countries had "first of all to acquire political supremacy" it "must rise to be the leading class of the nation." In short, the sense of this quote is almost the polar opposite of the one usually attributed to it.

The internationalism of the *Manifesto* lies in its assertion that the success of the coming revolution requires the victory of the working class in at least several of the leading European nations. A national victory was the first step in a European revolution. That first step could not be taken without taking into account the immediate issues facing specific national movements. It was just as obvious to Marx and Engels that a national movement that restricted itself to the first step was doomed to fail.

The *Manifesto* presents itself as the platform of an international revolutionary movement *manifesting* itself in different forms in different countries according to the different circumstances of each but still the *same* movement. The job of the communist vanguard is to emphasize the interdependence of the national movements and oppose the kind of national opportunism which ignores this interdependence.

The economic basis of this interdependence was most explicitly spelled out in one of Engels' two preliminary attempts at a manifesto. The *Principles of Communism*[43] was in the form of questions and answers which spelled out the basic principles of the communist "faith." It was consciously modeled on the catechism which was the elementary educational-propaganda device in both the Catholic and Protestant churches. Question 11 was "What were the immediate results of the industrial revolution and the division of society into bourgeois and proletarians?" Engels answered that the first consequence was the creation of a world market. That meant that "a new machine invented in England [threw] millions of workers in China out of work within a year." The political conclusion was that "if now in England or France the workers liberate themselves, this must lead to revolutions in all other countries, which sooner or later will also bring about the liberation of the workers in those countries."[44]

The *effect* of the European revolution, in the view of the *Manifesto* would be to speed up the process already begun by the economic activity of the bourgeoisie. That process led to increasing "uniformity in the mode of production and in the conditions of life corresponding thereto." The "political supremacy of the proletariat"[45] which, we have to remember, Marx and Engels then believed to be the inevitable and imminent consequence of a successful democratic revolution, would further accelerate this tendency to "uniformity of conditions." That was the tendency. The starting point was a world still far from such uniformity. That is why the revolutionaries in Cracow in 1846 had to fight for what was already the conservative program in France.

The idea is presented in the *Manifesto* as follows:

> Though not in substance, yet in form, the struggle of the proletariat with the bourgeoisie is at first a national struggle. The proletariat of each country must, of course, first of all settle matters with its own bourgeoisie.[46]

It is worth pointing out that in this passage the word country is a translation of the German *Land*. The term is simply the standard German for a geographical-political fact. It does not, like the word *Vaterland*, also imply a state of mind or political program.

The practical consequence of this perspective was that it made it the responsibility of the communists in the various countries to subordinate the immediate concerns of the national revolution to the European one.

One of the most striking statements of this view with respect to Germany is in one of the earliest issues of the *NRZ*. It is an axiom of Marx studies that the unification of Germany was the demand that formed the core of Marx and Engels foreign policy in 1848. And in general that was

War and the Democracy in 1848

true. Even this demand, however, was subordinated to the needs of the revolution. On June 25, 1848, Marx discussed the possibility that Prussia "the western province of Russia" would join forces with the Tsar. Marx proposes to counter the anticipated alliance between Prussia and Russia with an alliance of "Germany" and France:

> If the Prussians ally themselves with the Russians, the Germans will ally themselves with the French and united they will wage the war of the West against the East, of civilization against barbarism, of the republic against autocracy.

The common portrait of Marx as a kind of pan-German patriot whose foreign policy was *dominated* in 1848 (and perhaps after) by a desire for a united German state hardly squares with this kind of talk. Marx had not, however, abandoned the idea of a united Germany. He continues in the next paragraph:

> We want the unification of Germany. Only as the result of the disintegration of the large German monarchies, however, can the elements of this unity crystallize. They will be welded together only by the stress of war and revolution.[47]

The unification of Germany on a democratic basis and the maintenance of a revolutionary front of democratic nations also meant that purely *German* interests were sometimes secondary.

A little later in the year[48] Marx summed up his attitude towards the German revolution which, in its provincial narrow-mindedness, fell so far below the demands of the international movement. Marx's judgement of this Prussian revolution is at the same time an implicit statement of his view of what the revolution *should* have been:

> Far from being a *European Revolution* it was merely the stunted after-effect of a European revolution in a backward country. Instead of being ahead of its century,

> [like the seventeenth century English and eighteenth century French revolutions] it was over half a century behind its time. ... The Prussian March revolution was not even a *national, German* revolution; from the outset it was a *provincial, Prussian* revolution.⁴⁹

Because the German revolutionaries in 1848 were unable to think in international terms they were unable to solve even the most pressing national problems of Germany.

CHAPTER 2. "NON-HISTORIC" PEOPLES

From the time of its first issue in April of 1848 until its suppression in July of 1849, the *NRZ* made the liberation of the Poles, and later the Hungarians, from their German rulers a central feature of its propaganda. It was a vital task for the German national movement. Far more attention has been paid, however, to the *NRZ* articles in 1849 which appear to justify German (and Hungarian) suppression of the Czechs and South Slavs. Engels, and it was he who wrote these articles, seems to be contradicting everything else he wrote in 1848-49 and in the period immediately preceding the revolution.*

No writings of Marx and Engels have caused greater scandal. In them the Austrian Slavs are contemptuously dismissed as "non-historic" peoples who are incapable of forming viable national states. On the evidence of these articles Marx and Engels have been convicted as racists, Pan-Germans and even proto-Nazis.** A smaller sect of Marxologists, although perhaps a more important one, has used the arguments of these *NRZ* articles to justify the suppression of smaller nations in the interests of "civilization."[1]

Contrary to the assertions of both these factions, however, neither Marx nor Engels ever supported, either in these articles or elsewhere, the suppression of the national rights of any national group on the grounds that it was "non-historic" or "non-viable" when said nation actually proved its viability, its "historicity" by asserting its rights. In 1849, the *NRZ* was concerned with national movements which fought on the side of the Austrian and Russian empires *against nations which were in rebellion*. On occasion, in later years, Engels used similar language to describe similar behavior.

---

* The articles in question are almost all by Engels. They were published in the *NRZ*, however, under Marx's editorship and the same thesis appears, if anything more strongly stated, in a series of articles under the general title "Revolution and Counter-Revolution in Germany" which was published over Marx's byline in the New York Daily Tribune. Engels was usually in charge of writing material on military matters which is how these questions were treated. It was his field. There is no indication that Marx had any objections to the content of these articles.

** To discuss and refute all the wild accusations that have been made would require a separate book and not a very interesting one. Special note A is a cursory look at one of the more serious treatments of this material by another writer.

This is not to argue that these formulations by Engels are a guide to understanding the relation of the struggle for self-determination to revolution, democracy and socialism. They are not even a guide to understanding Engels' own position in 1848-9. They are a product of thorough confusion—and of rage.

1. Twenty Vendées

In order to understand what was behind this radical departure from everything else Marx and Engels wrote and said in this period, we have to recall the importance of the French Revolutionary war of 1793-4 for their thinking. One of the threats that weighed on their minds was that of a "Vendée," a peasant uprising led by the aristocracy and especially the clergy against the democratic republic.

For Marx and Engels, and every other democrat or liberal in 1848, this uprising in 1793 was inspired by an ignorant and bigoted fear of the modern world and there was certainly that element in the uprising. Defenders of the uprising were invariably defenders of the old régime. Here again, modern historians take a more nuanced view of the events.

In the early twentieth century, conservative defenders of the old régime and the uprising in the Vendée, apparently finding the defense of Church and King increasingly ineffective, began to question the standard interpretation of the uprising. Turning the intellectual weapons of the left against the traditional left republican and socialist defenders of the Jacobin government, these conservatives pointed to the considerable evidence that the social and economic roots of the uprising lay in peasant resentment of the new, bourgeois exploiters.[2] And there has been for some time a dissident left view of the Jacobin regime that tends to support this thesis. The government of the Committee of Public Safety that finally crushed the uprising—quite brutally—had already turned against the popular movement. It had become, with reservations and somewhat reluctantly, the government of that section of the bourgeoisie which had enriched itself at the expense of the defeated clerical and lay aristocracy. It could no longer claim to be the representative of the popular movement except demagogically.[3]

But Marx and Engels knew little of this history. Although they were more skeptical of the Jacobins than their contemporaries on the left, they did not at this time, or later, ever work up an extended treatment of the French Revolution or the terror. They referred to it as a model, a common reference point understood by all parties. To take one of many possible examples, Marx, quite incidentally, in an article on the crisis provoked by the resignation of the moderate Prussian government led by Ludolf Camphausen,[4] ridicules the conservatives who compared Camphausen's ministry and the Berlin Assembly to the Jacobins and the Convention. He goes on to predict that "If the Government goes on in the way it has been doing, we shall have a Convention before long ... a Convention which will have to use all means to cope with the civil war in our twenty Vendées and with the inevitable war with Russia."

In 1848 the twenty potential Vendées were not only the small backward German principalities with their differences of religion and tradition and even language, they were also the national groups and remnants of nations whose mutual antagonisms could be and were manipulated by the powers, especially Austria. And some national groups did respond to the revolution by enlisting in the Emperor's cause. The original enthusiasm combining national and social liberation tended to unravel. In some cases the republican and democratic impulse won out; in others devotion to the national cause overwhelmed the socially progressive tendency.

In 1849 Marx and Engels saw a Croatian soldiery under their leader Jellachich brutally suppressing uprisings in Italy, Austria and Hungary. They saw Czech nationalists openly repudiating the Frankfurt Assembly because it threatened the dissolution of the Hapsburg Empire from which the Czechs hoped to receive, as a gift from above, the liberal reforms the Hungarians fought for. They saw numerous ethnic groups, Slovaks, Rumanians, Transylvanian Germans, siding with the Austrians out of ethnic hatred of the Magyars. The mostly peasant population too often ended up collaborating in the destruction of those parties that actually fought for their rights. The image of the Vendée seemed to fit and certainly there seemed to be no recourse but arms.

In his article "The Magyar Struggle" Engels summed up the situation:

> The year 1848 first of all brought with it the most terrible chaos for Austria by setting free for a short time all these different nationalities which, owing to Metternich, had hitherto been enslaving one another. The Germans, Magyars, Czechs, Poles, Moravians, Slovaks, Croats, Ruthenians, Rumanians, Illyrians and Serbs came into conflict with one another, while within each of these nationalities a struggle went on between the different classes. But soon order came out of this chaos. The combatants divided into two large camps: the Germans, Poles and Magyars took the side of revolution; the remainder, all the Slavs—except for the Poles, the Rumanians, and Transylvanian Saxons, took the side of the counterrevolution.[5]

As a description of fact this statement contains a great deal of truth. But Engels makes more of it than that. This lineup was predetermined

> ...The division is in accordance with all the previous history of the nationalities in question.

In a later article[6] Engels characterizes the war whose current battlefield is Hungary as an international, revolutionary war:

> The coming European war will divide Europe into two armed camps, not according to nations or national sympathies, but according to the level of civilization. On the one side the revolution, on the other the coalition of all outmoded estate-classes and interests; on the one side civilization, on the other side barbarism.

Taken by itself this is a simple statement of the social and class character of the revolution. One could object to the imprecise language, the use of "the Germans," "the Poles," "the Slavs." Several critics have mounted their "Marxist" high horses to smite Engels for failing to make the necessary class distinctions within the various national groups. They miss the point. Engels, and Marx, had raised the class question often enough themselves. By the time of the Hungarian revolution, however, the lines had been drawn. In some national movements the democratic and republican tendency had won out. In others, it had lost. In any class struggle there are winners and losers. The winning side has the "right," if you will, to claim to represent the nation. At least for the time being. Engels' sketch of the lineup in 1849 was roughly accurate.

2. Hegel on "Residual Fragments of Peoples"

The problem with the "non-historic peoples" line is that it means, as Engels emphasizes several times, that the Austrian Slavs had no choice but to form a part of the "outmoded" world of barbarism. In the article titled "The Magyar Struggle" Engels quoted as his authority—Hegel!

> These relics of a nation mercilessly trampled under foot in the course of history, as Hegel says, these residual fragments of peoples always become fanatical standard-bearers of counter-revolution ...

Note the word always. The quote is typical of the kind of "Hegelianism" Marx and Engels had, a few years earlier, subjected to ruthless criticism and rejected. The historical observation that the national movements in question clung to the past and fought for counterrevolution at a certain time is turned into a supra-historical, metaphysical, cause of an equally metaphysical "backwardness." In 1848 the Czechs and Southern Slavs, or at any rate their leaders and spokesmen, did side with Austria and to a lesser extent Russia, because they feared absorption by Poles, Magyars and Germans. After all, these spokesmen were often good Hegelians too. They too decided that their national minorities were "non-historic" and opted for the maintenance of the Hapsburg dynasty.

Did these political leaders speak for the future of their national groups as well as their present and their past? After all, according to the Manifesto, all the nations, including the "historic" ones were being dissolved and absorbed into a European, indeed a world-wide, industrial civilization. Were not the minorities in the Austrian Empire capable of producing political currents that looked forward as well as ones that looked back?

A mere four years later, in the Crimean war crisis, Engels himself was to argue that the independence movements of the Serbs and Romanians represented a progressive force aimed against Russian Tsarism and Pan-Slavism as well as against Turkish rule. For that matter, the mere fact that a given nation fought for freedom in 1849 was no evidence, at least for non-Hegelians, that it would always do so. The Hungarians proved this in 1867 when they "dehistoricized" themselves. In that year they accepted the role of junior partner to the Hapsburgs that Czech and Croat politicians had unsuccessfully auditioned for in 1849.

3. The "Non-Historic" Czechs

This Hegelian pronouncement was not only no use for predicting the future behavior of the nations in question. It could not even "predict" the recent past. At the beginning of July 1848, in some of the earliest articles in the *NRZ*, the paper had supported the Czech rising in Prague and poured out the usual vitriol on the Germans and the Frankfurt Assembly for their refusal to support the Czechs' fight for freedom. The "non-historic" character of the Czech national movement was not apparent then. Instead, their case was amalgamated with that of the Poles and Italians.

Many of the writers who have discussed this material, including those most hostile towards Engels, have concluded that one of the things that turned Engels against the Austrian Slavs was the refusal of the Czech Pan-Slavist František Palacký to link the fate of the Czech national movement with that of the German revolution. Palacký, in the name of the Czech nation, refused the offer of the Frankfurt Assembly to seat him as a delegate.

Palacký defended his refusal in part on the grounds that the Czech nation had never considered itself part of the German Confederation. The Czech lands were part of the Holy Roman Empire and later of the German Confederation as a result of a purely dynastic arrangement between princes "of which the Czech nation and the Czech Estates, hardly wished to know and which they hardly noticed."[7] The bulk of this letter of refusal, however, concentrates on the Frankfurt Assembly's hostility to the Hapsburgs. In it

"Non-historic Peoples"

Palacký expresses his firm belief that only the Austrian Empire not a united Germany could defend Europe from the Russian threat. And then he explained to the Assembly why, as a Czech nationalist he was opposed to a united Germany.

> ... those who ask that Austria (and with it Bohemia) should unite on national lines with the German empire, demand its suicide, which is morally and politically meaningless; on the contrary, it would be much more meaningful to demand that Germany should unite with Austria, that is, that it should accede to the Austrian state under the conditions above mentioned.[8]

The conditions referred to are various liberalizing measures which Palacký recommends in place of the demand for independent republics of the subject peoples. Palacký bases his rejection of republicanism, or even a German constitutional monarchy, explicitly on the inability of the Austrian Slavs to maintain viable independent states especially when faced with German and Magyar competition. Here was a Slav nationalist arguing that the Austrian Slavs were "non-historic" peoples before Engels did. One would certainly expect Engels to come down hard on such a defense of the Hapsburg Monarchy and opposition to republicanism.

Only he didn't. He apologized for the decision of the Czechs, that is, of Palacký:

> And the Germans, after this,[the suppression of the Prague uprising] demand that the Czechs should trust them?
> Are the Czechs to be blamed for not wanting to join a nation that oppresses and maltreats other nations, while liberating itself?
> Are they to be blamed for not wanting to send their representatives to our wretched, faint-hearted "National Assembly" at Frankfurt, which is afraid of its own sovereignty?

> Are the Czechs to be blamed for dissociating themselves from the impotent Austrian Government,* which is in such a perplexed and helpless state that it seems to exist only in order to register the disintegration of Austria, which it is unable to prevent, or at least to give it an orderly course? A Government which is even too weak to save Prague from the guns and soldiers of a Windischgrätz?

Engels then proceeded to place the blame for the anticipated hostility of the Czechs towards the revolution squarely on the Germans and the Frankfurt Assembly:

> But it is the gallant Czechs themselves who are most of all to be pitied. Whether they win or are defeated, their doom is sealed. They have been driven into the arms of the Russians by 400 years of German oppression, which is being continued now in the street fighting waged in Prague. In the great struggle between Western and Eastern Europe, which may begin very soon, perhaps in a few weeks, the Czechs are placed by an unhappy fate on the side of the counterrevolution. The revolution will triumph and the Czechs will be the first to be crushed by it.
>
> The Germans once again bear the responsibility for the ruin of the Czech people, for it is the Germans who have betrayed them to Russia.[9]

---

* Engels refers here to the liberal cabinet that briefly held office as a result of the popular movement in Vienna. Like the Frankfurt Assembly, it accomplished nothing except to allow the Imperial Court time to regroup while the popular movement was beguiled by its debates and ultimately disillusioned by its inaction. Palacký repudiated this liberal administration's claims in favor of a liberalized monarchy.

Engels is describing here the reactionary consequences for the Czech movement of defeat not some metaphysical fate of "non-historic" nations and is blaming the German democrats for these consequences, not the Czechs. It could be argued that the consequences of the defeat of the revolution were reactionary all around. Reaction was strengthened in France, Germany, England and Hungary as well as among the Slavs. Engels, however, is not thinking, in this article or in any of the others he wrote in the *NRZ*, about the consequences of the defeat of the revolution. He is not speculating on the post-revolutionary future; he is concerned about the immediate prospect of a revolutionary war against Russia. He expected it "in a few weeks." In this crisis the Frankfurt Assembly had lost another potential ally.

4. "Counterrevolutionary Peoples"

What did provoke Engels to his neo-Hegelian outburst was the invasion of Hungary by the Croat nationalist leader Baron Jellachich. Jellachich was the only leader of a nationalist movement in 1848 who continued to serve as an army commander of one of the members of the Holy Alliance—there were plenty who were cashiered or resigned their commission to serve the revolution. What was worse the Croat mercenaries collaborated with the Austrians in the suppression of Italy and with the Russians in the defeat of the Hungarian revolution.

Historians are divided over the question of whether, and to what degree, the Hungarian Prime Minister, Count Batthyány, and his protégé, the future revolutionary leader Kossuth, attempted to compromise with the Croat demands.[10] There is no question of the Magyar contempt for the Slav populations they ruled over and there is no question that "Magyarization," that is the policy of insisting on Hungarian as the official language to be used in all public affairs, was a central demand of the liberals and especially of Kossuth. Some of the radicals to the left of Kossuth were even more adamant in their insistence on a monolingual, unified republic.[11]

On the other hand, the concessions made by the Hungarian radicals to local autonomy in language, deficient as they appear to us after a century and a half of conflict, armed and unarmed, over such questions, went much farther than anything the Hapsburg monarchy proposed let alone implemented. As the situation became critical, serious attempts were made to compromise the issue especially with the Croats. Jellachich rejected all such attempts.

There is very little dispute over the role played by Jellachich. His loyalty was to his Emperor and King first and only then to the cause of Croat nationalism. Perhaps it might be more fair to say that Jellachich saw no distinction between the two. In any case, all the evidence indicates that whatever compromises the Hungarian liberals and revolutionaries had been willing to make they would have been unacceptable to this principled defender of absolute monarchy. Under his leadership, Croat mercenaries became the Emperor's hangmen not only in Hungary, Vienna and Prague but also in Italy. At one point, Jellachich allowed his troops to be used to crush the Italians even when they were needed in Hungary where Croat national interests were directly involved. In his own way Jellachich was as principled an "internationalist" as Marx and Engels. He too was willing to subordinate immediate national interests to a greater cause. In his case the cause was that of counterrevolution.

This did not stop Jellachich and his defenders from using words like "freedom," and "the rights of the people." In 1848 all sides used that language. What Jellachich meant by those slogans, however, was the preservation or restoration of old, sometimes mythical, rights and privileges of the "nation" considered as an estate of the Empire. That was what Palacký meant also as he spelled out in some detail. It was what the Hungarian liberal nobility had aimed at, too, in the beginning. It was not the modern concept of the nation as an independent, constitutional state with well defined rights of all citizens under the law; it was not the kind of national freedom the Hungarians ended up fighting for. In Hungary, as elsewhere, that kind of freedom required an internal struggle against outmoded privileges within the national group. Within those national groups that Engels chose to describe as "non-historic" that struggle did not take place, or took place only sporadically. The road the Hungarian revolutionaries chose forced out the Esterházys. The Croatian national movement made Jellachich its hero.

That was not, however, a foregone conclusion. There is no question of Jellachich's popularity among the Croatians. Nevertheless, his leadership of the national movement was the result of something very much like a coup d'etat. In the beginning, Croatian nationalism in 1848 looked like every other national movement. There was the initial enthusiasm when everything looked possible. The Croatian assemblies were as liberal in their proposals as were their German and Magyar counterparts. Croatia's national assembly passed the usual resolutions calling for freedom of the press, the use of the "Illyrian" tongue as an official language, and the abolition of feudal obligations.[12] Some Croatian nationalists were also for some sort of accommodation with the Hungarians whose demands they initially endorsed.[13] And the Croatian border troops, ethnically Serb but great admirers of Jellachich, initially offered their support to the Hungarians.[14]

It was Jellachich, a national hero in a country where military service was a major industry, who campaigned to turn the Croatian national movement into one hostile to Magyar independence. The same assembly that voted the liberal measures also voted to make Jellachich Ban, the traditional military commander of the Croat nation. When the Emperor responded by appointing this former captain to a rank that rivaled that of Windischgrätz and Count Radetzky the two other generals of the counterrevolution, his popularity soared to such heights that he became unassailable.* Few noticed initially that the Emperor had not confirmed Jellachich as Ban, which is what the assembly had voted for, but merely elevated his rank in the Imperial army. Jellachich, himself, insisted that he would only accept the office of Ban from the Emperor and repudiated his nomination by the Croatian National Assembly as an illegal act.[15] The Croatian nationalists made no attempt to enlighten the Croatian people as to the realities of the situation. Jellachich's enormous personal popularity left him politically invulnerable. Croatian liberalism and the Croatian democracy withered on the vine and dropped off. And that meant that,

---

* This is a very condensed history. Jellachich was alternatively lauded as a hero and condemned as a traitor by the Court. His commission was awarded one day and taken back the next. In part, the attitude of the government was dependent on the shifting politics of the cabinet which was under pressure from the revolutionary movement in Vienna. But this shifting relation with Jellachich was also the result of a conscious policy of playing Hungarians off against Croats who were played off against Serbs and Romanians etc., etc. It was an old Hapsburg policy.

after the Croats had been used to defeat the Italian and Hungarian revolutions, they gained nothing.

In his dealings with the Hungarians Jellachich made one demand. They had to accept the proposals of the Emperor. These proposals meant the end of Hungarian independence and even the degree of autonomy that had existed up until then.

Engels gives no indication that he knew any of this. Neither he nor Marx had paid much attention to the Hungarians let alone the Croats, Serbs, Romanians, etc., prior to 1848. They knew something about Poland and Engels was to study the history and languages of Eastern Europe later, but in 1848 they were both learning on the job. It is something that is easy to overlook if Engels flat-footed statements are taken at face value by his defenders or his opponents.

But what Engels did know about the Croatian movement and that of the other non-Magyar peoples, or at any rate soon found out, should have been enough to have caused him to question the "historic people" formulation.

We have already mentioned one *NRZ* article that reported on the disaffection in the ranks of Jellachich's forces. There were others. I initially intended to do a statistical breakdown of Engels' articles in 1848-9 on the Hungarian revolution. By my count there are 76. About three-quarters of the way through I had found two which did not mention disaffection among the national minorities (including South Slavs) subject to the Hapsburgs. Nor was sympathy for the Hungarian Revolution lacking. What is more, Engels' reports (which are sometimes long excerpts from other papers or official dispatches) place great weight on this political warfare as a factor in the Hungarians' success. It should be kept in mind that, until the Russians intervened in April, just before the suppression of the *NRZ*, the Hungarians even though they were numerically inferior had driven back the Imperial forces.

Just one citation of many that could be quoted gives some indication of the kind of material that is in these articles:

> Everywhere the peasants and Jews have been driven into the arms of the Magyars by the Windischgrätz-Stadion tyranny. The Slovak peasants, who are indebted to

Kossuth for freeing them from feudal burdens, and upon whom Windischgrätz wanted to reimpose the former compulsory labor are enthusiastic supporters of the Magyars, ..."[16]

You have to imagine this multiplied more than 76 times to get the feel of these articles. One reason they are not more widely known is that this kind of observation is buried in articles that are otherwise concerned with military details designed to discredit the reports of the establishment press. The latter continually predicted the imminent collapse of the Hungarian government. Engels' military dispatches on "The War in Hungary" were of considerable polemical importance in combating this pro-Austrian tub-thumping in 1849 but the consequence is that the modern reader easily overlooks Engels' discussion of revolutionary political warfare.

Most modern historians do agree that the revolutionary program of the Hungarian government under Kossuth did have the effect of mobilizing the Magyar peasantry.[17] However, Engels's claims as to the effect on the non-Magyar peasantry has much less support. But there is evidence that there was some.[18] In any case, Engels was pointing to a growing tendency in what he expected to be a continuing revolution.

Whatever the truth of the matter, it is Engels' own reports that raise the following question. How did he square his accounts of political awakening among the non-Magyar peoples, and the sympathy he claimed they showed for the revolution of their traditional Magyar enemy, with his thesis that they were "non-historic" peoples? The claim was not just that the geographical dispersion, small numbers, and level of economic development of the Southern Slavs, Czechs, Romanians, etc., made it impossible for them to form stable nation states. That is a question of fact and is still open today. Engels' "non-historicity" thesis, however, required that this historical fact also condemn these ethnic groups to be tools in the hands of reaction. And his own articles refute that thesis. Engels modified his position in practice as we shall see in the next chapter, but he never repudiated the thesis explicitly.

The "non-historicity" of the South Slavs is an anomaly in Engels writings in 1848. In taking over this formula from Hegel, Engels contradicted everything else he and Marx were saying. In part, this was a cry of outrage against the behavior of nationalist demagogues like Jellachich but it was also a reaction to a kind of nationalism that was just beginning to emerge. A nationalism directed against the democratic and liberal demands of 1848. Some of Engels worst rhetorical and theoretical excesses as well as some of his clearest statements on the relation between nationalism, national liberation and revolutionary democracy were provoked by one early expression of this kind of nationalism in particular.

5. Bakunin's 'Völkisch' Nationalism

The occasion of Engels' two part article in the *NRZ* on "Democratic Pan-Slavism"[19] was the publication of "An Appeal to the Slavs by a Russian Patriot, Michael Bakunin, a Delegate to the Prague Congress." In this pamphlet Bakunin attempted to salvage the reputation of the democratic party in the Slavic speaking countries. It was not an easy job.

The Slavic Congress itself was dispersed by a Hapsburg army largely composed of Slav troops. This was after the congress had adopted a statement opposing independence, self-determination and republicanism and affirmed its support for a (reformed) Hapsburg monarchy. The loyalty of the Croatians to the Emperor and their brutal behavior in Italy and, since September, in Hungary had by the beginning of 1849 become notorious. By this time, the cause of the Austrian Slavs was not one that aroused much sympathy among democrats and liberals.

What was worse, Bakunin's own pan-Slavic sympathies had surfaced at the Prague Congress. According to the largely sympathetic Soviet editor of his works, I. M. Steklov, Bakunin and the circle of friends he had recruited at the Prague Congress had originally intended to attend a congress of "Young Slavs" in Agram (Zagreb) in September of 1848. When Bakunin was arrested a letter was found in his possession from Ludwig Shtur, a Slovenian pan-Slavist and opponent of Hungarian independence. The letter reproached Bakunin for not showing up in Agram as he had promised.[20] There is no indication that anyone knew anything at the time of Bakunin's links with the Southern Slav nationalists whose leader was so heavily involved in the suppression of the Hungarian,

Austrian and Italian revolutions. But Bakunin had not been shy about advocating pan-Slavism at the Prague Congress.

Bakunin authored three resolutions at Prague. "The Principles of a New Slavic Polity," "Principles of the Slavic Federation," and "Internal Relations of the Slavic Peoples."[21] What he outlined in as clear a form as had yet appeared was what was to become known later as a "völkisch" nationalism. That is he proposed a national identity based not on the equality of citizens in a more or less homogeneous linguistic and economic unit but on membership in a more or less mythical "volk." Such an entity had to be bound together then as now by hatred of the enemy. In Bakunin's case the enemy was the German and to a lesser extent the Magyar.

That race was the cement and not a common language or culture is apparent in an anecdote concerning Bakunin reported by a German left democrat, Alfred Meissner. In an article in the *Kölnische Zeitung* Meissner gave an account of a discussion with a "Russian émigré" while traveling to Prague. In his memoirs published later he identified his fellow traveler as Bakunin.[22]

Meissner was treated by Bakunin to a full blast of his racist Pan-Slavism. This kind of race-based nationalism was relatively new and Meissner, apparently not quite understanding what was really involved, replied as a democrat of 1848 might be expected to reply. He pointed out that the Slavs did not have a common language, one of the principle distinguishing characteristics of a "nation" as most liberals and democrats of 1848 understood the concept. Bakunin replied that all Slavs understood the phrase "Zarahbte niemce"; down with the Germans.

In this version of "völkisch" nationalism, as in the later models, racial solidarity against the outsider logically required the suppression of class struggle within the Slavic "tribes" as Bakunin calls them. At one point in his draft resolutions for the congress Bakunin took up the case of the Ukrainian jacquerie of 1846. This is the passage in which Bakunin addresses the "blind Tsar" whose claims to represent the Slav people is repudiated. It is interesting that the Tsar should even be considered for this role by a self confessed "democrat" given the political climate at the time.

In part, this was a question because there were pro-Tsarist pan-Slavists at the congress but as later events were to indicate, Bakunin was also debating his own pro-Tsarist tendency. At Prague, however, he raises this possibility only to refute it. The only real salvation for the Slavs is the peasant revolt conceived as a destructive assault on all order and civilization.

But for participants at the Congress, especially the Poles, the most recent example of such an uprising was the 1846 assault provoked by Metternich. Bakunin, for some reason which is unclear, places the blame for this action on the Tsar rather than the Hapsburg Emperor. In Bakunin's view the uprising was wrong because it was directed against freedom loving Slavs.

> Agreed, the peasant uprisings in Galicia were bad because at your [the Tsar's] instigation they were turned against a democratically-minded gentry sympathetic to freedom.[23]

This was the same Polish gentry so virulently condemned by Marx and Engels because their subordination of the national movement to their class interest amounted to a betrayal of the Polish national cause.

But there was no room in Bakunin's *Appeal* for an idea like "the main enemy is at home" because his "revolution" was a revolt against modernization by "freedom-loving" Slavs not a revolution that would destroy the remnants of feudal backwardness and bring the social order of the Slavic speaking peoples closer to that of the "decadent West."

Bakunin's scheme for a Slav federation was spelled out in a nine point "constitution" that centered on an all-powerful "Slavic Council." According to point nine:

> No individual Slavic tribe may form an alliance with any foreign people; that right belongs exclusively to the Council; nor may any individual tribe order Slavic armed forces into action against another people or a foreign state.[24]

This "Slavic Council" was, of course, to include the largest Slavic people, the Russians. Bakunin insisted in this version of Pan-Slavism that it would be a democratic Russia without being too clear on how the transformation from autocracy to democracy was to be achieved in the few months, or weeks, that remained before the Russian invasion of revolutionary Europe that all expected.

How would a democrat, especially a Polish democrat, be expected to respond to this kind of talk? It is not an idle question. The Prague Congress had been divided into three sections. The Northern section included the Poles and Ruthenes (Ukrainians), of whom there were sixty most of them Poles, and the Russians, of whom there were two, Bakunin and a priest of the heretical sect of Old Believers.

As we have seen the Poles tended to divide up into two political tendencies. The conservative faction sought to use the internal differences of the occupying powers to their advantage. In particular, they looked to Prussia as an ally which would be favorably disposed towards a Polish buffer state based in what was Prussian occupied Poland. The left placed its hopes in a social revolution and looked for allies among the German democrats and Hungarian revolutionaries. Polish officers were serving at that moment with the Hungarian army (without the permission of the "Slav Council.") The respective causes of the two nations were so close in the eyes of European public opinion that Engels could refer to "the Magyar-Polish ... revolutionary army." How would either left wing or right wing Poles be expected to react to the proclamation of a holy war of the "Slavs," including the Russians, against the Germans and Magyars?

The reaction of the Poles to Bakunin's pan-Slavism is probably the cause of one of those minor scandals that pepper the history of the radical movement. The Slav Congress was dispersed by counterrevolutionary troops on June 12, 1848. On July 6th the *NRZ* carried a report that a rumor was circulating among some Poles concerning Bakunin. According to the rumor the writer George Sand had evidence that Bakunin was a Russian agent. The *NRZ* invited Bakunin to reply, and printed his outraged response as well as George Sand's statement that she had no such information. On July 16th the *NRZ* printed a retraction. Later, the issue was raised again by Bakunin's supporters as ammunition against Marx during the fracas in the First International. It is in this connection that the rumor has repeatedly resurfaced. And it is often also used as an example of the notorious tendency of radicals to spread scurrilous gossip about one another. Bakunin's biographer E. H. Carr, no friend of Marx, concludes

67

that the editors of the *NRZ* in this case behaved correctly.[25] But neither Carr nor anyone else has treated this incident as anything more than a trivial personal quarrel.

What I have never found is any attempt to discover who the Poles were who were responsible for this rumor or why they were hostile enough to Bakunin to spread it. The timing would indicate that it was provoked by Bakunin's pan-Slavic stand at Prague. This was not the first time such rumors had been circulated. In 1847 Bakunin was persuaded to give a talk on Poland to Democrats in Brussels. According to Bakunin's own report the talk gave rise to some concern because in it, while full of enthusiasm for the freedom-loving Poles, he insisted on the necessity of an alliance with a (non-existent) Russian democracy.[26] Not realizing that Bakunin lived a good deal of the time in a fantasy world where all things were possible, the Poles were understandably suspicious of such a call for Slav unity.

The accusation that someone or another was in the pay of some foreign office or another was common enough. So was the inferential leap from the fact that someone took a pro-Tsarist position (or one that might be construed to be so) to the belief that the party in question was in the pay of the Tsar. Unfortunately, the politics behind the 1848 accusation against Bakunin never got through. Neither Marx nor Engels, at this time, read Russian or any other Slavic language (did George Sand?) and the deliberations of the Prague Congress were only selectively translated. When Bakunin's *Appeal* appeared six months later there was no one to see the connection; except, possibly, the Poles who had been burned by the earlier reaction to their spreading of an unsubstantiated rumor.

But in the *Appeal* we are not dealing with an isolated incident or temporary slip. There is further evidence of what Bakunin's race politics meant in practice. After his deportation to Russia and imprisonment Bakunin wrote his notorious *Confession* addressed to the Tsar. In this remarkable document he proposed that the Tsar place himself at the head of the democratic pan-Slavist movement. There is no evidence that Bakunin was induced by threat or bribe to write this manifesto. Undoubtedly, he was demoralized by the defeat of the revolution but, then, his biographer E. H. Carr demonstrates that he was pretty demoralized by the time of the Prague Congress and even more so by the time he wrote the *Appeal*.

In one section of the *Confession* Bakunin describes a conversation, perhaps imaginary, with a fellow passenger on the coach traveling to Strasbourg. The other passenger is surprised that his companion is a Russian revolutionary:

> At present all the Germans are denouncing Russia, praising the Poles, and preparing to march with them against the Russian Empire. Will you, a Russian, join them?

Bakunin replies:

> God forbid! If the Germans dare but set a foot on Slav soil, I shall become their irreconcilable enemy; I am going to Posen in order to resist with all my power this unnatural union of Poles and Germans.[27]

The *Confession* expands at some length on the need to encourage the philo-Muscovite tendency among the Poles. The Tsar could do this, according to Bakunin, by assuming the role of the protector of the Polish gentry from the wrath of the peasants they exploited. That is the Tsar should seize the opportunity presented by Austria's weakened condition and replace it as, in Engels' words, "the representative of barbarism, of reactionary stability in Europe."

What is revealing is *the continuity of ideas* behind the resolutions at Prague, the *Appeal*, the *Confession*, and the 1862 pamphlet *Pugachev, Pestel or Romanov*, in which the possibility of the Tsar putting himself at the head of the popular movement was considered seriously again.

None of this prevents people from continuing to portray Bakunin as the champion of the peasantry as opposed to the "urban" Marx who hated and distrusted them.

E. H. Carr has a particularly muddled discussion of this question.[28] It occurs almost immediately after he refers the reader to this very passage of Bakunin on the "democratically-minded" Polish gentry. Marx and Engels' 1847-8 statements on Poland, as well as the *NRZ* articles in which they emphasize and reemphasize that without an agrarian revolution the

Polish fight for independence was doomed, had been reprinted in the Russian version of the collected works. Carr refers often to this edition in other contexts but, apparently, he never bothered to check out what Engels and Marx actually wrote on the agrarian revolution in 1848.

6. Democratic Pan-Slavism

When Engels wrote his article the Pan-Slavism of the *Confession* was still in the future and remained a secret for decades after all participants in the disputes of 1848 were dead. The Prague resolutions were mostly unknown. The *Appeal* therefore came as a shock. Bakunin was known as a revolutionary. The *NRZ* articles refer to Bakunin as "our friend" and there is no hint of irony.* How to explain this article in defense of pan-Slavic nationalism at this juncture?

Engels took two different tacks. One more or less predominates in the first article and the other in the second. The first line of argument is a disaster. It goes much further than the "non-historic peoples" business. Engels attempts in this first article to counterpose his own materialist concept of nation and nationality to Bakunin's purely race-based one.

The problem is Engels was just beginning to sort through his own ideas at this time. We briefly touched on them in the earlier section which discussed the sketch in the *Manifesto* of the problem of nationality. For now, it is enough to note that Engels' thinking at this time was dominated by two propositions. The first was that the triumph of the bourgeoisie over the remnants of pre-bourgeois society was progressive, desirable, and represented the victory of civilization over barbarism. It was also the necessary prelude to the rise of a workers' movement. The second proposition was that this process required the creation of large, culturally unified states and the consequent destruction of the patchwork of small, backward remnants of medieval polities that covered central and Eastern Europe (including, especially, Germany) in 1848.

---

* Years later, Marx on at least one occasion defended Bakunin's reputation as a revolutionary and his role in the uprising in Dresden. And their meeting in 1863, after Bakunin's escape from exile, was, according to all accounts, cordial.

Engels' hostility to what must have appeared to him to be a variety of that "feudal socialism" denounced in the *Manifesto* led him to base the first part of his article on the struggle between "civilization" and "barbarism." In this first section, the question of class and even of democracy is pretty much forgotten. In one passage the argument borders on a defense of "Manifest Destiny":

> Or is it perhaps unfortunate that splendid California has been taken away from the lazy Mexicans, who could not do anything with it? That the energetic Yankees by rapid exploitation of the California gold mines will... create large cities, open up communications by steamship, construct a railway from New York to San Francisco ... ? The "independence" of a few Spanish Californians and Texans may suffer because of it ... but what does that matter, compared to such facts of world-historic significance?[29]

It would be a digression here to demonstrate why what Engels was getting at was not an early variant of what came to be called "Social Imperialism." For the same reason that the whole discussion is a digression in Engels' article. It is hard to see the relevance of the Mexican American War and John Charles Frémont's conquest of California to the fate of the revolution in central Europe in 1848. At best it is a debater's point which depends for its effect on the general sympathy felt by all democrats and liberals in 1848 for the North American republic, and an equally uncritical hostility to a Mexico dominated by the Church and the great landowners. Clearly, Engels' outrage over the glorification of a nationalist movement that was playing a cowardly and sycophantic role as the gendarme of the Holy Alliance led him to seize on any argument, however ill-thought-out, that could be used as a weapon to justify revolutionary war against these "reactionary peoples."

Unfortunately, this particular blunderbuss blew up in Engels' face and his wild statements in this article and in the revised version that appeared in the *New York Tribune*[30] have provided ammunition for anti-Marxists ever since. They were also subsequently used in a few cases to justify Social Democratic support for a colonialist policy even though Engels, as we shall see, explicitly repudiated any such conclusion from his premises (without, however, subjecting the premises themselves to a thoroughgoing reexamination.)

This theoretical disaster has completely overshadowed the second part of his article. This installment, published on February 16, is not only better journalism than the one of February 15 but is also an excellent statement of Engels' socialist internationalism that deserves to be better known.

Engels begins by repeating the gist of his "historic nations" thesis, mentioning once again the geographic and historic factors that make it impossible for "the Slavs" to form viable nations. He continues to speak of "the Slavs" even after making it explicit that he means the Austrian Slavs *not* the Poles, Russians and "possibly" the Slavs under Turkish rule, that is three-quarters of the Slavic speaking peoples. Then he proceeds to effectively repudiate the whole "historic nations" idea.

> All that, however, would still not be decisive. If at any epoch while they were oppressed the Slavs had begun a *new revolutionary history*, that by itself would have proved their viability. From that moment the revolution would have had an interest in their liberation, and the special interests of the Germans and the Magyars would have given way to the greater interest of the European revolution.[31]

The criterion is the same one Engels had used throughout 1848. A social revolution or at least a revolutionary movement is the test of a nation's viability not some metaphysical fate. But Engels forgets here that in at least one case, that of the Czechs, an Austrian Slav minority *had* begun "a new revolutionary history" in 1848. And the *NRZ* had welcomed them as members of the fraternity of revolutionary nations. Their revolution had been defeated by a combination of internal and external forces. The victory of Palacký's reactionary, pro-Hapsburg, nationalism was the consequence of this defeat not its cause as Engels had argued at the time.

"Non-historic Peoples"

In every case where Engels is called upon in 1848 to describe a real political struggle between "pure and simple" nationalism and a socially revolutionary national movement, whether that case be Hungary, Poland or Bohemia, the "historical nations" line disappears. For good reason. This idealist concept was of no use in analyzing a real movement. It appears only after the fact in cases where the democratic movement has been defeated or, as in Croatia, never really got off the ground. And then it is only a simple description of fact dressed up in Hegelian phraseology.

The "historical nations" line also disappears when Engels comes to grips with Bakunin's Pan-Slavism. He effectively counters this glorification of race by pointing to the recent history of the Germans. Again, it is the real political history that is discussed. The Germans, Engels points out, had for decades been the mercenaries used to suppress other nations fighting for their liberty. They were "unhistoric." Now it was "the Slavs" (by which he means the Croatians) who were the mercenaries. What made the difference? What turned the Germans into an "historic nation" in 1848? They had revolted against their own rulers. And in doing so they had to repudiate the kind of *völkisch* nationalism Bakunin was advocating for the Slavs:

> What would be said if the democratic party in Germany commenced its programme with the demand for the return of Alsace, Lorraine, and Belgium, which in every respect belongs to France, on the pretext that the majority there is Germanic? How ridiculous the German democrats would make themselves if they wanted to found a pan-Germanic German-Swedish-English-Dutch alliance for the "liberation" of all German-speaking countries! ... The German revolution only came into being, and the German nation only began to become something, when people had freed themselves completely from these futilities.[32]

The kind of fantasy that inspired the *Appeal to the Slavs* was appropriate only for nations which were not yet ready to fight for freedom in the real world. Engels went on to demonstrate that this kind of super-

73

patriotism often turned into its opposite. In Germany, in the 1830s and early 1840s this kind of romanticization of "German" values and the German *volk* had found its base in the *Burschenschaften,* the patriotic student societies. But their patriotism had evaporated when the question of German unity was put on the agenda by a revolution.

> ... in the long run the most pronounced counterrevolutionary frame of mind, the most ferocious hatred of Frenchmen, and the most narrow-minded national feeling, were to be found among the members of the German *Burschenschaften,* and ... later they all became traitors to the cause for which they had pretended to be enthusiastic...

The Pan-Slavism which dominated the Prague Congress and which was expressed in its most virulent form in Bakunin's resolutions and the *Appeal* was the expression of a national movement going in the opposite direction from that of the Germans.

> ... the democratic semblance among the democratic pan-Slavists [has] turned into fanatical hatred of Germans and Magyars, into indirect opposition to the restoration of Poland, and into direct adherence to the counter-revolution.[33]

Bakunin in a key passage had based the hopes of the Slav democracy on "a life-and-death struggle" by the Slavs against the Germans and the Magyars. Engels replied that the expected Russian invasion of Central Europe would almost certainly be supported by the Austrian Slavs in a war against the Polish, Magyar and German revolutions. And then:

> ... there will be a struggle, an "inexorable life-and-death struggle," against those Slavs who betray the revolution ... not in the interests of Germany, but in the interests of the revolution![34]

7. The Right of Self-determination

Engels continued to hold essentially the same views on national liberation and revolution that he held in 1848 throughout his life. And there is no evidence that Marx, who wrote much less on these questions, was aware of any difference between them on the subject.

On a number of occasions, however, Engels opened up a line of thought which, if followed through, could easily have led to a more modern view of the issue of self-determination.

In 1882, Engels wrote to Kautsky explaining why the Poles and the Irish had first to be nationalists in order to be good internationalists. The bulk of the article reiterates the stand of 1848. The viability of a nation depends on its ability to fight for its own independence rather than being used to suppress that of others. This in turn is determined by many factors, geographic and historic. Among these factors is the role played internationally by the oppressor nation.

In the course of the discussion, however, Engels makes the following argument:

> Now, it is historically impossible for a great people to even seriously discuss any internal questions as long as national independence is lacking. ... Every Polish peasant and worker who shakes off the gloom and wakes up to the common interest bumps right off into the fact of national subjugation ... Polish socialists who do not place the liberation of the country at the head of their program strike me like German socialists who refused to demand first and foremost the abolition of the Anti-Socialist Law and freedom of the press, organization and assembly. To be able to fight one must first have a footing—air, light and elbowroom.[35]

This is a note that Engels had sounded once before;[36] unfortunately, he never expanded on it or attempted to integrate it into a more rounded view of the question of self-determination. It was not until Lenin that a socialist propagandist was to make this point central to the discussion.

Still, this letter is not only Engels' finest statement on the relation of the struggle for national liberation to social revolution, it is one of the clearest statements on the subject anywhere. The argument here does *not* depend on the general role played by either the oppressor or oppressed nation historically or in the immediate struggle. The tendency of the national struggle to overlay the class struggle, to get in its way, was just as strong among, say, Croatians in 1848 as it was among Irish or Poles throughout the nineteenth century.

Whether an independent Croatia was desirable or possible in 1848-9 is beside the point as far as this argument was concerned. One could then, and should still, make the distinction between recognizing the right of self-determination, or cultural autonomy in some form or another, and advocating that a particular ethnic or linguistic group exercise this right.

To make clear what is involved we can try the following thought-experiment. Suppose in 1848 the Hungarian revolutionaries had acquiesced in the Croatian demand that they be allowed to use their own language in the Hungarian national assembly. Of course, the Hungarian government had already agreed to allow the use of Croatian in local administration (which was more than the Hapsburgs were prepared to do) and that had swayed neither Jellachich nor the Croatian National Assembly.

But consider what such a proposal could have meant as a weapon of political warfare against Jellachich's reactionary use of national demands. As Engels had stressed in his *NRZ* articles the Austrian Slavs showed considerable sympathy towards the Hungarian revolutionaries because of their agrarian program and because the split between Kossuth and the Magyar aristocracy allied with the Hapsburgs made clear what was at stake. Wouldn't the adoption of a more enlightened policy on the language question have furthered this process of disintegrating the pro-Imperial bloc?

The point of raising this possibility, of course, is not to give advice to participants in a revolution defeated a century and a half ago nor to judge them by a standard which has been constructed in the intervening period only after considerable theoretical debate and practical experience. It is, however, a useful way of illustrating what was wrong with Engels' *posing* of the question of national rights in 1848-49. The "historical peoples" slogan left him open to the accusation that he was for the forcible suppression of a people in revolt against oppression. The charge was, and is, demagogic. Neither Marx nor Engels ever argued for such a policy in 1848 or after but Engels' articles, endorsed by Marx, gave their enemies an opening.

CHAPTER 3. THE SIXTH POWER

By 1914, perhaps the best known of Marx and Engels' writings on war and its relation to revolution were the articles and pamphlets on the "Eastern Question."* While this "question" had many ramifications, it mainly concerned Tsarist Russia's imperialist designs in the Balkans and Central Asia where the disintegration of the Ottoman Empire created an opportunity. It was Russia's aggressive attempts to take advantage of the decline of the Ottomans and exploit the national revolts of the mostly Slavic and orthodox subjects of the European section of that empire that led to the Crimean War. And since that same Balkan policy of Tsarist Russia was a major factor contributing to the outbreak of World War I, these articles, suitably edited, were among the most important in creating the portrait of a fanatically anti-Tsarist Marx—a Marx eager to go to war over this "Eastern Question."

The decade of the 1850s was one between revolutionary moments. Although Marx and Engels confidently expected new revolutionary struggles to break out sooner rather than later, the Crimean War and the conflicts between the great powers in general sprang primarily from their own rivalries. Revolution appeared only as a cloud on the horizon or as a possible *result* of the conflict.

What is more, Marx and Engels had no publication of their own in which they could express their views freely as they had in the *NRZ* during the 1848 revolution. They did not even have the kind of platform they had after 1864 in the International Workingmen's Association.

Most of their writings of the time on the issues of war and peace were in the form of journalism, especially for Charles Dana's *New York*

---

* Eleanor Marx-Aveling (Marx's youngest daughter) and her husband Edward Aveling printed a collection of *NYDT* articles under the title *The Eastern Question: A Reprint of Letters written 1853-1856 dealing with the events of the Crimean War*, London, 1897. (Reprinted by Burt Franklin, New York, 1968.) The collection included articles attributed to Marx which most scholars now believe are not his. The aim of this collection was to counter the contemporary pro-Serb enthusiasm of French and British public opinion which was being whipped up by the press as part of the prowar campaign of the Entente. Since Russia by this time, as a consequence of the pre-World-War-I diplomatic game of musical chairs, was an ally of the French and British while the Ottomans had embraced the Hapsburg-Hohenzollern defenders of Western Civilization, Marx's exposé of Russia's war aims was useful ammunition against the prowar campaign in England. But it could also be used to bolster the anti-Tsarist campaign of the other side.

Daily Tribune. They were members of Dana's stable of "European correspondents." As the revolutionary ferment of 1848 receded into the past, there was increasing friction between Dana who wanted "objective" reporting and Marx and Engels who, as their correspondence indicates, found it a strain to tone down their political views. In some cases, the articles were edited to the point of outright misrepresentation.[1] Marx, in particular, regarded these writings as "hack work" which served to keep his family alive. That did not mean that he wrote things he did not believe or that he took this political platform lightly. It did mean that the articles were written with an eye to what Dana would accept and that he and Engels were not free to speak completely in their own voice. They were not writing for a revolutionary paper whose tone and policy they determined. The *New York Daily Tribune* was not the *Neue Rheinische Zeitung*.

Given these circumstances, it is obvious that Marx and Engels own views cannot be ascertained simply by quoting passages from the articles in the *NYDT* and prefacing them with "as Marx wrote." In these articles what Marx wrote cannot always be distinguished from what Charles Dana or an unknown copy editor wrote. The articles have to be supplemented by Marx and Engels' correspondence. Even here, while the two could freely state their views in their private letters as they often could not in the *NYDT*, those views were not expressed in rounded or detailed form and points of agreement were often assumed rather than stated.

Despite all this, the articles in the *NYDT* are clear enough. When Potresov or other prowar socialists traced their views back to Marx and Engels in this period, they were simply ignoring the record. The prowar socialists of 1914-1918 simply projected their politics back in time and foisted them off on Marx. Lenin, like most historians *without* a pro- or anti-Marxist axe to grind, was simply taken in.

1. Marx's "Russophobia"

Marx and Engels did not consider the Crimean War to be a conflict between two equally reactionary powers. They clearly looked forward to a Russian defeat which they believed, rightly as it turned out, would have revolutionary consequences inside Russia. The defeat of the revolutionary movements of 1848 had created a vacuum which, in their view, was inevitably filled by Tsarist Russia using panslavism as its political weapon.

As the first article on the subject of the impending war put it:

> Let Russia get possession of Turkey and her strength is increased nearly by half, and she becomes superior to all the rest of Europe put together. ... The maintenance of Turkish independence ... is a matter of the highest moment.[2]

Engels, who wrote this article although Marx's name was signed, concluded "In this instance the interests of the revolutionary democracy and of England go hand in hand."

This is just one of several articles in which Marx and Engels denounce the passivity and cowardice of the British government in the face of Russian "aggression." Marx, in particular, devoted two political pamphlets[3] to exposing what he was convinced was the betrayal of British national interests by several British administrations. Marx's anti-Russian sentiments are considered extreme and it is usual to treat them as a symptom of "eccentricity." His conviction, for example, that Henry John Temple, Lord Palmerston, had built a popular following by pandering to popular chauvinism while, in fact, pursuing a pro-Russian policy, is generally regarded as a personal crochet. The East German editors of Marx's works and other Communist scholars basically avoided discussing this question.[4] They apparently found it somewhat embarrassing that Marx's anti-Russian politics are treated as extreme even by bourgeois critics.

In several *NYDT* articles, the English working class is held up as the force that will carry out the anti-Tsarist policy that the bourgeoisie has abandoned. If you simply take these quotes and string them together you get a picture of Marx as a war-mongering monomaniac. At least one authority has done this. In *The Russian Menace*, a collection of Marx and Engels' writings on Russia including *NYDT* articles edited by Paul W. Blackstock and Bert F. Hoselitz,[5] this is the Marx presented.

In fact, Marx's analysis of the diplomatic maneuvering behind the war is much more complicated than this. For one thing, the French Empire of Louis Bonaparte was England's main coalition partner when war finally did break out and it was obvious from the beginning that the lines would be drawn that way. Marx and Engels were notorious for their hostility to Bonaparte. For another, they were not ignorant of the real character of the Turkish empire. War would facilitate social revolution on that side too.

A defeat for Tsarism was desirable. Marx and Engels "wished for its defeat" to use one of the formulas that Lenin used later when pressed to define his slogan of "revolutionary defeatism."[6] In the passage quoted above, Engels seems to be arguing that England would be doing the revolution's work and this theme was repeated by both Marx and Engels in their articles. But they *did not* see the anti-Tsarist coalition as their side in this war.

They supported what Engels called the "sixth power"—that is, the revolution. Despite their obvious anti-Tsarist tilt, they thought of themselves as being on the side of this "sixth power." They did not, however, present this line of thought as a startling breakthrough. It was certainly not a "theory." The criterion that determined their attitude, had they expressed it in a few words, was "what outcome (which might be the collapse of both sides with no clear-cut victory or defeat for either) will improve the chances of revolution." For them the criterion was not "which side is more progressive." And they would have been stunned to have been told they had to choose between two reactionary forces.

Since they were revolutionaries and had been revolutionaries for several years, this was all perfectly natural. It was so natural that they found no need to proclaim it as a discovery. It is the notion that revolutionaries should enroll themselves as auxiliaries in one or the other reactionary army that they would have thought needed explaining. When a couple of ex-revolutionaries did just that Marx denounced them—in *NYDT* articles that aren't usually included in the anthologies.[7]

It should be added that one of the things that helps to confuse the issue is that Marx and Engels had no occasion to issue any official statement of policy on the Crimean War. Even in their private letters there is no statement of position as such. Of course, it is possible that such a statement might have been made in letters that are no longer extant. As far as we can tell, however, in the 1850s they were writing as observers. In 1870-71 Marx and Engels had a platform and it is much easier to make the distinction between their personal views, opinions and speculations on the one hand, and the official policy they advocated for a workers' organization on the other. Of course, that does not mean such a distinction is always made.

As we will see later, just because Marx and Engels thought a Prussian victory in 1870 would have progressive consequences they did not therefore urge that the working class support Prussia. Quite the contrary. In the case of the Crimean War also, an objective evaluation of the conflict and its possible outcomes was not the same thing as a statement of position.

2. First Impressions

To begin with, Marx, at least, consciously abstained from any judgement. In a letter to Engels of March 10, 1853, at the beginning of the diplomatic crisis, he *apparently* regarded the contest with indifference.[8] The qualifier is necessary because what Marx is actually discussing is not the impending war so much as the problem of getting up articles for the *NYDT*. What Dana was interested in was the military aspect of the conflict. Marx tells Engels, whom he is nominating to write on this topic, that he will have to write on "haute politique," that is, the political maneuvering of the Powers not *his* political views. And, in fact, the analysis of this "haute politique" did provide much of the content of the articles sent in. It is hard to read these articles without getting the feeling of a lot of journalistic "color" in the form of geographical, historical and military commentary with revolutionary politics introduced when and where possible.

Marx goes on to say that this "high politics" concerns "the detestable Eastern Question," which "is primarily military and geographical, hence outside my °département°." That is, it is Engels' field. This paragraph winds up: "What is to become of the Turkish Empire is something I have no care about. I cannot therefore present a general perspective." Marx's advice to Engels is "to skirt the °question° as such in favor of its military, geographical and historical aspects ... ."

Part of the problem here is in deciding to what extent Marx is motivated by disinterest in the politics of the conflict (politics in *his* sense) and to what extent by the difficulty of adequately presenting his views in the alien and unfamiliar milieu of American bourgeois journalism. Nevertheless, there is no hint in this letter that Marx is concerned with "the Russian Menace to Europe." There is one vague remark that foreshadows his own attitude in the letter. "Should there be a general hullabaloo, Turkey will compel England to come in on the revolutionary side, an Anglo-Russian clash being inevitable in such a case."

3. The Revolutionary Side

What was the revolutionary side? The first article on the question by "the firm" of Marx and Engels[9] appeared on April 7, 1853 and began by making the observation that whenever the threat of revolution receded in Europe the "Eastern Question" thrust itself into the foreground. (This article is not included in the Blackstock and Hoselitz collection.)

Why? Why should the question: "What shall we do with Turkey?" have dominated the diplomacy of the Powers? In Engels' view, for it was he who wrote this section, the French Revolution taught the European governments one lesson. All their diplomacy had to focus on the maintenance of the *status quo*. Maintaining things as they happened to be by chance was the only alternative to revolution. As Engels put it:

> Napoleon could dispose of a whole continent at a moment's notice; aye, and dispose of it, too, in a manner that showed both genius and fixedness of purpose; the entire "collective wisdom" of European legitimacy, assembled in Congress at Vienna, took a couple of years to do the same job, got at loggerheads over it, made a very sad mess, indeed, of it, and found it such a dreadful bore that ever since they have had enough of it, and have never tried their hands at parceling out Europe.

Turkey, however, was "the living sore of European legitimacy." A polyglot empire of mostly Christian subject peoples ruled over by an Islamic minority, European Turkey was in a permanent state of decline. Maintaining the status quo there was in Engels' pungent phrase like trying "to keep up the precise degree of putridity into which the carcass of a dead horse has passed at a given time, ..."

In such a situation, the Orthodox Tsar of Russia appeared as the natural protector of the South Slavic population whose language was similar to Russian and most of whom adhered to the Orthodox faith. Engels, given his previous articles on the subject of panslavism, some of the most virulent of which had appeared in this same publication less than a year earlier,[10] might have been expected to veer off here into a denunciation of Tsarism and panslavism. There is plenty of that especially in later articles but not so much here. Instead he strikes a very different note which has largely been ignored by Marxologists and which was to become increasingly important in Engels' thinking. The political point made in this article is that to the extent the "Graeco-Slavonian population" becomes independent of Turkish rule it *also* tends "by and by [to] give birth to an anti-Russian progressive party." *

The specific example which Engels gives is that of the liberal party in quasi-independent Serbia headed by Iliya Garašanin. Party in this article, of course, is used in Marx and Engels' usual sense—that is, a political tendency, not necessarily an organization or electoral machine. According to the notes in *MECW*,[11] Garašanin was a mild reformer whose anti-Tsarism took the form of a pro-Anglo-French "tilt." His principle revolutionary blow in defense of independence was to get himself fired as Foreign Minister. It is not important for our subject to determine whether

---

* Engels had decided somewhat earlier that, in view of the importance of Russia as the gendarme of reaction and its influence among the Slavic-speaking peoples, "one of us should be acquainted with the languages, the history, the literature and the details of the social institutions of these nations ... ." (Engels to Marx, March 18, 1852. *MEW* 28:40.) This implies that the articles of Engels and the coverage of the South Slav question in the *NRZ* was *not* based on a thorough study of the matter. Indeed, Engels goes on to complain, referring to Bakunin's 1849 pamphlet, that "Actually, Bakunin has become something only because no one knew Russian."

There is no indication in Engels or Marx, at least in what we have, that they consciously changed their views on the viability of national movements among the Slavic peoples. Engels in this instance may not have been aware of any change. Perhaps, he simply felt he had learned more. In any case, as already noted, Engels had already left open the *possibility* of a genuine liberation movement on the part of the Slavs. In this sense, his line on the independence movement of the South Slavs in the Crimean War was a development of a line of thought he had already stated.

Engels' estimation of Garašanin was warranted or not. What is important is that the political side Engels supports in the Crimean conflict is that of the "Graeco-Slavonian" subjects of the Ottoman Empire. Their independence movement is inherently—"by and by"—anti-Tsarist as well as anti-Turkish. Engels also mentions the Wallachians and Moldavians—that is, the present-day Romanians—as an example of a people whose "semi-detachment" from Turkey led them in a democratic and anti-Tsarist direction. The "revolutionary side" in this article is the side of the "unhistoric peoples" who are in the process of becoming "historic peoples" by asserting their independence.

In this very first article on the Crimean War, Marx and Engels underline the argument that will characterize the whole series. All the powers, not just Russia, feared revolution. They all sought to maintain in so far as possible the decaying state structures they had cobbled together in 1815. Any movement, in any of the polyglot empires, by any of the oppressed nationalities, threatened them all.

4. The Peace Party in England

There is no doubt of the prowar "feel" of many of the *NYDT* articles on the Crimean War. One of the major themes in the series is the exposé of British military incompetence and the official policy of what we today would term "appeasement" of Tsarist Russia. What is more the articles are full of contempt not only for the administration but also for the "peace party."

This critical attitude to the peace party, in fact, pre-dated the crisis of 1853. It flowed from Marx and Engels' view of the class line up of the British political parties.

In an August 25, 1852 article on "The Chartists"[12] Marx tied the foreign policy of the Manchester Free Traders to their general hostility to the cost of government, whose commanding heights were dominated by their clerical and aristocratic opponents. A large standing army and national wars were linked in this article with royalty, the House of Lords, and a State Church. They all cost money and represented a tax on the "productive classes." From the point of view of the industrial bourgeoisie, England could exploit foreign nations more cheaply when she was at peace with them.

In this article, Marx was discussing the possibility of war arising out of the conflicts between Britain and Bonapartist France. War with Russia isn't the issue here, but the politics of the peace party exhibited the same contradiction that was to show up during the Crimean War. It was the liberal, anti-aristocratic party that counseled moderation and appeasement of a foreign despot even more strongly than their opponents who were in the government.

> It would be a great mistake to suppose that the peace doctrine of the Manchester School has a deep philosophical bearing. It only means that the feudal method of warfare shall be supplanted by the commercial one—cannons by capital. The Peace-Society yesterday held a meeting at Manchester, where it was almost unanimously declared, that Louis Napoleon could not be supposed as intending anything against the safety of England, *if the press would but discontinue its odious censures on his Government, and become mute!* [13]

For Marx the British government's floundering policy in the dispute between Turkey and Russia was a result of its being pulled in several different directions at once. On the one hand, the dismemberment of Turkey at Russia's hands not only threatened the status quo and the balance of power, it directly threatened England's interests in the Mediterranean and, ultimately, India. On the other hand, a general war would have all sorts of unpredictable consequences the *least* desirable of which would be the collapse of Russia as the guardian of order. England had counted on Russia to play that role since the French Revolution. Russian despotism on the continent was what made possible the "enlightened" pacifism of the Manchester School.

5. The Russian Menace

Given this perspective, Marx and Engels looked forward to a clash between Russia and England; for the same reason that the British bourgeoisie and aristocracy feared it.

Engels article "The Real Issue in Turkey,"[14] the second he sent in on the subject, began with a sweeping geopolitical survey of Russia as a great power and demonstrated the inevitability of its challenge to England's vital interests in the area. It is only at the end of the article that Engels tips his hand and reveals *his* interest in this conflict.

> Russia was the great, conquering nation until 1789 when a new antagonist appeared.
> We mean the European Revolution, the explosive force of democratic ideas and man's native thirst for freedom. Since that epoch there have been in reality but two powers on the continent of Europe—Russia and Absolutism, the Revolution and Democracy.

For *that reason* a Russian victory would be a calamity. For *that reason* "the maintenance of Turkish independence, or in the case of a possible dissolution of the Ottoman Empire, the arrest of the Russian scheme of annexation is a matter of the highest moment."

Engels concluded with the assertion that "in this instance" the interests of England and the revolutionary Democracy went hand in hand.

The reluctance of either the British governing party or its bourgeois opponents to defend their own interests meant that the country gradually became drawn into a war it could not prosecute successfully and the incompetence of the British civilian and military authorities in the administration of the war effort became a European scandal. To this day, it is the one thing for which the Crimean War is remembered.

Engels and Marx were as scathing in their attacks as anyone else but for them it demonstrated the impossibility of defending "European civilization" against barbarism by relying on the defenders of Order *because the men of Order themselves relied on that barbarism.*

> As for the British aristocracy, represented by the Coalition Ministry, they would, if need be, sacrifice the national English interests to their particular class interests, and permit the consolidation of a juvenile despotism in the East in the hopes of finding a support

for their valetudinarian oligarchy in the West. As to Louis Napoleon he is hesitating. All his predilections are on the side of the Autocrat, whose system of governing he has introduced into France, and all his antipathies are against England, whose parliamentary system he has destroyed there. ... On the other hand he is quite sure of the feelings of the Holy Alliance with regard to the "parvenu Khan."[15]

A new note is introduced in July of 1853 by Marx.[16] If the ruling classes are completely hopeless, then the working class will have to defend the common interests of England and the revolutionary Democracy. On July 7, the Manchester peace party held a rally in support of the foreign policy of the Aberdeen government. Marx notes that Queen Victoria was, coincidentally, entertaining members of the Russian royal family in the same week. Ernest Jones the Chartist leader who was organizing in the area at the time appeared at the meeting and proposed an amendment. According to Marx the amendment pledged the people to war and declared that before liberty was established peace was a crime. Marx reports that there was a furious debate but that Jones' amendment carried "by an immense majority." Marx makes no further comment on this resolution. Is he pledging *himself* to a prowar policy? We shall see later that Marx actually condemned those who did so. To anticipate that discussion, it has to be noted that what Jones proposed was an *antigovernment* resolution. It was not a motion of support for the government's policy but a condemnation of it. Marx and Engels were to emphasize more and more that "while an enlightened English aristocracy and bourgeoisie lies prostrate before the barbarian autocrat, the English proletariat alone protests against the impotency and degradation of the ruling classes."

What policy were Marx and Engels urging on the British government? Engels spelled it out as clearly as could be expected in the context of an "objective" newspaper article.

It begins with the head "What is to become of Turkey in Europe?"[17] The maintenance of the status quo—the continued Turkish rule over oppressed Christian Slavs—could have no other outcome than the growth of Tsarist political influence according to Engels. Turkey's power over its European possessions, therefore, had to be broken and a free and independent state of the Slav Christians had to be erected on its ruins. The Powers could not support such a policy. Hence, "the solution of the Turkish problem is reserved, with that of other great problems, to the European Revolution." At this point Engels still proclaims that England has to support this policy in its own interest but increasingly the emphasis is on the inability of an England, or a Europe, governed by the then ruling classes to oppose Tsarist absolutism.

What Marx and Engels were both proposing was what later came to be called a "transitional demand." The proposal to support an independent Slav state as against both the collapsing Ottoman Empire and the aggressive Tsarist one did not *directly* challenge the ruling classes in England. Indeed, it was consistent with their own ideology, propaganda and material interests. In fact, however, as Marx and Engels increasingly emphasized, these classes were no longer able to act effectively in their own interests or in defense of their own ostensible ideals. They could no longer defend the national interest. It was only the working class, the only real opposition party, that could actively pursue a progressive policy.

Marx crossed the t's and dotted the i's in a passage that sticks out like a sore thumb in an otherwise "objective" article.[18] He begins by ridiculing the anti-Russian monomaniac and conspiracy theorist David Urquhart:

> "There is no alternative. Either the laws of England have to be exercised in their penal rigour upon the persons of the four traitors,"(Aberdeen, Clarendon, Palmerston, and Russell), "or the Tsar of Russia commands the world." Such a declamation as this uttered in *The Morning Advertiser*, by D. Urquhart, is good for nothing. Who is to judge the four traitors? Parliament. Who forms that Parliament? The representatives of the Stockjobbers, the Millocrats, and the Aristocrats. And what foreign policy do these representatives represent? That of the *paix partout et toujours*. And who execute their ideas of foreign policy? The identical four men to be condemned by them as traitors, according to the simple-minded *Morning Advertiser*."

Marx's conclusion is:

> One thing must be evident at least, that it is the Stockjobbers, and the Peacemongering Bourgeoisie, represented in the Government by the Oligarchy, who surrender Europe to Russia, and that in order to resist the encroachment of the Tsar, we must, above all, overthrow the inglorious Empire of those mean, cringing and infamous adorers of the *veau d'or*.

What would Marx and Engels have done if the British ruling classes, pressed to the wall, *had* pursued the policy the two revolutionaries advocated? What if they had gone to war to defend an independent Slav state? Would Marx and Engels have supported that effort? And how? It is difficult to answer the question because *that* war never happened. One major reason was that Russia too feared a general European war and its unforeseeable consequences. The Russians too pulled their punches. In the war that did happen Marx and Engels were hostile to both sides.

When war did come both sides soon were bogged down in a series of marches and counter-marches, feints and counter attacks which were no less bloody for being meaningless and indecisive. As Engels noted "Napoleon the Great, the 'butcher' of so many millions of men, was a model of humanity in his bold, decisive, home-striking way of warfare, compared to the hesitating 'statesmen-like' directors of this Russian war ...."[19]

6. Two Ex-Revolutionaries

On at least two occasions Marx took the opportunity to condemn revolutionaries of the 1848 generation who took a position of support for the anti-Tsarist coalition similar to the one later historians have attributed to Marx and Engels themselves.

The first case was that of Louis Kossuth, the leader of the Hungarian revolutionary party in 1848. Kossuth, like other émigré revolutionaries of the 1848 generation, including Marx and Engels, looked for a way to use this crisis to advance his cause. In Kossuth's case this cause was not a European revolution but the narrower one of Hungarian independence. Kossuth, according to Marx's report,[20] suggested that Hungary ally itself with Russia if England supported Austria. Austria, was of course, Hungary's immediate enemy and, in Kossuth's narrow view, that justified his support even of Russian despotism as against liberty. It was Kossuth, it must be emphasized, who posed the question this way. It was he who was saying that in the interests of Hungary he would ally himself with despotism.

Given Marx's views on the threat of Russian Tsarism, and given the strong support the *Neue Rheinische Zeitung* had shown for Kossuth and the Hungarians in 1848 precisely because, in that conflict, they did not place their national cause above the interests of the revolution as a whole, Marx could be expected to come down hard on this stand by Kossuth. And he did. What wasn't as predictable was Marx's criticism of Kossuth's description of the war of the coalition against Russia as a war between liberty and despotism. That was "equally a mistake." For one thing, Marx pointed out, that would make Bonaparte a representative of liberty. But he went on to raise the more fundamental question of what the war was really about:

> ... the whole avowed object of the war is the maintenance of the balance of power and of the Vienna treaties—those very treaties which annul the liberty and independence of nations."[21]

Marx was to expand on this point in an article of July 10, 1855—almost at the end of the war:

> Russia's preponderance in Europe being inseparable from the Treaty of Vienna, any war against that power not proclaiming at the outset the abolition of the Treaty, cannot but prove a mere tissue of shams, delusions and collusions. Now, the present war is undertaken with a view not to supersede but rather to consolidate the Treaty of Vienna by the introduction, in a supplementary way, of Turkey into the protocols of 1815. Then it is expected the conservative millenium will dawn and the aggregate force

of the Governments be allowed to direct itself exclusively to the "tranquillization" of the European mind.[22]

Marx then cited documentary evidence which he believed proved that the Congress of Vienna itself considered that the maintenance of Turkey was "as much interwoven with 'the system' as the partition of Poland."

> [Bonaparte] is proving to the world that Napoleonism means war, not to emancipate France *from*, but to subject Turkey *to*, the Treaty of Vienna. War in the interest of the Treaty of Vienna and under the pretext of checking the power of Russia![23]

Can the position Marx outlines in this article be described as "supporting one of two equally reactionary powers"?

It is interesting that Blackstock and Hoselitz's *The Russian Menace* does not include Marx's attack on Kossuth. Neither does the collection published in England by the Communist Party called *Marxism, Nationality and War*[24] which purports to give the official "Marxist" line on the question. Eleanor Marx-Aveling and Edward Aveling *did* include this article in their collection. None of these collections, however, mentions the second occasion when Marx commented in the *NYDT* on a prowar stand by a revolutionary or in this case, as Marx insisted, ex-revolutionary.

Armand Barbès was a revolutionary of the pre-1848 generation. A long-time associate of Blanqui he broke with the later while both were in prison as a result of their participation in the revolution of 1848. They were treated more harshly than others because in the eyes of the public they were *the* representatives of the revolutionary working-class. For a time they were rivals in this respect. In October of 1854 Marx reported that "The *Moniteur* of the 5th October, announced that Barbès, for the last three years a prisoner at Belle-île, has been unconditionally freed by Bonaparte on account of a letter in which he expresses anxious feelings of hope for the success of Decembrist [i.e., Bonapartist] civilization against Muscovite civilization. ..."[25]

The background of this incident is sketched in a note in *MECW*.[26] According to the note Napoleon III's order of October 3 released Barbès from a life sentence. The authorities had intercepted a private letter of Barbès's written September 18 in which "he welcomed the war with Russia and wished the French troops success in 'the name of civilization.'" The papers carried the news on October 5. Barbès was released October 11. He then wrote a letter to the government organ that had published his letter acknowledging its authenticity and stating that "the greatness of France had always been his religion" but that he was still an enemy of the Bonapartist regime. This letter was published on October 13 and reprinted in many places. It was pretty obviously part of the deal that Barbès had struck in order to obtain his freedom while preserving at least some of his dignity. But Marx bases his article only on the first report. He may not have seen the Barbès letter of October 13 before he sent his article off. In any case, his response to this manifestation of prowar sentiment is cutting. After citing this incident Marx concludes that Barbès is no longer a revolutionist:

> From this moment Barbès has ceased to be one of the revolutionary chiefs of France. By declaring his sympathies for the French arms in whatever cause, and under whatever command they may be employed, he has irretrievably associated himself with the Muscovites themselves. Sharing their indifference as to the object of their campaigns. ... The fact of his letter and of Bonaparte's order decides the question as to who is the man of the revolution [Blanqui or Barbès] and who is not."

Once again, Marx explicitly condemns the position he is alleged to have held. Even more important, in this short notice, he makes the fundamental point that Lenin was to hammer home in World War I. The most important question to settle is: "What is the political aim [object] of this war on the part of the belligerents?" Marx clearly regarded any claim that the coalition partners were fighting for liberty to be demagogy. Their refusal to support the independence of the South Slavs and their attempt to patch up the Ottoman Empire made that clear. Neither side deserved the support of revolutionaries.

These two instances of Marx's antiwar position were long a matter of public record as they appeared in the same *NYDT* series which is the basis of the allegations that Marx and Engels supported the war. There is no excuse for leaving them out of the picture. Marx's correspondence with Engels, which has not been as easily available, adds something new. It documents Marx's *active* opposition to the war once it began. Marx *boasts* about this activity to Engels.

On November 22, 1854, Marx in a letter to Engels,[27] described an aborted plan by the German radical Karl Blind to hold an anti-Russian rally of German émigrés. Blind had been a left-republican in 1848 who in exile moved toward a garden-variety version of liberalism. Marx brags that he and Georg Freiligrath "frustrated" this plan although he does not say how. A preliminary meeting organized by Arnold Ruge, another 48er turned liberal, apparently blew up. Marx mentions that he was prepared to organize a rival meeting together with the Chartists if the German émigrés "should cause a stir with their meeting and unduly compromise 'Germany' by licking English boots . ..."

If Marx and Engels' position *after* the war began can be summed up in a phrase it would be "a plague on both your houses." Their general line was that the war had become a tragi-comedy of incompetence on all sides and the bigger the smash up the better because the general humiliation of the representatives of the old order could only increase the rage and contempt of the people.[28] There is a good deal of overlap, naturally, since Marx and Engels were working out their policy as events developed, but more and more as the war went on Marx and Engels' commentaries dwelt on the role of a general European War in opening up the path for the revolution—the sixth power.

7. The "Sixth Power"

The war aim of the allies, wrote Marx in August of 1853,[29] was "to maintain the status quo, i.e., the state of putrefaction which forbids the Sultan to emancipate himself from the Tsar, and the Slavonians to emancipate themselves from the Sultan."

Given this description, how could Marx have been expected to support the Western Powers? "The revolutionary party can only congratulate itself on this state of things. The humiliation of the reactionary western governments, and their manifest impotency to guard the interests of European civilization against Russian encroachment cannot fail to work out a wholesome indignation in the people who have suffered themselves, since 1849, to be subjected to the rule of counter-revolution."

The disgust of the working class occasioned by the corruption and incompetence of the government and its bourgeois opponents was real. It did not, however, as Marx and Engels expected or hoped, result in an immediate explosion which would have combined with unrest in the colonial and semi-colonial world to topple the old regime world-wide. In the next decade, however, the general disgust with bourgeois "politics as usual" led to the revival of the workingclass movement. The *International Workingmens' Association* played a major role in that revival. And one of the aims of that Association, Marx insisted, was to enable the working class to work out its own foreign policy independent of the possessing classes.

In February of 1854, Engels summed up "the firm's" perspective on the war:

> ... we must not forget that there is a sixth power in Europe, which at any given moment asserts its supremacy over the whole of the five so-called "great" powers [that is, England, France, Russia, Prussia and Austria] and makes them tremble, every one of them. That power is the revolution. Long silent and retired, it is now again called to action by the commercial crisis, and by the scarcity of food. From Manchester to Rome, from Paris to Warsaw and Pesth, it is omnipresent, lifting up its head and awakening from its slumbers. Manifold are the symptoms of its returning to life, everywhere visible in the agitation and disquietude which have seized the proletarian class. A signal only is wanted, and this sixth and greatest European power will come forward, in shining armor, and sword in hand, like Minerva from the head of the Olympian. This signal the impending

European war will give, and then all calculations as to the balance of power will be upset by the addition of the new element which, ever buoyant and youthful, will as much baffle the plans of the old European powers and their Generals, as it did from 1792 to 1800.[30]

This passage deserves to be better known. You could not ask for a clearer repudiation of the view usually attributed to Marx and Engels. What is more important, it is a glimpse into the origins of the antiwar and anti-imperialist tradition of the socialist and democratic movements of the late nineteenth and early twentieth centuries.

CHAPTER 4: PULLING THE PLUG

> When Louis Napoleon ... vaulted to a throne by perjury and treason, by midnight conspiracy and the seizure of the incorruptible members of the Assembly in their beds, backed by an overwhelming display of military force in the streets of Paris, the sovereign princes and great landowners, manufacturers, *rentiers*, and stockjobbers, almost to a man, exulted in his success as their own. "The crimes are his," was their general chuckle, "but their fruits are ours. Louis Napoleon reigns in the Tuileries; while we reign even more securely and despotically on our domains, in our factories, on the Bourse, and in our counting-houses. ... *Vive l'Empereur!*"[1]

Marx wrote these words in an article for the *New York Tribune* on the war crisis provoked by Louis Bonaparte in 1859. He goes on to describe the obsequious flattery addressed to this upstart adventurer and make-believe Napoleon by all the representatives of the *ancien régime* including the Pope and a French-hating British aristocracy. They thought they were using him. But then, at a stroke, Louis Bonaparte plunged this whole world, whose stability he had seemingly guaranteed by crushing the French Republic in 1852, into economic and political panic.

Seemingly out of the blue, with no provocation whatsoever, he deliberately challenged one of the major powers of the day, the Austrian empire, in its strategically vital province of Northern Italy.

Suddenly, Marx notes, "the royalties and bourgeoisies" realized that Bonaparte had been using *them*. He seriously intended, it seemed, to imitate his uncle and create a new French empire in which Italy was to become a "French satrapy" and Great Britain, Prussia and Austria were to be "merely satellites revolving around and lighted by the central orb France, the Empire of Charlemagne." [2]

Marx concludes:

> They know him now, what the peoples knew him long since—a reckless gambler, a desperate adventurer, who would as soon dice with royal bones as any other if the game promised to leave him a winner.[3]

Such sentiments may appear "un-Marxist" to those who insist that imperialist adventures and wars must have a more important cause than the character flaws of a particular leader. But neither Marx nor Engels were that kind of "Marxist." At one point, Marx goes out of his way to emphasize that one of the driving forces behind the war was Napoleon III's half-superstitious fear of assassination attempts by the secret society of Italian revolutionaries to which he had once belonged.[4]

There were, of course, more powerful forces at work. Bonaparte was driven forward not only by his own character but by his inability to resolve any of the domestic or foreign conflicts besetting French and European society. And both the traditional ruling classes and the upstart bourgeoisie relied on him because *they* had no solutions either. The domination of the continent by this nonentity was the direct result of *their* incapacity to govern.

In the event, Napoleon III was driven forward, like his uncle, until he had changed the face of Europe at the cost of his own throne. And the new Europe was a very dangerous place. The relative stability that followed the Congress of Vienna and had survived, somewhat shaken, the revolutions of 1848 was replaced by a Europe dominated by a Prussian militarism as reckless as Bonaparte himself but militarily and economically far more threatening. After 1870, as Marx and Engels immediately saw, this Prussian militarism had to bring into being a counter force—a Franco-Russian alliance. And the tension between these two forces created an unstable equilibrium that could only end in a devastating European-wide war.

One of the casualties of this new series of wars was to be the old politics of Marx and Engels on the question of war and peace. In 1848, war between the great powers was eagerly anticipated as the harbinger of revolution. In the Crimean War Marx and Engels also looked forward to a conflict between England and Russia for the same reason. But a new note began to creep into their public and private discussions of this new crisis. They did not change their views overnight. Traces of the old views lingered on and were not to be definitively abandoned until after 1870 as we shall see in the next chapter.

Pulling the Plug

1. The Demagogy of "National Revolution"

Bonaparte, like similar adventurers later on, cloaked his military project in the guise of a war of liberation. And, like many similar adventurers later on, he found it easy enough to do so. Austrian rule in Northern Italy *was* brutal by the standards of those days. Flogging was common and the regime was hated by the people especially in the towns. But the revolutionary movement was unexpectedly weak. Bonaparte found Italian collaborators in two quarters.

One was a minor Italian princeling with a liberal reputation—the King of Sardinia—who was happy to enhance his holdings and prestige with French help. In the end—why should anyone be surprised—he gained little land and his prestige was diminished. In a peace treaty at which the Kingdom of Sardinia was not even represented, Lombardy was ceded by the Austrians to Sardinia but, in return, France gained two provinces which had been part of the Kingdom of Sardinia—Nice and Savoy. The later province was the ancestral possession of the Sardinian dynasty. The Duchy of Venice remained under Austrian control. What was more important, the Papal States and large areas of central Italy remained for the moment under control of the dynasties established or re-established at the Congress of Vienna. The revolutionary committees that sprang up partly as genuine expressions of popular movements and partly as agents of the Sardinian government were dissolved with the aide of Austrian troops. The Sardinian prime minister, Camillo Benson, Count Cavour, who had been the driving force behind the French alliance and the ally, sometimes instigator, of the revolutionary committees was forced to resign.

Bonaparte's other Italian collaborator was the national movement itself. Like the Sardinian king, it was unable to make a bid for power unaided. Its fundamental weakness, in Marx and Engels' view, was its narrow social base. Reporting on the "cordial reception" given the Austrians in the region of Lomellina then a possession of Sardinia, Engels writes:

> ... the hatred of the peasantry in the Lomellina, as well as in Lombardy, against the landlords far exceeds their aversion against the foreign oppressor. Now, the landlords of the Lomellina (formerly an Austrian

101

province) are mostly *sudditi misti,* mixed subjects, belonging to Austria as well as Piedmont. All the great nobles of Milan have large possessions in the Lomellina. They are Piedmontese and anti-Austrian at heart; and, by contrast, the peasantry of the province rather lean toward Austria.[5]

There was a third, silent, partner in Bonaparte's camp. That was Prussia; or at least a political tendency within Prussia. From a narrow dynastic point of view, the humiliation of Austria would enhance Prussia's status within the German Confederation. For those who sought a "little German" solution to the question of German unity—that is, a Germany which excluded Austria and was, therefore, dominated by Prussia—Bonaparte's adventure provided an opportunity. As we shall see, Ferdinand Lassalle became one of the most outspoken champions of this view. But the German people were less enthusiastic.

There was, of course, the usual chauvinist response to a "French" attack on a "German" state. But there was more to it than that. For the smaller German states, especially in the south and west, Austria was their traditional guardian against French expansionism. There was a real fear, throughout Germany, that the real aim of the war was to force a defeated Austria to make concessions on the left, German speaking, bank of the Rhine. There was also a good deal of suspicion that Prussia was agreeable to such a settlement. The Kingdom of Prussia at that point, like the Kingdom of Sardinia, was willing to sacrifice national interests to its dynastic interests—in the name of protecting "Germany" of course. Both the fears and the suspicions of the German public were justified.

In general outlines the position of Marx and Engels was simple enough. They were for the unification and liberation of the German and Italian peoples through a revolution against all the dynasts. But that abstraction was not sufficient to decide what policy German socialists and democrats should take towards this particular war. What policy should be followed that would encourage a revolutionary outcome?

For Italian revolutionaries the path was fairly clear. All they had to do was to take advantage of Bonaparte's invasion to launch a revolutionary war against *all* the Italian dynasties, including ones that were, like the Papal

States, French client states. Mazzini's proclamation on *La Guerra* in the London magazine *Pensiero ed Azione* took just such a position and Marx translated it *in toto* for the *NYDT*, in effect, adopting it as his own.[6] This despite his lack of respect for Mazzini as a revolutionary statesman.

2. Po and Rhine

For many Germans, however, the French invasion represented not an opportunity but a threat. An Austrian defeat threatened *them,* not just the Hapsburgs.

Marx commented at length on the war in the columns of the *NYDT* but it was Engels who laid out their position in detail in two pamphlets — *Po und Rhine* and *Savoyen, Nizza und der Rhine* (*Po and Rhine* and *Savoy, Nice and the Rhine.*) Both Marx and Engels felt that, given the political climate in Germany, their views would not receive a hearing if presented openly as *their* views. It was only a few years earlier that former members of the Communist League had been the victims of a vicious witch hunt. Marx had been their main, practically their only, prominent defender. And this only reinforced his image as a wild-eyed revolutionary of the 1848 generation which was rapidly becoming a shameful memory for respectable Germans. All this accounts for the peculiar style of the two pamphlets, especially the first. Engels posed as an anonymous "military expert," presumably a military man. Like many of the *NYDT* articles by Engels, the pamphlets start out as what appear to be impartial technical analyses and only gradually lead the reader into the revolutionary politics. Engels was to use this dodge on later occasions too when the combination of government censorship and Social Democratic timidity made it impossible to start out with a clear statement of the politics. It worked for the most part because Engels really was well versed in the field of military science but the result is that, especially in the opening passages, the going is heavy for the modern reader.

In this case, Engels begins with an explicit statement of his opinion on the military question.

> Since the beginning of this year it has become the slogan of a large part of the German press that *the Rhine must be defended on the Po.*

> This slogan was fully justified in the face of Bonaparte's war preparations and threats. It was sensed in Germany, with correct instinct, that although the Po was Louis Napoleon's pretext, in any circumstances the Rhine could not but be his ultimate goal. ...
> In this sense the whole of Germany was indeed interested in the defense of the Po. On the eve of a war, as in war itself, one occupies every position that can be used to threaten the enemy and do him damage, without engaging in any moral speculations as to whether it is consonant with eternal righteousness and the principle of nationality. One simply fights for one's life.[7]

Engels then goes on to point out that this extreme emergency is *not* what military commentators had in mind when they argued that "the Rhine had to be defended on the Po." They meant that the Po—that is Lombardy and Venice, all of Northern Italy—had to be treated as "an indispensable strategic complement and, so to speak, an integral part of Germany."[8] The most fanatical defenders of this position were, naturally, German chauvinists who felt Germany could only be safe in an empire stretching from Alsace and Holland to the Vistula and including Italy and the Slavic lands as dependencies. But Engels dismisses this fantasy as irrelevant. The serious military question is "in order to defend its southwest border, does Germany require possession of the Adige, the Mincio and the Lower Po, with the bridgeheads of Peschiria and Mantua?"[9] Engels sets himself the task of refuting this opinion even though it is held "by military authorities ... among the foremost in Germany."

Almost the entire next section is devoted to defending his position strictly from the point of view of military science. The relevant volume of the *MECW* even has a nice map so you can follow the discussion more easily. In order to judge the validity of Engels' argument you would, of course, have to devote some time to studying other military authors of the time. Personally, I would rather take Engels' word for it.

Towards the end of this second section of the pamphlet the politics start to creep in. Why, asks Engels, should the Italians be expected to serve as a buffer against French rule when the Germans on the left bank of the

Rhine refused to provide the same service for the French? And, he emphasized, the real threat to Germany was its own disunity and weakness whose root cause was the German people's continued submission to the German princes.[10]

The entire third section is devoted to an exposition of the military reasons why the French had even more to fear from their exposed frontier on the Rhine than the Germans had to fear an unprotected southern flank. Why shouldn't the French have the right to occupy neutral Belgium if the Germans had the right to occupy northern Italy? Engels presciently argues that in any serious war Belgian neutrality "amounts to nothing more than a scrap of paper." [11]

> By now we have seen where the theory of natural frontiers advanced by the Central European great-power politicians leads us. France has the same right to the Rhine that Germany has to the Po. If France should not annex nine million Walloons, Netherlanders and Germans in order to obtain a good military position, then neither have we the right to subject six million Italians for the sake of a military position.[12]

Engels concludes by pointing out that German unity is the real key to the defense of the country and that with unity, the subjugation of foreign peoples, and the hatred engendered thereby, could easily be dispensed with. A contemporary reader would have understood the anti-Prussian thrust of this argument.

3. Lassalle's Appeasement Policy

Prior to this crisis Marx and Engels had been unaware of Ferdinand Lassalle's devolution into a pro-Prussian "kleindeutsch" democrat.[13] They still thought of him as a party comrade even though by this time they had come to consider him personally unreliable. They did know from Gustav Lewy of the suspicion entertained by many old comrades. In particular they accused him of flirting with the aristocracy. But his full blown pro-Prussian, pro-Bonapartist position came as a surprise to them.

Initially, Marx saw the coming war, a war basically between Germany and France even if fought initially on the soil of Austrian-occupied Italy, as having nothing but reactionary consequences In a letter to Lassalle on February 4, 1859 he frankly expressed his fear of the consequences if war came:

> The war would, of course, have serious, and without doubt ultimately revolutionary consequences. But initially it will maintain Bonapartism in France, set back the internal movement within England and Russia, revive the pettiest nationalist passions in Germany, etc., and hence, in my view, [have first and foremost a counterrevolutionary effect in every respect] its initial effect will everywhere be counter-revolutionary ...[14]

This was one of the earliest statements by Marx of a new outlook on the consequences for the revolutionary movement of war between the powers. In particular, Marx saw Bonaparte's use of the national aspirations of the Italians as pure humbug. He compared those veterans of 1848—including Kossuth and Garibaldi—whose anti-Austrian passions led them to endorse Napoleon III's pose, to pet monkeys.[15] But the national passion aroused both in Italy and in Germany threatened to turn the war into a real national war of liberation and Marx changed his mind.

A few weeks later he wrote Lassalle in another letter "I am now, °after all°, beginning to believe that the war might hold out some prospects for us as well." [16]

The statesmen of the potential belligerents also began to sense this revolutionary potential and that induced a sense of caution in their maneuvers. As earlier in the case of the Crimean War, the onset of war was delayed by maneuver and bluff, the conduct of the war when it did come was marked by costly and bloody blunders, and the resulting peace was humiliating to all sides.

Throughout this drawn-out and complicated diplomatic and military charade, Marx and Engels maintained a very simple line. A "red thread" ran through all their public and private comments. No support could be given to any of the governments involved without betraying the revolutionary aspirations of both Germans and Italians. Both peoples should seize the opportunity and take their destinies in their own hands.

And then Lassalle, known at the time as their political friend, a man who was then acting as their literary agent in Germany, published a pamphlet, without any warning to Marx or Engels, which proposed, not only to support Bonaparte's fraudulent liberation campaign but urged Prussia to enter the war itself—on the side of France and Piedmont. But Lassalle did not propose a direct declaration of war on Austria. Instead, Lassalle urged the King of Prussia to imitate Bonaparte and the King of Sardinia and "liberate" Schleswig-Holstein from the Danish monarchy in the name of German unity.[17] Since Austria also had some claims to this territory and in any case was a member of the German Confederation which alone, from a legal point of view, should have decided the Schleswig-Holstein question, this unilateral action by Prussia would have the effect of shoving German speaking Austrians out of Germany. Such a coup would also have had the effect of tying down the considerable number of troops Austria had stationed in Germany. In the event, the Prussian government did not yet have the initiative or imagination to carry out such a bold plan. Lassalle's soon-to-be political ally, Otto von Bismarck, was not yet Chancellor.

Lassalle used the very real atrocities committed by the Austrians to justify Prussian aggression against *Denmark*. The Napoleonic threat to the south German states was made light of, at least for the moment, because with the destruction of Austria, *Prussia* would become their "protector" against the "French menace." Lassalle's pamphlet on the war was based on the classic demagogy which has since been labeled "appeasement."

In the first place, everything was narrowed down to support for or opposition to one of the two sides in the war. Lassalle, in his correspondence, consistently accuses Marx and Engels of supporting the pro-Austrian parties in the war* even though they ridiculed these fanatics both in their *NYDT* articles and in *Po und Rhein*.[18] He even argued that their

---

* This slander has been repeated in most historical accounts. The source, acknowledge in some cases, unacknowledged in others is Mehring's biography. For a more detailed analysis of Mehring's biography see Special Note C in KMTR 4.

position led them to support Prussia's entry into the war on the Austrian side.

How could he get away with this? He resorted to the same dodge that has been used before and since in the same situation. Since all "practical" people understand that the only choice is between the governments, refusal to support the side the "hard-headed, practical" demagogue is supporting means you "objectively" support the other. The peculiar twist this takes in the case of an appeasement policy is that support for one side in the war takes the form of urging non-intervention on other great powers. Lassalle's pro-Bonapartist position took the form of opposing Prussia's entry into the war on Austria's side as the various proponents of a "Greater German Empire" advocated. Since Marx and Engels refused to endorse Bonaparte's phony war of liberation, Lassalle accused them of "objectively" supporting the "Greater Germany" policy of the pro-Austrian camp.

Quite typically, again, Lassalle made light of the threat to Germany represented by Bonaparte. This allowed him to denounce the anti-French agitation in Germany without reservation. His position appeared to be even more antiwar than that of Marx and Engels. But in fact it was the opposite. If your antiwar stance *depends* on minimizing the danger represented by an opposing power what happens when a war threat *becomes* serious? Lassalle died before Prussia made its move to unify Germany in a Prussian Empire and provoked a real war with Napoleonic France. His successors became ardent chauvinists who used the "French menace" for all it was worth.

4. Germany's Unification in "A Prussian Barracks"

Within a few years of the peace of Villafranca di Verona at which both the Sardinian king and the Hapsburg emperor were humiliated, the Prussian government embarked on the course which Lassalle had urged. It did take advantage of the military and diplomatic embarrassment of the Hapsburgs, first to force them into a war with Denmark which isolated them diplomatically from England and Russia, and then to use the ensuing imbroglio over the division of spoils (including the province of Schleswig with its large Danish-speaking minority) as a pretext for driving the Austrians out of Germany altogether. But the new Germany created on the ruins of the old federation was not a weak, economically backward, state like the new Italian monarchy. Under her new chancellor, Otto von Bismarck, a pupil in some sense of Lassalle's, Prussia seized the opportunity the Hohenzollern monarchy had been too timid to seize when Lassalle first proposed it.

5. Bismarck's Coup

Prussia, like most German states in 1860, was relatively weak militarily compared to the great powers that surrounded her: the French, Austrian and Russian empires. The dangers which threatened the country drove Wilhelm I, the recently crowned king of Prussia, to propose a sweeping, and expensive, military reform. The keystone of this proposed reform was a significant expansion of the system of universal conscription. The liberal majority of the lower House of the Prussian Diet responded with proposals of its own to restrict the powers of the monarch and his army. These proposals would have moved Prussia in the direction of a constitutional state with an effective parliament. Humiliated by this show of independence the king countered with a decree dissolving the Diet and calling new elections. What he got in return was a Diet with an even larger liberal majority.

With his back to the wall, the king called Otto von Bismarck to the chancellorship of Prussia. Bismarck's unusual combination of political intelligence and a Prussian Junker's conservative social outlook had long aroused suspicion and distrust among his colleagues; the liberals distrusted him because of his origins and his fellow Junkers distrusted him because of his intelligence. But it was just this combination that was required if the Prussian monarchy was to survive the tumultuous decade that ended with the unification of Germany.

As Lassalle had urged, Bismarck began by utilizing Bonaparte's "principle of nationalities" – the demagogic demand that the modern state should be based, not on dynastic claims, but on a more or less homogeneous, more or less imaginary, "nationality" – to demand the secession of Schleswig and Holstein from the Danish monarchy. With the secret acquiescence of Bonaparte, who effectively neutralized the Russian and British protectors of the Danish monarchy,[19] Bismarck forced Austria into a joint attack. After a brief and, from the German point of view, successful conflict the German Confederation was faced with the problem of administering the conquered territories. None of the statesmen, of course, considered the possibility of a democratic decision by the people inhabiting the two territories. It was never completely clear what Louis Bonaparte meant by the "principle of nationalities" but whatever it meant, it definitely did not mean the right of a population to choose its own constitutional arrangements. After all, Bonaparte never meant to extend that right to the very model of a modern nation—France.

At first, the two conquered provinces were administered jointly by the Austrians and the Prussians. Formerly the property of the Danish monarch, they now became the joint property of the Hapsburg and Hohenzollern monarchs neither of whose empires were based on the "principle of nationalities." After 1865 the Austrians ruled Holstein and the Prussians Schleswig. Obviously, this was an unstable arrangement which is what Bismarck intended. It gave him the opportunity of provoking a war which would drive the Hapsburgs out of Germany and make it, not a unified country, but a Prussian fiefdom.

Bismarck's campaign naturally included the usual diplomatic maneuvering. It was only fair that in return for standing aside while Bismarck drove the Hapsburgs out of Germany, Bonaparte should receive some compensation. In particular, France needed a more defensible border to its east. Bismarck kept offering Bonaparte Belgium and Bonaparte kept asking about Baden. But this kind of maneuvering was not what really decided the war. Bismarck more than any other statesman had learned from Bonaparte the art of manipulating public opinion in a new "democratic" Europe. Bismarck's fundamental solution to Prussia's foreign and domestic crisis was neither diplomatic nor military. What he did, what won him the victory, was to put the king of economically backward, socially conservative, politically reactionary, Prussia at the head of the movement for a united Germany. To the consternation of the Prussian king himself, Bismarck proposed that the question of German unification be decided by an all-German Diet whose delegates would be elected by universal, direct, equal, manhood, suffrage.

Outmaneuvered by this unexpectedly radical proposal of a conservative Junker, the liberals found themselves in a tight corner. Their majority in the Prussian Diet depended on an elaborate and very undemocratic electoral system. Delegates were elected, not directly, but by three bodies of electors. One body was elected by voters paying the most taxes, the second by those in the middle tax brackets and the third by those paying the least taxes. Each of the three electoral bodies elected one-third of the delegates to the Diet. Through this complicated mechanism the landed classes and the bourgeoisie were able to exercise a political power out of all proportion to their numbers. Even the most progressive liberals found it difficult to abandon a scheme in which they were not only over represented but in which they enjoyed an almost automatic majority. But this allowed Bismarck and his supporters to pose as the champions of democracy and the popular, even revolutionary, cause of German unification.

6. "The Prussian Military Question and the German Workers' Party"

Lassalle had preceded Bismarck on the diplomatic front; he had proposed using the distraction provided by the 1859 war between France and Austria to cover a unilateral seizure of Schleswig-Holstein by Prussia a good four years before Bismarck made his first move in that direction. But more importantly he also demonstrated the power of a demagogic campaign for universal suffrage. By the time Bismarck made his move, Lassalle was dead. His energetic successor, Johann Baptist von Schweizer, however, proved more than capable of completing his work. Mainly through his control of the newspaper, the *Social-Democrat*, Schweitzer took over the main Lassallean organization—the ADVA (Allgemeine Deutsche Verein der Arbeiter or General Association of German Workers)—and steered in an openly Prussian direction. Marx and Engels had originally agreed to write for the newspaper despite their suspicions of Schweitzer. But the latter not only openly campaigned for German unification under the Prussian monarchy, he refused to print Marx and Engels' opposing views. They were to supply the "theoretical" and "philosophical" weapons against the capitalist system; "practical" political questions—like whether or not to attack the precapitalist landed classes which were the base of the Prussian monarchy—was to be left to people in Germany. Like Schweitzer.

Under the circumstances, Marx and Engels had no choice but to resign from the *Social-Democrat* and publish their views independently.

In 1865 Engels published a pamphlet in which he explicitly attacked the campaign for universal suffrage then being waged by Schweitzer's

AVDA. This was not an ill-considered, off the cuff, minor piece by Engels. Although little known today, this was a joint product in which Marx and Engels defended their public break with the pro-Prussian politics of the ADVA and its spokesman. And it was Marx who, prior to the break, first proposed the idea to Engels as a way of opening up an attack on the pro-Prussianism of the Lassalleans.[20]

Engels' opposition to the AVDA demand for universal suffrage had nothing in common, however, with that hostility to universal suffrage and "bourgeois democracy" that has become a badge of honor for many self-styled "Marxists" since at least 1895 when Engels died. As volume three of this work demonstrated Marx and Engels were familiar with this kind of "leftist" hostility to popular rule from the beginning of their political careers. From the early 1840s, when their political views on most major issues jelled, until Engels' death in 1895, they were outspoken in their hostility to this kind of "leftism." In 1865, in Prussia, their opposition to universal suffrage meant at least a qualified *defense*, not even of bourgeois democracy, but of bourgeois liberalism.

The Prussian government was offering universal suffrage to the working classes as a plebiscitarian device to blunt the half-hearted assault by the liberals on the prerogatives of the absolute monarchy. What Schweitzer was advocating was an alliance with the monarchy *against* the liberals. Engels pamphlet was a qualified—heavily qualified—argument for a limited united front with the liberals instead.

According to Schweitzer's biographer, Gustav Meyer, Lassalle's campaign for universal manhood suffrage met with real enthusiasm in his working class audience. Schweitzer made explicit the promonarchical politics of this campaign. Whether Bismarck could have defeated the liberals without the weapon of working class support cannot be known. Certainly, bourgeois public opinion soon rallied to his side and liberal opposition collapsed. At the very least, however, the agitation of Lassalle and the AVDA neutralized working class opposition to the monarchy and allowed Bismarck to appear before the bourgeois public as a man who could rally the "dangerous classes" to a united, powerful, but socially conservative, Germany.

Now, obviously, what the Prussian liberals should have done in this situation was to put *themselves* at the head of a movement for a unified, democratic and constitutional Germany. They should have combined their demands for constitutional restrictions on royal authority with the demand for universal suffrage, beginning with Prussia itself.[21] Bismarck's Achilles heel was that he had no intention of replacing *Prussia's* three-class electoral system with one based on universal suffrage. A representative body elected on such a basis would have represented a serious and direct threat to the Prussian monarchy which was not what he intended. But the German bourgeoisie, including its liberal wing, had made clear in 1848 that it had no desire to unleash a popular and potentially revolutionary movement for constitutional government.

7. Engels on Universal Conscription

Engels' pamphlet is divided into three sections. In the first section, he raises an issue on which he was to elaborate at length later. And that is: the fundamental contradiction between a citizen army intensively trained for a short period but liable to a long period of reserve service and an army based on a caste of professional soldiers alienated from the civilian population and disciplined to unquestioning obedience. Engels believed that the first type of army had proved its superiority militarily in the French Revolution and then in Prussia's national uprising against Napoleon. No country could do without such an army. At the same time such an army was worse than useless against the "enemy within."

In this article this political point is very much obscured for the modern reader because Engels spends most of his time on the technical details of military reorganization.* In particular, he goes into great detail to prove that the reforms proposed by the conservatives did not add up to real universal conscription. In fact, he argues, the monarchy could not introduce real universal conscription.

Engels' conclusion is that the mess the Prussian army was in was a result of an attempt to combine two contradictory organizational forms.

---

* In part, the obscurity of the first section is intentional. Too direct an attack on the Prussian government could have led to the confiscation of the issue of the *Social-Demokrat* for which the article was originally intended. It was Marx who suggested to Engels that the first section take the form of a technical discussion by a "military expert." The politics could be concealed under this guise.

The emphasis on parade drill—Engels found the goose step a particularly ridiculous excrescence[22]—and a humiliating, at times brutal, discipline aimed at breaking in recruits the way horses are broken to the saddle, could only demoralize civilians and further alienate them from their officers. Civilian reservists, who in an emergency would comprise the overwhelming majority of the troops under the system of universal conscription, simply would not follow officers who relied on these methods. Engels does admit that there must be an exception made for the cavalry since years of experience are required before a cavalryman is completely at ease on horseback. Engels discussion of this issue is particularly revealing.

> We shall be criticised by members of the [liberal] opposition on the grounds that this would mean a cavalry made up exclusively of mercenaries who would lend themselves to any coup d'etat. We would reply: that may well be. But in present conditions the cavalry will always be reactionary ..., just as the artillery will always be liberal. That is in the nature of things. ... cavalry is useless on the barricades anyway; and it is the barricades in the big cities, and especially the attitude of the infantry and artillery towards them, which nowadays decide the outcome of any coup d'etat.[23]

What Engels, and others, were anticipating in this crisis, then, was an attempt by the monarchy to suppress the Diet by force. And the outcome of such an attempt would be decided by an army heavily weighted with civilian draftees from the bourgeoisie and the working classes. In hindsight, we know that this confrontation did not take place. But that is because the liberals collapsed. No coup d'etat was necessary.

8. A Bourgeois Bluff

In the second chapter of his pamphlet, Engels addresses this question himself. Carried away by their own rhetoric, the liberals had overreached themselves he argues. By refusing the monarchy the military means required to pursue the grandiose foreign policy which the Prussian liberals themselves supported, and even demanded, of the government, the liberals had themselves created the crisis. But, since 1848, they had tried to avoid just such a split with the monarchy.

> By overestimating its own strength, the bourgeoisie has got itself into the situation of having to use this military question as a test-case to see whether it is the decisive force in the state or nothing at all. If it wins, it will simultaneously acquire the power of appointing and dismissing ministers, such as the English Lower House possesses. If it is vanquished, it will never again achieve any kind of significance by constitutional means.[24]

Engels concludes this section as follows: "We fear that on this occasion too the bourgeoisie will have no scruples in betraying its own cause."

9. The "Workers' Party" and Universal Suffrage

It is in the last section—on the appropriate response of the workers' party* to this crisis—that Engels takes up the issue of universal suffrage and what the response of the workers' party should have been. He begins by emphasizing the greater significance of universal conscription.

> The German proletariat will never have any truck with Imperial Constitutions, Prussian hegemonies, tripartite systems and the like, unless it be to sweep them away; it is indifferent to the question of how many soldiers the Prussian state needs in order to prolong its vegetable existence as a great power. ... On the other hand it certainly cannot remain indifferent to the question of whether or not universal conscription is fully implemented. The more workers who are trained in the

---

* Engels does not mean here the AVDA with whose leader he and Marx had already broken. "Party" here is to be taken in the much broader sense that he and Marx often used.

use of weapons the better. Universal conscription is the necessary and natural corollary of universal suffrage; it puts the voters in the position of being able to enforce their decisions gun in hand against any attempt at a coup d'etat.[25]

This was the big difference, the deciding difference, between universal suffrage as a plebiscitarian device—what Wilhelm Liebknecht was going to call a "fig leaf covering the nakedness of absolutism"—and universal suffrage as a means by which the people really effect their will. For the rest of his life Engels was to connect universal conscription in this way with universal suffrage. Without the former the later was a safety valve, a means for rallying the people to a preconceived project of the authorities. In the Prussian case, Engels argued, an assembly and an electoral system established by royal decree could just as easily be abolished by royal decree.[26]

And, Engels insisted, in the constitutional crisis of 1860 it was the bourgeois liberals who, in their half-hearted fashion, were attempting to *impose* a limited form of representative government on the semi-feudal monarchy by exploiting its momentary weakness. In doing so they were fighting for the interests of the working class even more than their own.

10. "Bourgeois Freedoms"

In Prussia the aristocracy and the bureaucracy had little need for representative government. The army and the civil service were in their hands and that was sufficient for their needs. But the working class and the bourgeoisie could only exercise power through parliamentary representatives with real power; especially power over the °purse strings°. What was the point of universal suffrage if it gained the working class entry into an assembly with no real influence?[27] If the Prussian liberals were defeated that would be a victory for Bismarck not for the workers who would lose more than the bourgeoisie. Without freedom of the press and association, without local self-government the bourgeoisie "can get along passably" but the working class "can never win [its] emancipation" without these freedoms.[28] In another passage Engels describes these "bourgeois freedoms" as providing "the environment necessary for its [the workers' party's] existence, ... the air it needs to breathe."[29]

These sweeping statements are based on a general analysis of the position of the wage worker in modern society, but there were further difficulties with Bismarck's sham assembly which were peculiar to Germany in 1865. Two thirds of the German working class were directly exploited not by capitalists but by the aristocracy. Day laborers and tenants were dependent on their masters in this patriarchal economy to a degree that the urban worker was not. And nowhere was this more true than on the estates of eastern Prussia where Bismarck's fellow Junkers ruled. These rural workers, lacking the right to organize, poorly educated, systematically indoctrinated by the clergy of a state-established church, and, given the absence of a free press, isolated from the larger world, would be nothing but voting cattle herded to the polls by the village curate and the bailiff.[30] Even in the France of the Second Empire, where the peasantry had long since freed itself from this kind of aristocratic and clerical tutelage, universal suffrage had done little for the worker in the absence of freedom of the press and association.

> The battle against feudal and bureaucratic reaction—for the two are inseparable in our country—is in Germany identical with struggle for the intellectual and political emancipation of the rural proletariat—and until such time as the rural proletariat is also swept along into the movement, the urban proletariat cannot and will not achieve anything at all in Germany and universal suffrage will not be a weapon for the proletariat but a *snare*.[31]

So important did Engels consider this point that he concludes his pamphlet with the statement that even if, in the worst case scenario, the bourgeoisie itself gave up, the working class would have to fight on alone to win these "bourgeois freedoms."[32] Meanwhile, the interests of the working class lay in supporting the liberals, indeed of driving them on, in their fight with the monarchy. If the bourgeoisie should win the workers' party would win a greatly expanded field in which to carry on its struggle against its capitalist *and* aristocratic exploiters. If the monarchy should win the proletariat would gain nothing. The monarchy might demagogically exploit the resentment of the proletariat against the bourgeoisie but it would not deprive the bourgeoisie of political freedom only in order to turn around and grant it to the working classes.[33]

We can only note in passing that the German Social Democracy never did abandon the Lassallean project and fight the bureaucratic state. In particular, it never did make a serious attempt to organize the rural laborers of East Prussia against their Junker overlords.

11. Engels as "Military Expert" in 1866

We have mentioned before, and will have cause to mention again Engels' deserved reputation as a student of military science. But this reputation was not well served by Engels' articles and letters at the beginning of the 1866 war between Prussia and Austria. He consistently overestimated the abilities of the Austrian General Staff and predicted a Prussian debacle. Only late in the day did he acknowledge his mistake. It is one of the clearest examples of Engels' tendency to let his political enthusiasm overwhelm his critical faculties.

In a five-part series under the title "Notes on the War in Germany" written for the *Manchester Guardian*, Engels claimed, in the opening paragraph of Note I, to be commenting "impartially, and from a strictly military point of view, upon the current events."[34]

The rest of Note I is spent disparaging the capabilities of the Prussian forces and in particular their commander-in-chief "a parade soldier of at best very mediocre capacities, and of weak, but often obstinate character."[35]

> This much is certain: Monsieur Bismarck has ridden into a morass with which neither he nor any of the present regime can cope. If things are settled peaceably, he will have burnt up the available funds and therefore he will no longer be able to help himself, and if there is a war, he will have to *Acheronta movere* [set those below in motion EH], who will certainly consume him. In these circumstances, even a direct victory of the Chamber-

burghers will be revolutionary in character and is bound to lead to other things.[36]

Engels' articles and correspondence of this period are full of predictions of Prussian defeat and reports on popular outbursts of anti-monarchical sentiments in Prussia.[37] But this rebellious spirit to the extent it existed at all, never represented a serious threat to the Prussian army.

Engels, in his comments on the war, almost up until the end failed to realize the degree to which Bismarck had managed to exploit the hostility of the German people against the petty dynasts who kept the country divided and weak in the interests of one of those dynasties, namely, the Hohenzollern.

But Engels did come to realize this by the end of the successful Prussian campaign and he was to spend the rest of his life trying to work out a political response to the new and dangerous Europe divided into belligerent, and well-armed, nation states.

CHAPTER 5. "THE DESPOTS OF *ALL* COUNTRIES ARE OUR ENEMIES"[1]

The prevailing view, you might even call it the unopposed view, is that Marx and Engels together with the majority of the German socialist movement were at least reluctant, and often enthusiastic, prowar patriots during the Franco-Prussian war.[2] If you were to ask what is the single most important work in the literature, the one that did the most to entrench this view in the history books, the answer would have to be a brilliant Lassallean anti-Marx polemic that masqueraded as a sympathetic biography of Karl Marx. The polemic was called *Karl Marx, The Story of His Life* and the author was Franz Mehring—a prominent left-wing journalist and author, leader of the prewar Social Democracy and cofounder of the German Communist party.[3]

1. The 1870 Split in the German Social Democracy

Mehring describes the division in the German socialist movement at the beginning of the war, a division which split the party into three factions, in very simple terms.[4] On the one side were August Bebel and Wilhelm Liebknecht who, isolated from and opposed by their own closest comrades, abstained from voting war credits. Mehring ridiculed this act as "but a moral protest which ... was not in accordance with the political exigencies of the situation."[5] On the other side were not only the Lassalleans but also the leading committee and the majority of Bebel and Liebknecht's own party. Marx and Engels, according to Mehring, led the theoretical assault on Liebknecht.[6]

But, contrary to Mehring, the record, which no one so far has tried to look at as a whole, presents us with a much more complicated picture. There were really not two positions but three-and-a-half. At one pole were the orthodox Lassalleans, organized in the *Allgemeine Deutsche Arbeiter Verein* or *ADAV* and led by Johann Baptist von Schweitzer, a man who receives very favorable treatment in Mehring's book. They took an unabashed, prowar and pro-Prussian stand. That was nothing new for them.[7] Liebknecht, at the other pole, treated the war as simply a dynastic conflict whose outcome was of no consequence for the people or working class of either country.[8] The Executive Committee of the party to which Liebknecht belonged, the *Sozialdemokratischer Arbeiterpartei* or *SDAP*, dominated by former dissidents who had left the Lassallean group over issues unrelated to the one at hand, took a stand that "split the difference" between Liebknecht and Schweitzer. (That makes two-and-a-half positions.) Marx and Engels differed from all of the above. And, at one point, they disagreed with one another. (Does that make three-and-three-quarters positions?)

What Mehring did, by selectively quoting from Marx and Engels' private correspondence which was not generally available[9] and ignoring their public statements, was to portray them as defenders of Schweitzer. It was part of his campaign to prove that Marx's criticism of Lassalle and Schweitzer was largely personal and there were not really substantial political differences between the two factions.

The irony is that Mehring wrote this book in 1913 at a time when he was moving rapidly to the right, back to the pro-Prussian, pro-Lassallean stand he had defended before he joined the Social Democratic Party. But, when the war came, his disgust with the useless slaughter pushed him back to the left. He became an opponent of the war and, as we said, a cofounder of the Communist Party.

After the Prussian state Mehring had spent a great part of his political life defending collapsed in 1918, his biography of Marx could finally be published. This pro-Prussian polemic was accepted as a left wing defense of Karl Marx, a revolutionary opponent of the Prussian state since his youth. Mehring's political evolution after he wrote the book is almost certainly responsible for its general acceptance later as a standard biography of Marx, if not *the* standard biography. A cofounder of the German Communist Party a pro-Prussian patriot as late as 1913! Who could believe it? No wonder the historical record is so confused.

The next prominent, sympathetic, biography of Marx was written by Boris Nicolaevsky, a Russian Menshevik, in collaboration with Otto Mänchen-Helfen.[10] While he quoted two of the many anti-Prussian statements of Marx, Nicolaevsky pretty much echoed Mehring's assessment. Adding only the by now standard, and unsupported, assertion that Marx considered war an engine of historical progress and believed that the proletariat could not be "indifferent" to which side won. Nicolaevsky states that Marx "rejected the idea of anything in itself being 'reactionary.'"[11] Nicolaevsky is so confident that this is what Marx believed that he doesn't even feel the need to refer to anything specific the man wrote. This is, of course, nothing more than a repetition of the line used by all sides in the debates between prowar and antiwar socialists in World War I. All agreed without evidence that Marx supported "even reactionary governments" at times.[12] Not a whisper of Marx's antiwar position in 1870 from the first day on can be heard in this book.

James Guillaume's *Karl Marx Pan-Germaniste* differed from the biographies of Mehring and Nicolaevsky in that it was openly hostile to Marx—from a 'libertarian' point of view. As such it is often referred to as a 'left' criticism of Marx. Since its main thesis reinforced the accounts by sympathetic social democrats—'Marxists'—it strengthened the general impression that "everyone knew" about Marx's pro-Prussian sympathies. But Guillaume, Bakunin's organization man in the political attack on Marx (and the *International*) and floor leader of Bakunin's faction in the *IWMA* Congress at the Hague in 1872[13] had, by 1915, become an ardent French chauvinist. The avowed purpose of the pamphlet was to provide a 'left' defense of the French government in World War I. It is, in fact, a bizarre slander arguing that Marx was Bismarck's conscious agent whose aim was to turn the International movement into a shill for Prussian imperialism.

In his campaign against Marx, Guillaume charged that Marx in 1870 had believed that the immediate cause of the war was an attack by Louis Bonaparte on Germany. That was true. Marx did believe that Bonaparte sought to reverse the unification of Germany that had followed the defeat of Austria in 1866. And he did concede that Germany had a right to defend itself. Guillaume, of course, ignored the fact that Marx only shared the view of most people at the time. This included the French section of the *IWMA*. By the time Guillaume wrote his book the evidence that Bismarck had deliberately provoked the French attack was very strong and well known. In large part, it was well known because of the investigative reporting of the German socialists and in particular Wilhelm Liebknecht.

When the First World War broke out and the socialist movement split over the question of whether or not socialists should rally to the side of their respective governments in order to 'defend the nation' both sides had to deal with the fact that Marx had clearly stated that the war in 1870 was one of self-defense on Germany's part at least to begin with. Prowar socialists attempted to use this as support for their policy of abandoning all activity that might hinder the war effort. They tried to show that Marx would have chosen their course and suspended the class struggle for the duration. Antiwar socialists tried by various shifts to explain Marx's clear and unambiguous statements away.[14] Both sides quoted selectively and with no regard for the context. Nobody has been interested in the real history of political developments inside the movement in 1870.

There is one exception to this statement. One book does attempt a rounded treatment of the whole episode. That is Heinz Beike's *Die Deutsche Arbeiterbewegung und der Krieg von 1870/1871*.[15] This is the most thorough single reference on the political dispute in the German movement. Its interpretation is confused, however, because Beike, whether from conviction or necessity, writes as if Marx and Engels were not only infallible but also always in agreement with one another. And, of course, being infallible, they never had to change their minds about anything. Beike, therefore, has to present flatly contradictory statements side by side and at least pretend not to notice the contradiction. This hagiographic methodology is especially misleading in this instance because the only way to make sense of Marx and Engels' discussion of the war policy of the German section of the *International* in this crisis is to understand that they disagreed at a crucial juncture on what the party's position should be.

The result of all this is that from this large, tendentious and polemical body of literature it is almost impossible to get a coherent picture of what was really going on inside the German socialist movement in 1870.

2. Marx and Engels' 'Defensism'

There is no question that both Marx and Engels initially saw the war as one of self defense on the part, not so much of Prussia, but of Germany. That was the view of most observers at the time.

The German Empire created by the Prussian victory in 1870 was to become the most aggressive and powerful imperialist state in Europe through 1945. We know that. In 1870 no one did. In 1870 the 'aggressor' was not Prussia but the Second French Empire. It was France that declared war. The French *casus belli*—the 'insult' offered the French Emperor when Prussia toyed with the idea of accepting the offer by a revolutionary Spanish military junta to install a Hohenzollern Prince as Spanish monarch—was a traditional dynastic one. The demand that the North German Federation make territorial concessions was justified on similar grounds. On the French side at least there was none of the democratic rhetoric that has been required by militarism since the beginning of World War I. There was no pretense that the German people were being delivered from a tyrannical government. That Bismarck desired the war and waged an active campaign to provoke the French to declare it was a fact not as well known then, and certainly not as well-documented, as it has since become.* [16] But there was a more general consideration behind Marx's characterization of the war as one of defense on Germany's part.

In Marx and Engels' view, but not only theirs, Louis Bonaparte's exploitation of the Napoleonic tradition domestically and the maintenance of a large standing army, also for domestic proposes, created a constant pressure driving him to military adventures. At the same time both Marx and Engels had a low opinion of the real fighting ability of this imitation of the Napoleonic *Grande Armée*.[17] Certainly, by 1870, the French army represented no revolutionary threat to the stability of the monarchies, except in so far as war in general has the potential of provoking revolution. Bonaparte's policy in Europe was one of shifting alliances aimed at preventing the growth of any serious opponent. In particular it meant keeping Germany in a state of disarray with Prussia dependent on Russia and the south German states dependent on Austria. Although he cloaked himself in the mantle of Napoleon, Bonaparte's aim, and only hope, was to maintain the division of Europe settled on at the Congress of Vienna.

---

* There were those who were suspicious of course. Marx *may* have been one of them. The minutes of the February 14, 1871 meeting of the *GC* report a long speech by Marx. In the course of it he summed up his view of the causes and progress of the war. The general line is the same as that in the two addresses he wrote for the *GC*. The war began as a defensive war but after Bonaparte's defeat at Sedan this was no longer so. He then goes on to say "I know that Bismarck worked as hard to bring about the war as Napoleon, the defense was only a pretext. But after Sedan he wanted a new pretext."
Unfortunately, we cannot be sure that Marx actually said this because at the next meeting on February 21 he repudiated the minutes *in toto*. He claimed that the minutes were so inaccurate that he could only correct them by repeating the whole speech.[16] There is no way of knowing whether he repudiated this particular sentence or not. There is certainly no other statement private or public in which either Marx or Engels denied that the war was initially a war of defense on Germany's part. On the other hand, the argument that *Bismarck* was using the war as a pretext for his annexationist plans is perfectly consistent with everything Marx and Engels wrote.[17]

Karl Marx's Theory of Revolution: V5

A defeat for Louis Bonaparte, the Napoleonic legend, and French chauvinism was almost as important for Marx and Engels as the defeat of Tsarist Russia. Indeed, since both powers worked to preserve the same system, a defeat for either amounted to the same thing. Given this view of the historical evolution of the European state system, it was natural that the war was seen as a defensive one on Germany's side. It was not only a question of who was 'the aggressor,' although, obviously, Marx's response to the war was conditioned by the almost universal belief that Bonaparte was playing that role.

What political conclusion did Marx draw from all of this? Marx did not welcome a war. And he certainly did not endorse either side. In the *First Address* on the war which he drafted for the General Council of the *IWMA*, he *conceded* that the war was defensive in nature on the German side. He then proceeded to heavily qualify the concession, urged the members of the *IWMA* to oppose the war, and held up as examples the antiwar activity of both the French and German sections.

This was not a new departure for Marx. He had struck the same note in 1868 in his advice to his political allies Johann Georg Eccarius and Friedrich Lessner who were delegates to the Brussels congress of the *IWMA*. The context was a proposed resolution of the *IWMA* on war put forward by J. P. Becker, who was also a political friend of Marx. Becker's resolution presented on behalf of the German delegation stated that "any European war, and especially any war between France and Germany, must be regarded today as a civil war mainly for the profit of Russia ..."[18] Marx's advice was:

> The decision to be adopted on this question seems to be simply this: that the working class is not yet sufficiently organized to throw any substantial weight into the scales; that the Congress, however, protests in the name of the working class and denounces the instigators of the war; that a war between France and Germany is a civil war, ruinous for both countries and ruinous for Europe in general. A statement that war can only benefit the Russian Government will scarcely win the endorsement of the French and Belgian gentlemen.[19]

This was the line Marx was to follow throughout the war crisis in 1870. Hostility to the 'instigators' of the war by the *IWMA* as a power independent of and opposed to all belligerents was the political emphasis in Marx's statements on the war, private as well as public. His comments, especially his private comments, on the relative merits of the two sides, on the reactions of the French and German workers and the non-working class populations of the two countries, his hopes as to the outcome of the war, even his prognostications as to the outcome of the war, have all been mined by Marxologists trying to dig out Marx's 'real' position. Usually, these comments are used to 'prove' that Marx was 'really' a pro-German patriot. The attempt has met with some success because most commentators simply ignore Marx's explicit statements to the contrary.

What is especially interesting about this 1868 incident is Marx's advice to his friends to *tone down* the anti-Tsarist language of the proposed resolution. Obviously, Marx shared Becker's hostility to Tsarism. But, he wanted an antiwar resolution that would unite rather than divide this newly formed movement.

3. Marx and Engels' 'Change of Position'"

The conventional explanation for the ambiguities and contradictions in the statements on the Franco-Prussian war by Marx and Engels holds that they changed their position after Bonaparte's surrender at Sedan on September 2, 1870. Before then they supported Germany and after they supported France.[20] This is a convenient schema and Engels himself is partly responsible for its spread for reasons that will become clear later.[21] All sides in the debates of the socialist movement before, during and after World War I accepted the proposition. But the record indicates that Marx declared his opposition to *Bismarck's* role at the very beginning of the war and praised the German section of the *IWMA* for what Marx alleged was its antiwar stand.

One reason for the ambiguity in Marx's *public* pronouncements is that in them he was performing a diplomatic balancing act. The trick was to write a defiant antiwar address hostile to both governments which would carefully avoid, as much as possible, anything that could provide ammunition for the inevitable chauvinist backlash against the national sections of the *IWMA* or undermine their mutual solidarity. Recall that, in the 1868 letter to Eccarius quoted above, Marx was already advising his friends not to include a direct attack on Russia in the *International* resolution on war not because *he* disagreed with such a statement but because a fight over the issue with the French and Belgians would make it difficult to pass an antiwar resolution.

This is an easy thing for most commentators to miss. The overwhelming majority of Marxologists are academics with little or no organizational experience in the labor movement or any mass movement. They simply don't understand how easy it is to blow up a promising organization by insisting that every 't' be crossed and every 'I' dotted. In a period where even the best people are under tremendous pressure, as all were during the crisis of the Franco-Prussian war, it required enormous tact to work out a public stand that sections of the *IWMA* in the different belligerent countries could adhere to and defend. Marx explicitly stated the problem in a letter to Engels accompanying a copy of the draft of the *Second Address* of the GC:

> You must not forget that the General Council has to deal with °susceptibilities from all sides° and hence cannot write the same way we two can in our own name.[22]

Yet, the addresses of the General Council drafted by Marx are often treated as if Marx were stating his own position without restriction.

His *private* comments, where he could more freely express his own opinions, were less readily available. However, even before World War I there was enough evidence to make clear that the alleged 'change of position' after Sedan simply didn't happen.

From the day the war broke out Marx urged both the French and German sections of the *IWMA* to organize against their own governments. Even at this date, when public opinion, especially in England, sympathized with Germany, Marx warned of *Bismarck's* annexationist plans. In the meetings of the General Council Marx reported on every sign of opposition to the war on the part of the German and French sections. The public addresses of the *GC* which he drafted also emphasized this opposition to both sides. With one exception, Liebknecht's refusal to vote

The Despots of ALL Countries ...

for war credits in the Reichstag, both Marx and Engels unreservedly supported such actions.

In the case of Liebknecht, Engels at one point did express private reservations concerning the Reichstag vote. Engels' letter in which he attacked Liebknecht was used by Mehring and is still used to argue that *both* Marx and Engels repudiated Liebknecht and urged support for the German side before Sedan. But Marx, before and after Engels' criticism, not only endorsed Liebknecht's action but also used it frequently as evidence of the hostility to *Bismarck's* war on the part of the German working class. In a report to the *GC* at the first meeting after the vote he mentioned it as one of a number of antiwar demonstrations by the German section.[23] Marx always boasted of this particular act of protest by the German section of the *IWMA* and Engels very shortly came around to this view of Liebknecht's behavior himself.

4. Marx's 'Pro-Prussianism'

In order to buttress the case for Marx's alleged pro-Prussianism at the beginning of the war and associate him with Engels' attack on Liebknecht resort has to be made to his private correspondence. That is because there is no evidence for this alleged pro-Prussian sentiment in Marx's public statements as spokesman for the *GC*.

The French declaration of war on July 19, 1870 happened to fall on the same day as a regularly scheduled meeting of the General Council of the *IWMA*. The Paris Section of the organization had already published an antiwar declaration on July 12 calling on the French, German and Spanish workers to unite in opposing the political ambitions of the ruling classes. In particular, they opposed any division between French and German workers which could only "result in the complete triumph of *despotism* on both sides of the Rhine." [24] Marx read a translation of this declaration into the minutes. He also read excerpts from a "private letter" (from Paul Lafargue) which reported on the lack of war feeling in the provinces and the manufactured enthusiasm in Paris.[25]

Unfortunately, the sections of the *IWMA* in France were weak and disorganized, in large part because of police persecution, and Marx was well aware of the real strength of French chauvinism. Popular support for Bonaparte swept over the country. In a letter to Engels the day after the

GC meeting in which he had reported on the antiwar manifesto (July 20) he noted that in the same journal, *La Réveil*, in which the declaration of the Paris section had appeared the lead articles by the editor, Charles Delescluze, took a generally prowar line—while continuing to oppose the government, of course. Delescluze was an old and honorable Jacobin revolutionary (nonsocialist) from 1830 on, a courageous opponent of Louis Bonaparte, and a man shortly to die a hero's death in the defense of the Commune. If even he was succumbing to the outpouring of popular prowar sentiment things were in a bad way in France.

This recrudescence of chauvinism among the French people, and in particular in the French left, provoked an outburst from Marx. In this letter Marx sounded a theme which he and Engels were to repeat throughout the war in their *private* communications.* Partly as a result of Bonapartism *and the capitulation to it* of that section of the French left (the largest section by far) which looked back to the old tradition of 1793, Marx and Engels came to believe that the French had ceded the leadership of the revolutionary movement, at least temporarily, to the Germans.

> ... the paper [*La Réveil*] is also interesting on account of the leading articles by old Delescluze. Although he opposes the government [he represents] the fullest expression of chauvinism, *car la France est le seul pays de l'idée* (namely, the ideas it has about itself). These republican chauvinists are put out only by the fact that the real expression of their idol—Louis Bonaparte ... does not correspond with their fanciful picture of him. The French need a thrashing. If the Prussians win, then the centralization of the state power [will be] useful for the centralization of the German working class. German predominance would, furthermore, shift the center of

---

* Engels *after* the war was to repeat a similar theme in two public statements. His pamphlets on *The Housing Question* and *The Program of the Blanquists* were directed in large part at the outlived tradition of French radical nationalism. By this time, however, the issues which had occupied public attention before the fall of the Empire were ancient history.

> gravity of the Western European working-class movement from France to Germany, and one has only to compare the movement in both countries from 1866 till now to see that the German working class is superior to the French theoretically and organizationally. Its predominance over the French on the world stage would at the same time mean the predominance of our theory over that of Proudhon, etc. ...²⁶

This passage is the strongest evidence for Marx's 'pro-Prussianism' and the one most often used to convict him of being a supporter of the war. He wants to see the French "thrashed!" He looks forward to a *Prussian* victory because it would assure his theoretical ascendance! The background, the explosion of French chauvinism, is ignored.

A much more balanced analysis appeared in a letter the same day, July 28, to Paul and Laura Lafargue. Marx included two clippings from *Der Volkstaat* (Liebknecht's paper) and commented "You will see that he and Bebel behaved exceedingly well in the Reichstag." Then he outlined, in softer tones than the earlier letter to Engels, his speculation on the beneficial effects of a Prussian victory:

> For my own part, I should like that both, Prussians and French, thrashed each other alternately, and that—as I believe will be the case—the Germans got *ultimately* the better of it. I wish this because the definite defeat of Bonaparte is likely to provoke Revolution in France, while the definite defeat of the Germans would only protract the present state of things for 20 years.²⁷

Both of these passages should be compared to Marx's 1859 letter to Lassalle in which he warns of the *reactionary* consequences of a war between France and Germany. And there are other statements in 1870 on the reactionary results of a German victory which have to be taken into account if one wants a balanced view of Marx's speculations on the war. Engels, especially, in later years emphasized the reactionary consequences of the victory and, as we shall see shortly, even in the very first stages of the war Marx made opposition to the annexation of Alsace-Lorraine, which he and Engels anticipated, a key point in the resolutions of the *International*. What is clear from these letters is that Marx and Engels were thinking out loud about the war as it was developing. This 'thinking out loud' did not, however, determine what official policy Marx urged on the *IWMA*.

But it is not only Marx's public antiwar statements that are ignored. Those private letters which express his contempt for the Prussian king, for Bismarck and for German nationalism *at the very beginning of the war* also disappear in most accounts.

In his July 28 letter to Engels, barely a week after the war began, Marx expressed his deep contempt for the Prussian side. His remarks were provoked by the contrast between the "opening ceremonies" of the war on the respective sides. In France, naturally, the *Marseillaise* was the background music. It was parody Marx said "just like the whole Second Empire." But at least "that dog" knew he couldn't get away with his favorite imperialist hymn "On to Syria." Wilhelm I and Bismarck, however, had no need of "such tomfoolery" because of the backwardness of German public opinion. They sang an old Protestant hymn reminding the world that the soon-to-be German Empire was not only not a republic but was not even a modern nation state. It was the fiefdom of a Protestant dynasty whose ideology was not only alien to the increasingly secular society of nineteenth century Europe but offensive to the large number of its subjects-to-be who were Catholic.

Marx commented on the enthusiasm which greeted this display:

> The German philistine seems absolutely delighted that he can now unabashedly give vent to his innate servility. Who would have thought that 22 years after 1848 a national war in Germany would take on *such* theoretical expression![28]

The good news was that the working class was not taken in:

The Despots of ALL Countries ...

> ... fortunately the war of classes in both countries, France and Germany, has developed to such an extent that no war abroad can seriously turn back the wheel of history.

Marx could be accused here of overestimating the strength of the working class opposition to the war (although in light of the subsequent explosion of the Commune his optimism may have been based on better judgement than the cynicism of the manipulators of public opinion) but he cannot be accused of pro-Prussianism.

5. The "Neutrality Spirit'

If Marx at first 'wished for' a Prussian victory as the most desirable outcome, he never wavered in his conviction that the *International* and the organized working class had to oppose both sides. In the very same week in which Marx expressed his violent reaction to French chauvinism he continued his campaign of *public* support for and emphasis on the antiwar activity of the French and German working classes. At the second meeting of the *GC* after the war began, this was on July 26, Marx presented the draft of *The First Address of the General Council of the International Working Men's Association on the War*. At this same meeting he reported on the arrest of Tolain and 15 other members of the *International* by the Paris police, a peace demonstration at Lyons suppressed by the military, and a strike by miners in Alsace "who cared nothing about the war." It was at this meeting also that he reported on the refusal of Bebel and Liebknecht to vote for war credits in the Reichstag of the North German Confederation. There is not a hint in public of any pro-Prussian sentiment. What is more to the point, there is no hint that the conviction that the war was at least partly a war of defense meant that Marx thought the *International* ought to support the German side in some way. Even the statement in the *First Address* that the war *began* as a war of defense for the Germans did not lead to any call for support to the German side. Quite the contrary. But there was more. In the very letter to the Lafargues in which he expressed his wish that the Prussians "ultimately" prevail Marx explained what he was trying to do in the *IWMA*:

> As to the English workmen, they hate Bonaparte more than Bismarck, principally because he is the aggressor. At the same time they say: "The plague on both your houses," and if the English oligarchy, as it seems very inclined, should take part in the war against France, there would be a "tuck" at London. For my own part, I do everything in my power, through the means of the *International*, to stimulate this 'Neutrality' spirit and to baffle the '*paid*' (paid by the 'respectables') leaders of the English working class who strain every nerve to mislead them.[29]

That certainly makes it clear enough. But there is another issue raised in this letter which has been overlooked and should be mentioned before we leave it. That is the war that did not happen. Namely, the English intervention on the German side which Marx anticipated. Just before the passage quoted above Marx expanded on this threat:

> The English upper classes are full of indignation against Bonaparte at whose feet they have fawned for 18 years. Then they wanted him as the savior of their privileges, of rents and profits. At the same time, they know the man to be seated on a volcano the which unpleasant position forces him to trouble peace periodically ... Now they hope that to solid Prussia, protestant Prussia, backed by Russia, will fall the part of keeping down revolution in Europe. It would be for them a safer and more respectable policeman.[30]

This is not an isolated observation. Marx had made the same point in the letter to Engels of the same day and he repeated it again in a letter to Engels of August 1.[31] There he applauded the hostility of the English working class public to "That damned German dynasty of ours" which "wants for family reasons to involve us in the continental war. ..." This hostility was widespread despite the fact that Bismarck "has duly bought up part of the London Press." Marx reported to Engels that one of these,

Reynold's, was demanding the dismemberment of France. His comment on this sudden abandonment of Bonaparte by the English establishment? "These swine manage their flipflops crudely."

As an explanation of the pro-Prussianism of English public opinion at the beginning of the war this is interesting. But things did not turn out the way Marx originally thought they would. The unexpected, overwhelming victory of Prussia and the exposure of France's weakness pushed England and Russia into an alliance with France *against* the new German Empire. And it soon became clear to Marx and even more to Engels that this was going to be the pattern that dominated the future. Nevertheless, at the very beginning of the war, when Marx still saw it as a war of defense on Germany's part he was prepared to lead a fight against English intervention. His speculations about the war, even his recognition of the superior claim of one side did not lead him to advocate support for any of the governments involved. He bent his efforts to maintaining and asserting the independence of the international workers' movement.

6. The Trouble With Wilhelm Liebknecht

The refusal of August Bebel and Wilhelm Liebknecht to vote for war credits on July 20, 1870 was one of those acts that define a political party. As we have seen Marx immediately seized on it as a symbol of working class antiwar resistance in Germany and continued to use it as such in all public statements. After the war, at least up until 1914, the majority of German socialists pointed to this dramatic demonstration of intransigent opposition to Bismarck with pride. This was how socialists were supposed to act. Marx certainly endorsed that view. At the time, however, the action was highly controversial in the German party. And Engels also opposed it briefly.

The Lassallean delegation to the Reichstag, headed by Schweitzer, enthusiastically voted for the credits. A lead article in the Lassallean paper, *Social-Democrat*, declared that "every German who throws himself against the breaker of the peace [Bonaparte] fights not only for the Fatherland ... [but] for Liberty, Equality and Fraternity."[32] This confusion of Wilhelm the First, King of Prussia, with Robespierre came naturally to the Lassalleans since their whole policy was based on an alliance with the Prussian monarchy against the bourgeois liberals. They had no qualms or difficulties to overcome and welcomed the chance to put themselves forward as the most patriotic party.

More problematic was the prowar response of members of Liebknecht's own party, the *SDAP*. Reluctance to face up to the wave of popular chauvinism sweeping the country played a role, of course, but part of the problem was the existence of a significant number of ex-Lassalleans within the party. These dissidents had broken with Schweitzer over his insistence on maintaining his personal dictatorship over the party and the infant trade union movement (*à la* Lassalle himself). When the opportunity for merger presented itself in 1869, less than a year before the war broke out, Liebknecht and his friends, shrinking from a confrontation over the matter, ignored the pro-Prussianism instilled in their new comrades by Lassalle and Schweitzer. (The same pattern was repeated in 1875 when the two parties united and the issue was never resolved right up to 1914 when the party split over it.)

The pro-Prussian, patriotic tendency of most members of the executive committee of the *SDAP* residing in Brunswick* quickly surfaced. They called a public meeting on July 16, just before the declaration of war, and passed a resolution regretfully accepting the "war of defense as an unavoidable evil."[33] Four days later they informed Liebknecht that he was to align the editorial policy of his paper, *Der Volkstaat*, with that of the Brunswick resolution. On July 24 they amplified their position in a leaflet committing the party to the defense of the fatherland as long as the country was menaced by French troops, supported the "striving of the German people for national unity" and "hoped" that the new state would be a social democratic People's state rather than a dynastic, Prussian one.[34]

What created more of a problem for Liebknecht was that when he attempted to use the *First Address* of the *GC* as a weapon against the Executive Committee the latter sought the advice of Marx and Engels—and Engels tended to side with the Brunswickers at least in so far

---

* The Germans call this town *Braunschweig*. But in all the English translations of Marx and Engels' writings the Cental Committee is referred to collectively as "the Brunswickers." To avoid confusion I will use the English term.

as their criticism of Liebknecht was concerned. The letter that was sent in reply bore Marx's signature but it was written with Engels' collaboration.[35]

The position outlined in this joint letter differed significantly from both the Executive Committee position and that of Liebknecht. While the Brunswick committee *identified* the defense of Germany with that of Bismarck's war and Liebknecht denied that there was anything involved *except* a dynastic conflict, Marx and Engels saw a more complicated pattern. What they saw was Bismarck *using* the real issue of German unity as a pretext for his dynastic-imperial purposes. The *main* task of the German working class—and this repeated the theme of the *First Address*—was to frustrate Bismarck's annexationist designs on France.

But if Germany's national integrity really was threatened, shouldn't socialists have supported the war at least up to a point?

In his letter to Marx on the matter Engels sharply attacked Liebknecht's statement to the Reichstag and, however indirectly, the line taken in the *First Address* by Marx himself. Marx, in response, defended Liebknecht only lukewarmly.

What was agitating Engels was a longstanding dispute between the Londoners and Liebknecht over a number of issues combined with a generally low opinion of Liebknecht's political acumen. As we saw in the last chapter, while Marx and Engels had come to the conclusion—reluctantly—that German unity was to come at the hands of Bismarck, Liebknecht refused to accept that fact. Liebknecht paid lip service to the 1848 ideal of a Germany united by a democratic revolution but, since that was not in the cards, in practice he flirted with the South German liberals, who hoped to counterbalance Prussian might by shoring up the petty princelings, and even with pro-Austrian clerical reactionaries.

Marx and Engels would have nothing to do with such politics. They wanted to see an aggressive, independent socialist party use the new united Germany as a battlefield; a far more favorable one for the working class movement than the old semi-feudal *German Confederation* had been. Judged by this standard, Schweitzer and his Lassalleans were often closer to the mark than Liebknecht, even if Marx and Engels opposed Schweitzer on more basic principles.

In this case we have an instance of a general pattern. While far more sympathetic to Liebknecht at a fundamental level, Engels feared that his blindness to the real benefits of German unification would lead him to bungle the attack on Bismarck's annexationist schemes. And, in Engels' opinion, Marx had helped mislead Liebknecht.

7. Engels' Attack on Liebknecht

In order to straighten out the tangled politics of the German party Engels had to think through his own position on the war. Marx, in his capacity as political leader of the *General Council*, had been required to come up with a minimum statement that all sections of the *International* could support. What he and Engels were now called on to do was to elaborate a political program for a workers' party in a country involved in the war and facing political isolation. How could the party regain the initiative and reverse the wave of chauvinism that threatened to overwhelm it?

Engels' attempt, outlined in detail in a letter to Marx on August 15, was the first, and only, statement by either man that contemplated support to one side in the war. He proposed to support the German side while opposing the Prussian government. His target was what he called Liebknecht's "abstention."[36]

The principle argument advanced by Engels was similar to the one he was to make later in the letter to Kautsky of 1882 which was quoted in an earlier chapter.[37] It was the same argument that Lenin was to make the basis of his defense of the right of nations to self determination. Engels concluded that if the war was one for national existence then Germany's defeat would set back the workers' movement because the national question would overlay and suppress the social question. The German party therefore had an obligation to support this war of self-defense up to a point:

> Germany has been driven by [Bonaparte] into a war for national existence. If [Bonaparte] defeats her Bonapartism will be strengthened for years and Germany broken for years, perhaps for generations. In that event there can be no question of an independent German working class movement either, the struggle to restore Germany's national existence will absorb everything. ... If Germany wins French Bonapartism will be smashed, the endless

row about the establishment of German unity will at last be got rid of, the German workers will be able to organize on a national scale ... and the French workers, whatever sort of government may succeed this one, are certain to have a freer field than under Bonapartism.[38]

Like the Poles and the Irish, the German workers needed national independence to give them "footing—air, light and elbow-room."[39] Engels asked sarcastically how a nation that allowed itself to "suffer kicks and blows" could be expected to make a social revolution. Given this starting point Engels had to oppose "total abstention *à la* Wilhelm."* After a sentence or two emphasizing the chauvinism "of the mass of the French population" and the impossibility of peace until this chauvinism is "knocked on the head," he gets down to what he proposes against Liebknecht:

> 1) join the national movement—you can see from Kugelman's letter how strong it is—in so far and for so long as it is limited to the defense of Germany (which does not exclude an offensive in certain circumstances, until peace is arrived at);
> 2) at the same time emphasize the differences between German national and dynastic-Prussian interests;
> 3) work against any annexation of Alsace and Lorraine—Bismarck is now intimating an intention of annexing them to Bavaria and Baden;
> 4) as soon as a non-chauvinistic republican government is at the helm in Paris, work for an honorable peace with it;

---

* It is not clear whether Engels at the time he wrote this letter was aware that the declaration made to the Reichstag was actually Bebel's and not Liebknecht's.
Liebknecht had originally intended to oppose the motion to vote war credits. Bebel convinced him to abstain on the vote instead precisely because a "no" vote could be made to look like backhanded support to Bonaparte.

5) constantly stress the unity of interests between the German and French workers, who did not approve of the war and are also not making war on one another;[40]

The key to this proposed program is the emphasis on Alsace-Lorraine. For Engels, opposition to the annexation of this region of France by Prussian militarism had to be part of the policy of German socialists. It was the key to a working class alliance against both Prussian militarism and French revanchism. Engels emphasized its importance throughout the war and for the next couple of decades—until the end of his life. It was the issue which in practice separated the dynastic-Prussian and national-German interests. As opposed to what he saw as Liebknecht's attempt to hide a policy of abstention behind revolutionary rhetoric (something Liebknecht had done before and would do again) Engels proposed to attack Bismarck at a political weak point.

It should not be supposed, however, that Engels was advocating support for the Brunswick committee. His position was as far from theirs as it was from Liebknecht's. The Executive Committee had not distinguished its prowar policy at all from that of the government except in so far as its support for the war was reluctant rather than enthusiastic. The Brunswick declarations had not opposed Bismarck's annexationist plans. Indeed, they had not even hinted that such plans existed.[41] But, then, Bebel and Liebknecht had not made anything of this issue either.

Engels tactic made sense given two conditions. The first was that a Prussian defeat remained a real possibility. In that case she would have been thrown back into an alliance with Russia (a danger Marx had warned against in the *First Address*) and Germany would have reverted back to its pre-1866 state. The second condition, related to the first, was that Bismarck continued to hold the high ground politically as against the increasingly isolated Bonaparte.

And that is what is the most interesting, and confusing, feature of Engels' letter. In the second half of it, after a couple more paragraphs spent bashing "Wilhelm," he shifts gears and begins to describe what is going on in France. It is clear that Engels understood that, by this time, Bonaparte was well on the way to losing the war. That is, the situation in

The Despots of ALL Countries ...

which Engels' proposals made sense was past, or at any rate, very close to being so.

At the start of the war Engels had contracted with a London journal, *The Pall Mall Gazette*, to write a series of articles reporting on the military operations of the two armies. The series lasted from July 29, 1870 to February 18, 1871 and consisted of some 52 articles. By mid-August Engels was describing in detail to his readers just how bad a shellacking the Bonapartist armies were taking. The second part of his letter to Marx is a snapshot of the situation as he saw it.

> The debacle in France seems to be frightful. Everything squandered, sold, swindled away. The *chassepots* are badly made and miss fire in action; there are no more of them and the old flintlocks have got to be hunted out again. Nevertheless a revolutionary government, if it comes *soon*, need not despair. But it must abandon Paris to its fate and carry on the war from the South. There would then still be a possibility of its holding out until arms have been brought and new armies organized which would gradually force the enemy back to the frontier.[42]

This is a most peculiar letter. In its first half Engels goes as far as either he or Marx ever had towards openly supporting the German side in the war. In the second half he writes as a military partisan of the French revolutionary government he expected and hoped to see soon *against* the same Prussian armies which were defending Germany's national existence only a few short sentences before.

The cause of this jarring transition has to be sought in the rapid pace of events. This letter was written less than a month after the war began. Engels, along with Marx, found himself drawn into an internal debate in the German movement which arose in the first days of the war. As usual his old friend Liebknecht, who was often seen as his and Marx's contact and even representative in the German movement, had taken a position which was too close to being right to be denounced but not close enough to being right to be endorsed. This is the problem Engels was asked to solve and the first half of the letter attempts to solve it by outlining what

141

Liebknecht's position *should have been* in the beginning when all believed that there was a real threat to Germany. But by mid-August, as Engels knew better than most, the threat to Germany, if it ever had been serious, was so no longer. As a consequence, the letter looks in two directions. One toward the beginning of the war, the other toward the present and the immediate future.

In the meantime, the Executive Committee of the *SDAP* awaited the reply from London to their letter.

8. Marx's Reply to Engels

Marx clearly recognized that Engels was criticizing not only Liebknecht but his own enthusiastic and unqualified endorsement of Bebel and Liebknecht's Reichstag vote. In a sense it was the *First Address* of the *GC* written by Marx that had sparked off the debate in Germany. Liebknecht had translated the address (badly Marx claimed) and reprinted it in *Der Volkstaat*. Its forceful antiwar phrases and its hostility to Bismarck—something that was lacking in the Brunswick Committee's original resolution—lent credit to Liebknecht's claim that it was he and not the Brunswick Committee who represented the view of the international movement.*

Furthermore, Liebknecht's publication of Marx's statement was not an isolated incident. It was part of a campaign. In order to get around the Executive Committee's insistence that he edit *Der Volkstaat* in accord with the party policy it had set, Liebknecht had taken to filling his columns with "news reports" of every manifestation of antiwar sentiment among German workers he could dig up. Apparently, there were a good many.[43]

---

* There is another aspect to this fight. The main reason the Lassallean dissidents had split from Schweitzer was his dictatorship over the *ADAV*. In particular, he wrote what he pleased in the paper without regard for the opinion of the majority of his party. Now Liebknecht was using the main paper of the *SDAP* to agitate for his antiwar position while the elected leadership of the party was prowar. The ex-Lassalleans accused Liebknecht of setting up the same kind of intra party dictatorship that Lassalle and Schweitzer had. Of course, they had not been elected to their positions on a prowar platform. Neither they nor Liebknecht had any mandate to speak for the party as a whole.

Now, in fact the *First Address* had not openly taken a stand on the internal German party dispute. It did not advocate any practical policy for the German party—beyond protesting the war—any more than it did for the French. But it was obviously written with the debate in Germany in mind.

It began with a quote from the *Inaugural Address* of the *IWMA* which denounced "piratical wars," proceeded to an attack on Louis Bonaparte and his "war plot" and then strongly emphasized the opposition to the war and to Bonaparte by the French section of the International. Only then, half-way through did it mention that the war was one of self-defense on Germany's part. But it was a qualified endorsement of that view:

> On the German side, the war is a war of self defense, but who put Germany to the necessity of defending herself? Who enabled Louis Bonaparte to wage war on her? *Prussia*! It was Bismarck who conspired with that very same Louis Bonaparte for the purpose of crushing opposition at home, and annexing Germany to the Hohenzollern dynasty. ... The Bonapartist regime, which till then only flourished on one side of the Rhine, had now got its counterfeit on the other.[44]

This whole passage was an indirect reference to the quarrel between Bebel-Liebknecht and the Brunswick Committee. Marx was quoting Bebel and Liebknecht here and not only their statement to the Reichstag. The same anti-Bismarck language characterized a declaration issued in Chemnitz by a regional congress of the *SDAP* hurriedly organized by the two Reichstag deputies on July 20. This was their response to the Executive Committee's prowar rally of July 16. The antiwar resolution passed by the congress was, of course, published in *Der Volkstaat*.[45] Who could question its newsworthiness?

Marx also reprinted the section of the Brunswick Committee's resolution of July 16 which expressed its sorrow and grief over having to fight a war of self-defense but he coupled it with excerpts from the diametrically opposed resolution of the Chemnitz congress. That assembly had declared the war "exclusively dynastic" and swore never to forget "that the workmen of *all* countries are our *friends* and the despots of *all* countries are our *enemies*."[46] And this is the section Marx chose to quote in the *First Address*.

But Marx made no mention of the Bebel-Liebknecht Reichstag vote in the *First Address* although he certainly knew of it by then and had already publicized their protest at the July 26 meeting of the General Council.[47] It is hard to avoid the conclusion that he included excerpts from *both* the Brunswick and Chemnitz resolutions in the First Address because he wanted to stress that *all* sections of the German movement opposed the government and, in some sense, the war. For the same reason, Marx may not have mentioned the vote because he knew it was a point of contention and he did not want to emphasize the differences in the German section. A split of the German section into a prowar majority and an antiwar minority would have undermined the *International* and destroyed the new German party as well. In order to avoid that, Marx had to win over the Brunswick Committee not drive them out. His inclusion of a passage from the Executive Committee's official resolution that sounded at least mildly critical of the war was a way of associating them indirectly with his own antiwar stand.

What then was the responsibility of the German working class? To prevent the war from degenerating into one against the French people according to the *First Address*. This political point was the specific contribution of Marx and Engels. Its strong antiwar thrust was more consistent with Bebel and Liebknecht's stand in the Reichstag than the Brunswick Committee's reluctant commitment to the war of defense. One could even argue that it was a sharper and better focused attack on Bismarck than the Bebel-Liebknecht resolution because it directly challenged his pose as innocent victim of aggression. Certainly, Bismarck took this challenge as a hostile act.

All and all, even if the Reichstag vote was not mentioned directly, it was obvious that, in style and substance, the *First Address* was closer to Liebknecht and Bebel than it was to that of the Brunswick Executive Committee. Liebknecht had every right to appeal to it in his defense.

We also know that, in private, Marx had already expressed his reservations about the Brunswick resolution in a letter to Engels of July 20. He enclosed with that letter a copy of the resolution and added that he agreed with Kugelman's criticism of its undiplomatic insistence that the French workers overthrow Bonaparte as a proof of their solidarity.[48]

As for Schweitzer, Marx had dismissed his followers as inconsequential in his letter of July 28 to Engels: "The working class [of Germany] with the exception of the direct supporters of Schweitzer, takes no part in it."[49] [By it Marx refers to the chauvinist demonstrations of the German bourgeoisie]. The important thing for Marx was that the majority of the German movement, including the Brunswick committee, was suspicious of Bismarck and reluctant to join in the national prowar euphoria. He was trying in the *First Address* to encourage this "neutrality spirit."

Engels obviously disagreed. Although he did not argue that the position of the *International* should be changed, his letter was a warning to Marx that the *First Address* had sent Liebknecht the wrong signal. The stick had to be bent the other way.

Marx defended his actions in moderate tones but he did not change his view. He could not simply ignore Engels' criticism of Liebknecht. It was too close to his own view of the man and he had too often been politically embarrassed himself by Liebknecht. But he also couldn't avoid thinking of the *international* repercussions of the fight in the German movement. The French sections, sharing the general French indifference to the politics of foreign countries, couldn't have cared less about the disputes between South German particularists and pro-Prussians. For them an emphasis, such as Engels proposed, by a German party could be seen as a concession to German chauvinism.

What Marx told Engels was that it was not "a question of Wilhelm but of *directives on the attitude* [toward the war] *for the German workers*."[50] He then distanced himself from Liebknecht on the grounds that 1) Liebknecht's use of the *First Address* as a buttress to his position was dependent on the latter's first translating it into "Wilhelmese" and 2) his endorsement of the Bebel-Liebknecht stand on war credits in the Reichstag could not be taken as an endorsement of Liebknecht's general position. The second point is particularly confused in the letter:

> That was a "moment" when sticking for principle was *un acte de courage,* from which it does not follow at all that the moment still continues, and much less that the position

of the German proletariat on the war which has become a national war is comprehended in Wilhelm's antipathy to Prussia. It would be just as if, because at the appropriate moment we had raised our voices against the "Bonapartist" liberation of Italy, we should want to reverse the relative independence which Italy obtained as a result of this war.[51]

The problem with this argument is that the timing is all wrong. Actually, the timing is backwards. *At the beginning of the war*, when Bonaparte still had to be taken seriously and was taken seriously by everybody, Engels' criticism of Liebknecht had some merit. But it was precisely then that Marx himself had made so much of the protest by the two Reichstag deputies. By mid-August, when these letters were being written, Bonaparte's military prowess was revealed to be the hollow boast it probably had always been. In hindsight, we know that *Bismarck* had never been that worried about the military potential of the French. For that matter, Marx himself, in the *Second Address*, claimed that "even before war operations had actually set in, we treated the Bonapartist bubble as a thing of the past."[52]

As far as German unity and independence were concerned, by this time Prussian victories had already decided the issue and Liebknecht himself soon accepted the new political reality imposed by Bismarck's triumph. In fact, for the next couple of decades Marx and Engels, and then Engels alone, found themselves fighting Liebknecht's tendency to adapt himself and the party to this new reality. Just as they had previously had to fight his tendency to accommodate the provincial prejudices of the South German liberals.

However confused Marx's reply to Engels was in detail, the main thrust of his argument was clear. *Liebknecht's follies are not that important.* Engels' objections to Liebknecht *on this matter* were passé by the time he wrote his letter to Marx and they apparently did not show up in the reply to the Executive Committee in Brunswick. The letter to the Brunswick Committee which Marx and Engels wrote over the next couple of weeks was if anything more hostile to Bismarck and Prussia than anything they had written before.

The Despots of ALL Countries ...

In one sense Engels was proven right. The definitive victory of Prussia in the war laid the question of German unity to rest. For the German movement there was now one clear enemy.

9. The Letter to the Brunswick Committee

The letter that Marx and Engels worked on between August 22 and August 30 is not extant. However, a substantial section of it was quoted verbatim in a leaflet issued by the Brunswick Committee on September 5, 1870 and published in *Der Volkstaat* on September 11, 1870.[53] The dates are significant. While the leaflet was published after Bonaparte's humiliating surrender at Sedan on September 2 Marx and Engels' letter was written when the issue was still in doubt. But even then it was not much in doubt. Engels wrote two articles at the same time he was working on the reply to the Brunswickers. The first on August 27 and the second on August 31.[54] Neither of these articles say explicitly that the French army is through but both clearly anticipate a defensive war by the French. For the next several months, through the middle of February 1871, Engels' articles—despite his pose as 'objective' military expert—are frankly pro-French. The issue that had divided the *SDAP* was no longer relevant.

Marx and Engels' letter, as excerpted in the Brunswick leaflet, did not mention the defense of Germany against the Bonapartist threat. That doesn't mean it wasn't in the original. Since Bonaparte had surrendered three days before it was written and probably more than a week before it was published[55] it is certainly possible that the Committee excised any reference to Germany's self-defense as yesterday's news. But it doesn't seem likely that there was any reference to 'defensism' in the letter given what Engels was writing in *The Pall Mall Gazette*.

Other sections of Engels' letter to Marx of August 15 are strongly reflected, however, in the Brunswick leaflet. The main thrust of the leaflet was a blast at the growing popular enthusiasm in Germany for the annexation of Alsace and Lorraine:

> ... The military camarilla, the professoriat, the citizenry and pothouse politicians maintain that this [the annexation of Alsace-Lorraine] is the means of forever protecting Germany from a war with France. On the contrary it

147

is the best-tested way of turning this war into a *European institution*.*

Neither in their July 16 address nor in any other public pronouncement had the Brunswick committee raised the issue of annexation. When they included this excerpt in the September 5 leaflet it was a first. Bebel and Liebknecht, of course, had attacked Bismarck's aggressive designs from the beginning.

Echoing their denunciations of Prussian policy in 1848 Marx and Engels predicted that Alsace-Lorraine would become "a Poland of the west" that is, not only a forcibly oppressed country but "the surest way of perpetuating military despotism in the rejuvenated Germany."

What was worse the natural reaction of "a viable people" would only encourage the growth of French chauvinism as the Prussians ought to have learned from their own experience under Napoleon's occupation. The letter even argues that a chauvinist reaction in France was partially justified:

> If French chauvinism, as long as the *old state* system existed had a certain material justification in the fact that since 1815 France's capital Paris, and thereby France herself, has lain defenceless after a few lost battles, what new nourishment will this chauvinism not imbibe as soon as the border runs at the Vosges mountains on the east and Metz on the north.[56]

The danger that chauvinism and the thirst for *revanche* would become *permanent* features of French politics as a result of the annexation of Alsace-Lorraine preoccupied Engels for the rest of his life. Prior to the Franco-Prussian war imperialism and militarism had appeared to Marx and Engels primarily as a product of dynastic ambitions. Whether traditional dynasties

---

* *MECW* 22:260 mistranslates "diesen Krieg" of *MEW* 17:268 as "war." But war had been a "European tradition" for a couple of millenia. It is the conflict of German and French chauvinisms that Marx and Engels are concerned about here not war in general.

with more than one foot in the feudal past like the Hapsburgs, Hohenzollerns and Romanovs, or upstart pretenders like the Bonapartes, they had some difficulty presenting themselves as defenders of the people and the nation. Their quarrels were not the peoples' quarrels.

What loomed ahead were "peoples' wars," wars in which the nation itself was threatened or felt to be threatened. Such wars would cut the ground out from under the trend towards international solidarity and provide a powerful political weapon against militant class struggle at home. The attention Engels devoted to this phenomenon in the last decade or so of his life as World War I incubated will be the subject of the next chapter. I mention it now because it is easy for us to underestimate how new this problem was for Marx, Engels and the socialist movement. For us, unfortunately, it is all old hat.

Since the war was not over—it was going to go on until mid-February and was in fact not nearly half over—there was still time for French military resistance and German working class opposition to forestall the annexation of Alsace-Lorraine and the disasters that would follow.

The letter to the Brunswick committee put the choice starkly before the German movement. As we well know, the choice was, indeed, as fateful as Marx and Engels stated it.

> Anyone who is not entirely deafened by the clamor of the moment and who has no *interest* in deafening the German people, must perceive that the war of 1870 is pregnant with a *war between Germany and Russia* just as necessarily as the war of 1866 was pregnant with the war of 1870.[57]

If the Germans "grabbed" Alsace-Lorraine then France would fight alongside Russia in the war which Marx and Engels saw coming. "It is unnecessary to point out the disastrous consequences." On the other hand if an honorable peace were concluded then France's legitimate national claims would not cover for Russia's dynastic pretensions. In that case, and with the important proviso that social revolution in Russia might derail the oncoming war, the results of a confrontation between the new Prussian Empire and Russia would be generally progressive:

> ... then that war will emancipate Europe from the Moscovite dictatorship, will bring about Prussia's dissolution into Germany, will allow a peaceful development in the western part of the Continent, and finally will help the breakthrough of the Russian social revolution ...[58]

This leaflet was far closer to the militant antiwar stance of the Bebel-Liebknecht statement to the Reichstag and the *First Address* than to the July 16 resolution of the Brunswick committee. In fact it is the first *antiwar* statement of the united party. If the Brunswickers now joined Bebel and Liebknecht in opposition to the war and the government it was not because they no longer need fear a popular backlash or government prosecution. The German people were more intoxicated with chauvinism not less after the smashing victory at Sedan and the government shortly indicted the Brunswick committee for treason and shipped them off to an East Prussian fortress in chains. Bebel and Liebknecht were soon to be indicted for treason also. The explanation for the complete political capitulation of the Brunswick leadership has to lie partly in the prestige of Marx, Engels and the *International* and in the convincing force of Marx's letter. But political reality had changed too. As the letter went on to say:

> The present war opens up a new world-historical epoch because of Germany's proof that, even excluding German Austria, she is capable of going her own way, *independent of other countries*. The fact that she is finding her unity in *Prussian barracks* is a punishment that she richly deserves. But *one* result has been immediately gained, by this very fact. The petty trivialities, like for example, the conflict between the National-Liberal North Germans and the South Germans of the People's Party, will no longer stand uselessly in the way.[59]

This last was a parting shot at Liebknecht whose dalliance with the People's Party was well known and used against him by the Lassalleans. This not only put Marx and Engels on record as opposing Liebknecht's policy where it was wrong but also, undoubtedly, made it easier for the

Brunswick committee to accept a statement on the war which was much closer to the Bebel-Liebknecht position than their original one.

Finally, this was their way of saying that German unity was a step forward but that what was most progressive about it was that it was already finished. The issue had been, in Engels' words, "got rid of." There is no reason to doubt that Bonaparte's declaration of war had aroused real fear for Germany's safety in the leadership of the *SDAP*. This letter said: that is over and done with. And so is your dispute with Liebknecht.

The most serious consequence of the war and of German unification, according to the letter, was the increased responsibility it placed on the German movement. "This war has shifted the center of gravity of the Continental working-class movement from France to Germany" Marx claimed. The Germans therefore had a greater responsibility to raise their voice against "the knaves and fools" who wished to continue their "mad game."

10. What Changed at Sedan

We can now see just how oversimplified the usual claim that Marx and Engels changed their position after Bonaparte's collapse is. Certainly, the European balance of power was significantly altered by Bonaparte's defeat and Marx and Engels recognized that as soon and as clearly as anyone else. But the claim is that Marx and Engels both supported the German *government* until Sedan and only opposed it after Bonaparte's defeat. And that is what is not true. Marx never, in public or in private, urged any practical course on the German party or any other section of the *International* other than opposition to the war policy of its own government. His early and enthusiastic endorsement of Liebknecht and Bebel makes that clear. Engels may have been right to insist that if Germany were threatened with dismemberment as all believed initially then Liebknecht's position was a mistake, however honestly made. And, by this line of reasoning, Marx was wrong to support him so uncritically. The abstention of Bebel and Liebknecht in the Reichstag, again following out Engels' line of thought, did lay them open to the demagogy of the Lassalleans and Bismarck and did place the party in an untenable position. We cannot know what course this discussion between Marx and Engels might have taken had the war lasted longer. As it was, the matter was simply dropped.

What changed at Sedan, and even before Sedan, was not Marx's position on the war but the relevance of Engels' objection to it.

Engels himself apparently realized this. In December of 1870, he wrote to Liebknecht's wife, Natalie, in response to the news that Bebel, Liebknecht and Adolph Hepner had been arrested:

> It [the arrest] is the revenge of the Prussians for the moral defeats suffered by the Prussian Empire at the hands of Liebknecht and Bebel even before it was born. We all rejoiced here at the courageous behaviour of both of them in the Reichstag under circumstances where it was really no small achievement to put forward our views freely and defiantly. ... in view of the really admirable reaction of the German workers which has even compelled that swine Schweitzer to acknowledge the leadership of Liebknecht and Bebel, this *coup de force* may well completely miss the target ...

11. Postscript

Marx was furious at the publication of some of the excerpts from his letter in *Der Volkstaat* and their clear attribution to him. He complained to Engels that he had sent the letter as a set of political guidelines expressed in frank language (Marx uses the adjective "brutal") that was not meant to be published.[60] The only specific objection he makes is to the inclusion of the passage describing the shift of the center of gravity within the workers' movement from France to Germany. This was meant to "spur them [the Germans] on" but should never have been published because of the possible inflammatory effect on the French. Engels thought little harm had been done since that is the only point that could be objected to in the leaflet.[61]

In the meantime, the French section, legal now and able to function openly and freely for the first time since the war began, had sent out a manifesto appealing to German workers' to withdraw immediately "back to the Rhine" or face a war in which "we will have to shed your blood."[62] Even ignoring the braggadocio—the French army had just suffered a smashing defeat after all—the letter was objectionable because it was likely to inflame German national feeling. The left bank of the Rhine had been German-speaking for centuries.

To top it off both the Germans and the French had translated their respective manifestos into the other's language and sent copies to the appropriate addresses. Liebknecht duly published the French leaflet in *Der Volkstaat*. Marx had every reason to fear an outburst of chauvinist recriminations on both sides which was just what he had been trying to avert since day one.

But nothing happened. Partly, it was because both sides were used to ringing declarations whose specific political content was not meant to be scrutinized closely or taken too seriously. Partly, it was because, as Engels pointed out in his reply to Marx, the French had other things on their mind as they faced the German invasion and occupation of their country.[63] For that matter, the Germans were undoubtedly preoccupied as well by their upcoming treason trial. In the end the witch-hunt that descended on the socialist and labor movements, not only in Germany and France but in all of Europe, united the militant sections of the labor movement despite their political differences. You could not very well accuse foreign comrades of a lack of solidarity as their own government carted them off to prison.

12. "How to Fight the Prussians"

Neither Marx nor Engels ever spelled out what political consequences followed from their conviction that the war in Germany's case was defensive to begin with. Had Bonaparte put up a better fight perhaps they would have. One might infer from Engels' attack on Liebknecht that he thought something along the lines of an amendment to, or substitute for, the government motion should have been made in the Reichstag. The *SDAP* could have agreed to the voting of war credits but with restrictions that would have prevented the government from carrying on the war beyond the point where it ceased to be a defensive one. Such an amendment or substitute motion would certainly have been voted down—probably it would have been howled down—but Bismarck would have had to show his hand. The *SDAP* would have turned the tables on him politically, demonstrating its willingness to defend Germany's legitimate national interest while exposing "the purely dynastic policy" that lay behind Bismarck's machinations. This is the kind of parliamentary tactic Engels was to urge on the German Party in the future.[64] But this is all speculation.

We do not have to guess, however, what specific actions Marx and Engels would have proposed during the remaining five and one-half months of war. Engels' articles in *The Pall Mall Gazette* which Marx, as we know from his correspondence, followed closely and collaborated on, comprise a little textbook on guerilla warfare. Their common theme is summed up by the title he gave to his article of September 17, 1870. The article was called *How to Fight the Prussians*.

The irony is that the furious debate over Marx and Engels' alleged 'defensism' centers on their *qualified* characterization of the war as one of national defense from the German side in the beginning. Everyone ignores their *unqualified* support of the war of the French Republic against the Prussian invasion from September 4 until the end in February 1871. They were active in the attempt to gain recognition for the new Republic by other European governments and especially the government of England. Engels' articles were intended partly to advise its defenders. If you wanted a precedent for a 'defensist' position in the First World War these unambiguous articles would be far more useful than the earlier material. But for a number of reasons they have largely been ignored.[65]

In the first place, these articles were written *before* the revolt of the Paris Commune. The Republic whose military cause they championed and in whose interest they were written was the same Republic in whose name the defenders of the Commune were massacred. Many of the members of the first administration of the new Republic were responsible for the assault on the Commune and the subsequent murder of prisoners and other atrocities. Even without this, the dramatic events surrounding the fall of the Commune would have overshadowed the Republic's war against the Prussian invaders.

In the second place, there were problems with these articles for both sets of prowar socialists in 1914. On the one hand, in France, Marx's writings had never been treated with the same reverence as they had in Germany and French 'defensists' in the First World War found the tradition of 1793 a more useful ideological tool. Besides, there was the aforementioned reputation of the Third Republic as the butcher of the

Commune. On the other hand, for German prowar socialists, Engels' 'defensist' articles in *The Pall Mall Gazette* which praised French guerrillas who were sniping at "German boys" and damned the Prussian invaders would not have been all that useful.

The fundamental difficulty with these articles, however, was that Engels based his whole series on the thesis that the Prussians could only be beaten by revolutionary means which would seriously threaten the bourgeois republic itself. And in fact that is what happened in Paris. The insurrection began when the Parisian population took the defense of the city into its own hands and found that the politicians of the Third Republic preferred defeat at the hands of the Prussians to victory as the leaders of a revolutionary movement.*

Prowar socialists in 1914 were not interested in that kind of precedent. They wanted a precedent that endorsed their policy of collaboration with the military government and the suppression of all independent activity by the working classes for the duration. The articles by the "military expert" of *The Pall Mall Gazette* were clearly the wrong place to look for that.

13. Treason

This much neglected series of articles by Engels deserves some treatment at length because its approach to the whole problem of the relation between war and revolution is at the base of Engels' thinking throughout the next couple of decades. We will turn to that issue in the last chapter. But a little postscript to this chapter is in order. There was a byproduct of these articles which was to cause some embarrassment for

---

* Much has been made of Marx and Engels' repeated warnings that a workingclass uprising was premature. Some have attempted to use these warnings to demonstrate that they were not 'really' in favor of the Commune. They have often been used by reformists to show that Marx and Engels were as frightened as they were of a 'premature' revolution. A 'premature' revolution being defined by reformists as any revolution occurring in their lifetime.
All that Marx and Engels were doing in these letters, however, was expressing their distrust of the bourgeois politicians leading the defense of the country against Prussia. They feared just the kind of betrayal that did happen.

the German Social Democratic Party later. It is worth mentioning both for the light this episode throws on Engels' reputation as an alleged pro-German patriot and for the light it throws on the subsequent evolution of the Social Democracy especially in Germany.

Toward the end of 1870 Engels apparently drew up a plan for the defense of the French Republic against the Prussians based on his study of the Prussian military system. Engels' qualifications in this field were apparently quite real and his writings were actually studied by Prussian students of military strategy and tactics themselves.[66] This is not a case where a political leader's alleged talents in diverse fields are 'puffed' by his sycophantic followers.

According to Engels' biographer, Gustav Mayer, a rough draft of this plan was found in Engels' papers by his literary executors, Eduard Bernstein and August Bebel (in a later incarnation), and they burned it. Mayer attributed this action to a fear that the party could be charged with treason even though no one but Engels was actually responsible for this document or even knew about it. Confirmation of this report by Mayer, which was based on several conversations with Bernstein from 1920 on, can be found in the Engels archives where the following note was found: "Packet no. 38 was destroyed today, by joint decision, by A. Bebel, Eduard Bernstein, London, July 24, 1896."[67]

Boris Nicolaevsky also looked into this question.[68] He too interviewed Bernstein and dated the memorandum (Bernstein's word) to the winter of 1870-71.*

---

* Nicolaevsky stated in his 1933 biography *Karl Marx, Man and Fighter* that "Bernstein refused to discuss the matter during the whole of his lifetime...", p.339. While the book was published in 1933, twenty years before the IRSH article, the interview with Bernstein had to have taken place at least a year earlier since Bernstein died in 1932. Maybe the manuscript was completed before the interview but the book clearly implies that Bernstein is dead. Since the IRSH article agrees with Mayer's account, it would seem to be more reliable. But why would Nicolaevsky remember twenty years later an event he had forgotten within the year? There is no political point to be made since Nicolaevsky does not question Mayer's account. It does indicate just how blurry the line between fiction and non-fiction can become.

As for the content of Engels' plan, there may be an indication in a document written by Engels much later, at the beginning of 1877. This is a long note to page 29 of Lissagaray's *History of the Commune*.[69]

This whole affair was silly. Why Bernstein and Bebel thought they could conceal the 'treasonous' attitude of a man who went around publishing articles titled "How to Fight the Prussians" in well-known and easily obtainable journals by burning an untitled memorandum found in his private papers is something of a mystery. For that matter the *Second Address of the General Council*, signed by Marx, was pretty 'treasonous' itself. It denounced the war as now nothing more than an attempt to dismember France and expressed fear that the opposition to the war might not be immediately successful. Certainly, Bismarck considered such language treasonous as Bebel of all people ought to have known. He spent time in prison for his antiwar protest in 1870. You can only make sense of what Bebel and Bernstein did if you realize how nervous the heritage of Marx and Engels made even the best of the Social Democratic leadership.

CHAPTER 6. BURYING THE 'TSARIST MENACE'

Engels' writings on war and its relation to revolution in the 1880s and 90s are best considered as his contribution to the dispute that split the Socialist International in World War I. This is not just because all sides in that dispute appealed to his authority. Engels himself was obsessed with the danger this threatening war presented for the socialist movement and practically everything he wrote from the late 1880s on touched on the question. After some rethinking, he ended by definitively burying the "Russian Menace" in his writings on two controversies with the leadership of the Social Democratic Party that marked his last years.

1. The Danger of War

The defeat of Louis Bonaparte at Sedan in 1870 and the subsequent humiliation of the French nation did cause a radical change in the political approach of Marx and Engels to war and its relation to revolution. But it was not a change from a position of support for one or other of the governments involved to one of opposition. They could not abandon a position they had never held. What then was the change?

As late as 1866 Marx and Engels had continued to look at international conflicts as they had since 1848. War was a threat to the established order. The conflicts between the powers created internal strains which popular movements could exploit. They treated the war between Prussia and Austria in 1866, for example, much as they had treated the Crimean War. It was a bloody farce that could only disgust the people and expose the incompetence and hypocrisy of the military and political establishment. And that was a prospect they welcomed. Consequently, while they did not display the callous disregard for human life that often characterizes arm chair analysts of military affairs, they did treat the conduct and outcome of the conflict as a matter for dispassionate analysis rather than anxious concern.

At first, that is how they looked at the Franco-Prussian war too. But a new note began to creep in, at first largely in their private correspondence. To one another they frankly discussed their mutual fear that the chauvinist passions unleashed might pose a threat, not to the established order, but to the growing working class movement. And that was the main political thrust of their letter to the Brunswick committee in September of 1870. In that document the emphasis is on the duty of the working class, in this case the German working class, to counter the chauvinism that was sweeping the country.

Karl Marx's Theory of Revolution: V5

In the years following Marx's death in 1883, Engels became the major spokesman for the international left of the socialist movement and his fear of the threatening world war dominated his thinking. Contrast the following quote taken from a letter by Engels' to Bebel in 1882 with Marx's letters at the beginning of the Franco-Prussian war quoted in the previous chapter:

> I think a European war would be very unfortunate; this time it would really be serious, it would inflame chauvinism everywhere for years to come because each people would be fighting for its own existence. All the work of the revolutionaries in Russia, who are on the eve of victory, would be rendered useless and destroyed; our party in Germany would be temporarily overwhelmed in a flood of chauvinism and broken up, and the same would happen in France.[1]

As the century wore on, Engels also became increasingly concerned about the devastating consequences of modern warfare for European civilization itself. In a once well-known introduction to a pamphlet by the German socialist Sigismund Borkheim, Engels wrote:

> And in the end, for Prussia-Germany no other war is possible any longer except a world war, and indeed a world war of an extensiveness and fierceness undreamed of up to now. Eight to ten million soldiers will be at each others' throats and thereby strip all Europe bare as no swarm of locusts has ever done. The devastation of the Thirty Years War ... famine, pestilence, general degeneration of civilization ... irremediable disorganization of our artificial machinery ... ending in general bankruptcy; breakdown of the old states and their traditional state wisdom, such that crowns by the dozens will be rolling in the streets and no one will pick them up; absolute impossibility of foreseeing how all this will end and who will emerge the victor ...[2]

At one point, admittedly in a private letter and not in a public statement, Engels concluded a passage in this vein by describing his position as "peace at any price."[3] Whatever one thinks of this as a political slogan, it emphasizes just how grim the world situation appeared to the usually sanguine Engels.

2. The Tsarist Threat

In the 1880s the threat of a general European war seemed to Engels, and to many others, to come from the bizarre alliance between the French Republic and Tsarist absolutism. Bismarck's policy had, as Marx and Engels predicted, led to Germany's isolation internationally. Domestically, the Prussian military and the court party around the belligerent and none-too-bright monarch would certainly use the war crisis as a pretext to destroy the movement; but a victory of Tsarist Russia in alliance with a viciously anti-workingclass French Republican bourgeoisie would pose the same threat. There was only one way out for the workingclass and for Germany as a united nation. The socialist movement would have to save itself and the nation from both internal and external enemies. What Engels had in mind was the revolutionary defense of the French nation in 1793 by the mobilization of the people. This was a familiar model of revolution for Marx and Engels and for the European left; it was a model for Marx and Engels long before they became socialists.

But this model evoked for Engels a whole series of memories of 1848 which were no longer relevant. For one thing, the 1848 pattern required Engels to see Bismarck and Prussia as dependent on Russia. In any serious confrontation, the Tsar would hold the balance between Germany and France. He would dictate the terms.

Quotes like the following can be multiplied:

> What Mohr said in the Circular to the International in 1870, that the annexation of Alsace etc., has made Russia *l'arbitre de l'Europe*, is now at last becoming evident. Bismarck has had to cave in completely, and the will of Russia has to be done. The dream of the German Empire, the guardian of European peace, without whose leave not a cannon shot can be fired,

> is dispelled, and the German Philistine finds that he is as much a slave of the Tsar as when Prussia was "das fünfte Rad am europäischen Wagen."⁴

In a long letter to Lafargue in 1886⁵ Engels emphasized the *irresponsibility* of the great power game. English Liberals and French Republicans were not only hypocrites who used the slogans of freedom and self-determination to glorify nationalist passions that were being manipulated, in Engels' view, by their new ally the Tsar for imperialist aims; they were risking the future of the continent for essentially petty ends.* Throughout the last years of his life Engels regularly used the image of the reckless gambler to describe the statesmen. Over and over, he uses the phrase *va banque* (go for broke) to describe their behavior.

Nevertheless, Engels himself was obviously aware that the Europe of 1848, a Europe dominated by the Holy Alliance against revolution, was past. There were echoes of that past everywhere, not just in Engels' head. Nevertheless, they were just echoes and fading ones at that. The following excerpt from a letter to a Social Democratic editor, is just as typical of Engels in this period.

> I too have, since 1848, frequently made the statement that Russian Tsarism is the last bulwark and the greatest reserve army of European reaction. Nevertheless, much has changed in Russia in the last 20 years. The so-called emancipation of the peasantry has created a thoroughly revolutionary situation. ...⁶

Engels goes on to describe the growth of capitalism in Russia and simultaneously of a revolutionary movement. (Which movement Engels expects will produce very soon a bourgeois revolution.) One consequence of this is the increasing financial dependence of Tsarism on European states. In the case discussed in this letter, it is Bismarck who is bailing out

---

* For an extended discussion of this aspect of the prewar situation in Europe, see *The Balkan Socialist Tradition,* by Dragan Plavsic and Andreja Zivkovic.

the Tsar. "Bismarck thereby put his yoke on Russia, which even now gets no money without his say-so, ..." [7]

Later, as we shall see, it is the French Republic which comes to the rescue of the Tsar. Throughout this period, despite the echoes of 1848 and the Holy Alliance, Engels more often portrays Tsarism as a "paper tiger" rather than the powerful "evil empire" of 1815.

In part, Engels' confused picture reflects his contemporary reality more accurately than our anachronistic view. For us, looking backwards from a post World War I (and even post World War II) vantage point, the division of Europe into two rigid camps is a given. But in the 70s, 80s and even 90s of the nineteenth century it was by no means obvious to the statesmen themselves what the line up would be in the war they were all expecting. Italy, we have to remember, took so long to make up its mind which side it was on in World War I that it almost missed the event entirely.

Despite the confusion, in reality and in Engels' head, one major difference between his 1848 position and his post 1870 stands out. In 1848, Marx, Engels and radicals of all political shades looked forward to a war by revolutionary Germany, under the leadership of bourgeois democratic revolutionaries, against Tsarist Russia. Marx and Engels, after 1870, did not desire a war with Russia. They feared it. And they were adamant that they would not support any of the governments in such a war. They were for using the crisis of war to replace the governments in all countries be they republics or monarchies.

The most striking statement of this position came from Engels in 1888. It occurred in a letter to Ion Nadejde, the editor of a new social-democratic newspaper in Roumania called *Contemporanul*.[8] This was not a personal letter but a public one to the editor congratulating the Roumanian socialists on their new publication.

What he sent to the editor was not a routine letter of greetings, but a survey of the state of Europe as it faced world war. Before citing the conclusion of this survey-letter, it should be made clear that this letter was as vehemently anti-Tsarist as ever; there was not the slightest evidence of any increasing softness about the Russian autocracy: "Since Russia enjoys a strategic position almost impervious to conquest, Russian Tsarism forms the core of this alliance ['the old Holy Alliance of the three assassins of

Poland'], the great reserve of all European reaction. To overthrow Tsarism, to destroy this nightmare that weighs on all Europe—this is, in my eyes, the first condition for the emancipation of the nationalities of the European center and east." And there was more of this kind of stuff. This letter is one of the clearest examples of the hold the politics of 1848 still exercised over Engels. Indeed, Engels informed Laura Lafargue that one of the purposes of the letter was to dampen any enthusiasm the Roumanian socialists might have for Tsarist-sponsored wars of liberation.⁹

Did this mean, to Engels himself, that workers should give political support to war by the "progressive" west against this reservoir of world reaction? That is where the logic of the letter seems to lead. But the statement ended with the following political conclusion, in view of the fact that war seemed "imminent":

> I hope that peace will be maintained; in such a war, one could not sympathize with any of the combatants; on the contrary one would wish them all to be beaten if that were possible.

As was the case in the Crimean War, the "special Russian position" did not lead Engels to support the anti-Tsarist alliance.

Nevertheless, the myth persists that Engels favored a war of defense against Tsarist Russia. The evidence for this myth stems mainly from an 1891 article by Engels called *Socialism in Germany* and the controversy that led up to its publication.

3. Engels' 1891 "Prowar" Aberration

In the period between the French defeat at Sedan in 1870 and his death in 1895, Frederick Engels worked out an antiwar position that was in all essentials that of the Lenin-Luxemburg resolution passed at the Stuttgart congress of the Second International in 1907 and of the Zimmerwald left in the midst of World War I. That position was: 1) war, especially a war between France and Germany, would be a disaster for the workingclass movement and European civilization; 2) none of the belligerent governments could be supported in any way; 3) the role of the socialist movement was to seize the opportunity of the war crisis and overthrow the governments and the old society which they represented and defended; and, 4) the threat of such a revolutionary movement was the only credible and effective deterrent to the "mad game" of the governments. Engels, of course, had no confidence that a pacifist, non-violent, resistance could ward off the danger of war.

There was one partial exception to this trend in Engels' writing. For a brief period in 1891-92, Engels reverted to, or seemed to revert to, the politics he and Marx had held *before* 1870. In 1891, Engels clearly argued the view that the war that threatened to break out *immediately* as a result of the newly formed alliance between Tsarist Russia and republican France would be a war to dismember Germany and crush the German socialist movement. In such a war, the German working class would have to defend the right of Germany to exist. Worse. At one point, Engels, *in a private letter to Bebel*, accepted the possibility that the Social Democratic Party might have to break with its long standing tradition and vote for the war budget. Publicly, Engels outlined his position in an article written in French for the *Almanach du Parti Ouvrier pour 1892*[10] and translated later into German, with a new introduction and conclusion, for *Die Neue Zeit*.

This article was the precedent used in 1914 by the prowar socialists, especially in Germany, but not only in Germany, to justify their betrayal of the antiwar resolutions of the International. After all, it appeared quite likely that, whichever side lost the war, the defeated countries would be threatened, if not with dismemberment, then certainly with economic disaster and political humiliation. And the working class movement would bear the brunt of those disasters. Economically the working class in the defeated countries would be forced to pay for the indemnities and reparations exacted by the victors, and politically the organized working class in all countries would be threatened by the inevitable chauvinist backlash. Engels, himself, had admitted that in such a case the working class had to defend the nation, hadn't he?

All the voluminous material in Engels' other writings on the coming war, public and private, from 1870 until 1895 were ignored. This article itself was bowdlerized since, unlike Engels private communication to Bebel, it did *not* envision possible support of the German *government* in this invasion which did not happen. It rejected such support clearly and explicitly.

There are other difficulties with the misuse of this article, along with some of Engels' letters written at the same time, to create a 'prowar' Engels. As usual, contrary evidence is ignored. Other writings of Engels during this period, especially his letters, indicate that he was uncomfortable with the idea to begin with. What is more, Engels insisted that the only possible defense had to be a revolutionary one; the Poles and Alsatians would have to be offered their freedom, the standing army would have to be subordinated to the popular militia and dissolved into the militia as quickly as possible, and the repressive legislation of the Prussian state had to be repealed.

In 1914, prowar socialists openly abandoned all political opposition in favor of civil peace, the notorious *Burgfrieden*, but here Engels proposed to intensify revolutionary political agitation as a means of rallying the working class to the defense of the nation. A Prussian government with its back to the wall *might* be forced to accede to these demands. If it didn't it would be pushed aside. Engels, in short, was thinking of a Germany in the same sort of predicament that France had found itself in after the defeat at Sedan. For that matter, the 1793 analogy required there to be a revolutionary crisis (or opportunity) which was caused by the military collapse of the old regime. Engels, of course, didn't use any slogan or formula remotely comparable to those used later by Lenin *calling* for the defeat of "one's own" government by the enemy. But he certainly was saying that the imminence of defeat by the enemy presented the revolutionary party with the opportunity *and obligation* to take over.

It is worth noting that Rosa Luxemburg, in her magnificent polemic against the prowar socialists, the "Junius" pamphlet, quoted these very sections of Engels' article *Socialism in Germany* [11]. And they fit in quite nicely. But the most significant fact is this: Engels dropped this idea of 'revolutionary defense' *even under a bourgeois government* almost immediately and, in at least one letter,[12] excused his article on the grounds that it was occasioned by a specific set of circumstances and was not to be used to construct a general position of 'revolutionary defensism.' To the German edition of this article, published in *Die Neue Zeit* in January 1892, Engels appended concluding remarks in which he announced that the war danger had evaporated and Tsarism no longer represented an immediate threat to Germany.

4. The Tsar Learns to Sing the Marseillaise

What were the specific circumstances that provoked this change of line on Engels' part? In 1891-92, the political alliance between France and Russia that Engels had feared and predicted since before the French defeat at Sedan, was consummated. The preliminary approach came in July of 1891, when the Tsar himself welcomed a French squadron to the naval base at Kronstadt. The Tsarist military band played the *Marseillaise*, the same revolutionary anthem Napoleon's soldiers had sung when they marched on Moscow. That the Tsar, the policeman of reaction for most of the century, should welcome a French fleet with this ceremony was a good indication of how seriously he took the rhetoric of the bourgeois Third Republic.

The enemy, for Engels, however, was *not* primarily Tsarism as his letters and his article make clear. It was French chauvinism. Already by the mid-1880s Engels was writing as if the relationship between the Tsar and the conservative western powers had been reversed.[13] Tsarism had been seriously wounded by its defeat in the Crimean war. Its economic, and, therefore, its military weakness had been revealed. And there was now, in Russia itself, a growing revolutionary movement. There is no doubt that Engels, with his usual optimism, overestimated the strength of the *Narodnaya Voliya* and of the bourgeois revolutionary pressures he believed they reflected and represented, but his principal claim—that the old, medieval, Russia was done for—was certainly sound. And what followed was that the Tsar needed a western ally, whether Bismarck or the French Republic, at least as badly as that ally needed him.

At the same time, in France, the republican tradition had been thoroughly compromised by the experience of the Third Republic. Its leading figures were involved in one financial scandal after another. And the midwife of this republic had been the alliance of Bismarck, defeated Bonapartist generals, bourgeois Republicans, and French monarchists who had joined together to crush the Paris Commune. That the memory of the massacre of the Communards did not fade with time was not only because the workingclass nursed its historic grievances. Republican governments were as hostile to the growing workers' movement as the traditional right. Strikes were regularly broken by the military.

In the 1880s, the traditional monarchist right in France had found in new movements, in Boulangism[14] and antisemitism, the popular base it had previously lacked. And the cement that held it all together was anti-German chauvinism; the Jew for French antisemites at this time was a stand-in for the German as well as a scapegoat for the sins of the republic of bankers and swindlers. This was the same poisonous mixture that was to explode in the Dreyfus case a few years later.[15]

The possibility that disgust with a corrupt republic would lead, as it had in 1851, to the victory of an authoritarian movement dedicated to restoring of France's lost military glory was what was bothering Engels. Only this time, such a victory would immediately be followed by an attack on Germany, and that would precipitate just the catastrophe he feared.

Engels wrote his article on *Socialism in Germany* in October of 1891. The ceremonial welcoming of the French naval squadron by the Tsar had taken place in July, and soon, in August of 1892, a pact calling for mutual consultation was signed. The military adventurer Boulanger had committed suicide for the second time at the end of September 1891,* but there were now organized movements to take his place. And even ordinary republican politicians had discovered how effective chauvinism could be as a means of diverting public attention from the state of the country and public anger from themselves. Engels was worried that the French socialists would be tempted to appease this growing mood. He had not been encouraged, as volume 4 of this work demonstrated,[16] by their response to Boulanger's agitation and he would not have been surprised (or pleased) by the confusion in their ranks had he lived a few more years and witnessed the Dreyfus affair.

Engels wrote this article *reluctantly*. As he wrote to Laura Lafargue on July 12, 1891, he did not think that an article or interview for the French press would be a good idea:

> I should have to remind them of the fact that by their submission, for twenty years, to the adventurer Louis Bonaparte they laid the foundation for all the wars that

---

* See KMTR volume 4 for an account of this remarkable feat.

have come over us since 1850, including the Franco-German War; that that war had originated, *en dernier lieu* [in the last analysis], in their claim to interfere in German internal affairs, a claim they even now they think they have a right to make ... All this might be very useful to tell them , but will they even listen to it ... ?[17]

Engels clearly did not want to take on French chauvinism himself. He thought the French socialists ought to have done that.

5. The Dispute With Bebel

There was something else, however, pushing Engels in the direction of openly espousing "revolutionary defensism." In 1890, Engels had begun his long-planned offensive against the right wing of the German Social Democracy. It can easily be demonstrated that, at least from the time of the dispute over the steamship subsidy in 1884,[18] Engels had intended to force this fight with the intention of driving the right wing out of their positions within the party even if that meant a split. The details of this important and neglected incident will be discussed in the next, and last, volume of this work; what is relevant to our present investigation is that Engels had counted on the support of August Bebel as he had counted on his support against the right wing throughout the 80s.

But Bebel backed away. And it was Bebel who, in 1891, was sounding the alarm and warning of an impending Russian invasion of Germany. Bebel began what amounted to a campaign against this alleged threat with a *Vorwärts* article on September 27, 1891. Engels was faced with the task of countering Bebel's prowar politics without driving him further away. He responded to Bebel's article in a letter written on October 1, 1891.[19] In it Engels outlined his view of the Russian threat. The bulk of the letter is spent debunking, very diplomatically, Bebel's article. Engels' argument can be summed up as follows: Tsarism does not want war; it only hopes to achieve its diplomatic aims by bluster, by threatening war; if war actually breaks out that will be a defeat for Tsarist diplomacy; what Russia is trying to do is finesse some small gains in the east and when that is accomplished all the French chauvinists will get is "a poke in the eye;"

Tsarism is facing revolution in the near future and a famine right now. And the letter goes on in this vein at some length.

Engels then, in the concluding paragraphs of the letter, turns to the threat from France, which he considers more important. In these notes it is not at all clear whether Engels is describing the conduct of a war by a revolutionary government or the conduct that the socialist movement will force on the Kaiser's government. In fact, it appears that Engels isn't clear on that point himself. It is Engels who is confused, not just the writing. What *is* clear is that Engels emphasizes the war must be waged by "revolutionary means." The specific measures mentioned in this letter have to do with renouncing German claims to Alsace-Lorraine and Poland. Engels concludes:

> This much seems to me certain: If we are beaten, then for years to come every door in Europe will stand wide open to chauvinism and a war of revenge. If we win, then our party comes to power. The victory of Germany is therefore the victory of the revolution, and, if it comes to war, we must not only wish victory but further it by every means.[20]

This is a letter. Engels is thinking out loud and not writing for publication. Even so, how can Engels conclude that the *only* way Germany could conduct the war would be in a revolutionary way? Who is the "we" that is the subject of the last sentence? Is it the German Party or just Germany? Is Engels saying that the Social Democracy should "further" the war "by every means" even if in the coming world war operations on the German side were to be conducted, as they in fact were, by the General Staff and the regular army using reactionary means? Unfortunately, as we will see, Engels' article did not answer this question either. In both cases, Engels insists that the war can only be won by revolutionary means but is equally adamant that Germany must win or else ... disaster. It is easy to see why prowar socialists should have seized on this precedent. It is also probably the reason that Engels began backing away from this line of argument even in his article.

In a reply to Engels on October 9, Bebel continued to press his point that a Russian attack was imminent.[21] What was implied was that the party ought to be gearing up its agitation for this imminent development. Bebel underlined that by referring Engels to a *Vorwärts* article he had written the same day. In it Bebel mentioned that "you—Marx and you—always put forward the same views [as I, Bebel, am putting forward now? EH] on Russia." Bebel is here quite consciously laying the groundwork for what was to be the party's prowar line in 1914. Engels countered on October 13:

> ... From this [Engels' description of the state of affairs in Russia] it seems clear to me that you would be vulnerable if you willingly put credence in the assurances of our military budget advocates when they count with certainty on war in the spring. Just as it is the function of Russian diplomacy to prepare for war all the more actively the less they are heading in that direction, so too it is the task of the General Staffers to humbug you by saying that war is certain by April '92. ...
> If we are convinced that it will blow up in the spring, then we can hardly be against these requests for money *in principle*. And this would be a rather nasty situation for us. All the toadying parties would exult that they had been right and now we had to trample under foot our twenty-year-old policy. And such an unprepared-for change of front would also arouse a tremendous amount of friction inside the party. And internationally too.[22]

Engels' way out of this dilemma was one we have seen him use before. He suggested a series of demands and proposals which Bebel and the rest of the party leadership could make which would allow them to shift political responsibility for the war threat on to the government and its parliamentary supporters. If the voting of the military budget was made contingent on the government's acceptance of the Social Democracy's demands for democratization of the army, and if the party's agitation centered on the renunciation of the annexation of Alsace-Lorraine as the key to thwarting the Tsar's political offensive, then one of two things would happen. Either the government would oppose these demands and the party could refuse to vote for the budget without appearing callous in the face of a real threat to the nation, or, if the country were attacked and faced defeat, the government would have to accede to demands which would weaken it. In either case, the socialists could use the crisis to undermine the government.

In this instance, I think there is more to Engels' customary tactic than the usual attempt to counter the government's offensive. I think a close reading of Engels' correspondence with Bebel supports the thesis that he was also looking for a way to let Bebel back down from an impossible position.

More serious, in Engels' view was the problem of dealing with French chauvinism. How would the French socialists react to what could only appear to them as Bebel's tub-thumping support of German war preparations?

Engels concludes his letter to Bebel:

> I will give the French some preparation for the war contingency; it is, however, damned hard not to do more harm than good, these people are so sensitive. ...
> In my opinion, the war contingency—if you believe with such certainty in its breaking out in the spring—should be discussed at the party congress at least in the corridors.[23]

Is Engels here warning Bebel that he faces a fight over his prowar turn in the German party as well as in the international movement? The general drift of this correspondence is certainly clear. Engels is trying to bring Bebel back down to earth without openly attacking him. Engels obviously doesn't really believe in an immediate war threat.

Engels' article for the French press begins with the assumption that the French bourgeoisie wants war. He agrees that:

> There is no doubt: in relation to this German Empire, the French republic as it is now represents revolution, the

bourgeois revolution to be sure, but still revolution. But the instant this republic places itself under the orders of the Russian Tsar it is a different matter entirely. Russian Tsarism is the enemy of all the Western nations, even of the bourgeoisie of these nations.[24]

In the event the German Social Democrats come to power, Engels goes on to say, the issue of Alsace-Lorraine, as well as that of Poland and Schleswig, will be settled "in the twinkling of an eye," but for the "patriots of Alsace-Lorraine" to gamble on a war in which France and Germany fight to the death while Russia waits to pick up the pieces: is that game worth the candle?

Engels then goes on to outline the consequences of a German defeat. He is particularly worried about the consequences for the German socialist movement. If Germany were crushed militarily it would be politically overwhelmed, at least for some time, by a wave of chauvinism. In short, Engels argues that the war being planned by the French chauvinists is the mirror image of the one plotted by Bismarck in 1870. And the German socialists would have to react as the French republicans did after Sedan.

Engels repeats the argument he made to Bebel:

> A war in which Russians and Frenchmen invaded Germany would be, for Germany, a war to the death, in which, in order to ensure its national existence, it would have to resort to the most revolutionary means. The present government, certainly, would not unleash revolution, unless it were forced to. But there is a strong party which would force it to, or if necessary replace it.[25]

Again Engels simply avoids the question of what socialists ought to do in the event that German militarism fought the war in its own way and refused to be forced into a revolutionary defense of the nation. He simply rejects the possibility. It is just assumed that in such an eventuality the government will be overthrown. However, Engels does add one note here that was lacking in his discussion with Bebel:

> No socialist, of whatever country, can desire victory in war, either by the present German government or by the French bourgeois republic; even less by the Tsar, which would be tantamount to the subjugation of Europe. That is why socialists everywhere demand that peace be maintained.[26]

Engels concludes with his by now familiar warning that this war would be devastating for all. In the German edition of the article, he added the concluding remarks I referred to earlier. In this new conclusion he states unequivocally that the war threat is over:

> But then a powerful check was imposed on the Russian war-monger. First came the news of harvest failure at home, with every reason to expect a famine. Then came the failure of the Paris loan, signifying the collapse of Russian state credit.[27]

And Engels ends his German article with the following paragraph:

> For Europe it means peace for the time being. Russian war-mongering is paralysed for a good many years to come. Instead of millions of soldiers dying on the battle-fields, millions of Russian peasants are dying of starvation. But its effects as far as Russian despotism is concerned remain to be seen.[28]

There is only one thing to add to complete this story. In the passage just quoted and in letters to Adolf Sorge and Paul (Panajionis) Argyriades,[29] Engels emphasized the Russian famine as the factor which made war impossible for some time to come. But he had already argued that the famine made war unlikely in his first letter to Bebel! Indeed, he had stated flatly as early as August 17, in a letter to Laura Lafargue, that peace was assured because of the Russian famine.[30] No further evidence is required to prove that Engels had talked himself into taking this particular war threat, as opposed to the general threat, more seriously than it deserved in order to avoid an open break with Bebel.

Engels' recognition of the *weakness* of the Tsarist power is especially interesting in light of Rosa Luxemburg's later attempt to defend his 1892 article.[31] She emphasized, rightly, the change in the European state system effected by the revolution of 1905. The emergence of the working class as an independent and powerful force made the old 'special Russian position' obsolete. Tsarism was no longer the static, 'Asiatic,' relic of the past. It was no longer the reserve force of counterrevolution. It was no longer 'special.'

But Engels' letters make clear that he already realized this in 1892. And his concluding paragraph in the German edition of *Socialism in Germany* explicitly and publicly rejected the old politics based on Tsarism's "special" features. Until that old politics was revived in 1914, the concept of Russian "specialness" had disappeared from the foreign policy resolutions of the Second International.[32] And Engels', in this article of 1892, was the one who explicitly dropped it.

6. The French Reaction

Engels was just as eager to avoid a head on collision with the French socialists as he was to avoid one with Bebel. As he said in his letter to Argyriades, his main concern throughout this episode had been "preventing, insofar as it lay in my power, any possibility of a misunderstanding between the German and French workers ... ."[33]

That Engels was not as successful as he might have liked in this effort was demonstrated by the aftermath. Those French socialists most closely associated with Engels and most alienated from the republic and its chauvinist defenders, people like Paul Lafargue and Jules Guesde, found themselves on the defensive as a result of Bebel's pronouncements and Engels' apparent endorsement of them. In an exchange of letters with one of their critics, Charles Bonnier, Engels complained that no German socialist would even think of denying the French the right to defend their country against a German attack and French socialists had the obligation to defend Germany's right to self-defense.[34] The problem with this line of argument is that each side in any war that broke out would claim to be acting in self-defense and, given the calamitous consequences of defeat, would have some justification for the claim.

Like Lenin later, Engels in this dispute started with a clear but mistaken position of support for one side in a war based on an inappropriate analogy. But this was not a position he could live with. As he recognized in practically everything else he wrote at this time, no government could be supported in the coming war. Even in this article, he emphasized that the defense of legitimate national interests required a revolutionary assault on the government. Why then use language like "defense of the country" which ignores just this point? It sounded like a 'hard' line against French chauvinism which is what Engels intended but in practice it gave aid and comfort to both German and French chauvinism.

7. A New Stage of Capitalism?

In his first letter to Bebel on October 1, Engels had minimized the war danger represented by the *Tsar* and the Tsarist government, weakened as they were by famine and threatened by revolution. But, he went on to say, there was a more serious long range threat of war. The Russian *bourgeoisie*, not Tsarist despotism, had an interest in war. This bourgeoisie, Engels wrote, had developed out of a class of independent farmers (he uses the Russian word *kulak*) who had made their money by distilling and selling vodka and out of government contractors. It depended on Tsarism. But it did have an interest in war:

> If regard for *this* bourgeoisie is a pressure tending towards war, that is only because it has turned Panslavism into something material or rather has revealed its material foundation: expanding the internal market by annexations. Hence the Slavophile fanaticism, hence the wild hatred of Germany—till 20 years ago Russia's commerce was almost exclusively in German hands!—hence the Jew-baiting. This scurvy, ignorant, bourgeoisie which cannot see beyond the end of its nose certainly desires war and agitates for it in the press.

Engels then goes on to write that the bourgeoisie represents the only real threat to Tsarism, since the nobility is no longer able to challenge the regime and the proletariat is not yet able to do so:

> ... And a palace revolution or a successful *attentat* could today bring only the bourgeoisie to power, no matter by whom the blow was struck. This bourgeoisie would certainly be capable of hurling itself into war even more readily than the Tsar.[35]

This argument is a digression in Engels' letter since he is arguing in *it* only that Bebel's fear of *Tsarist* aggression is exaggerated, at least in the short run. But it is too bad that Engels did not think this argument through. Not only is its portrait of the class alignment in Russia in World War I remarkably accurate—the bourgeoisie *was* far more eager for war than the dynasty and its supporters—but this line of thought might well have led Engels out of a serious dilemma that was in part responsible for the ambiguous position he took in his dispute with Bebel.

For Engels, and for Marx before him, it was dynastic, pre-capitalist, imperialism that was the main cause of wars and threats of war. From 1815 through 1870, the dynasties strove jointly to suppress revolution while each sought to expand at the expense of the others. And Tsarist Russia was the most dynamic of these dynastic imperialisms. The bourgeoisie, on the other hand, was torn between making a revolutionary appeal to the people against the dynasts and grudgingly accepting the latter out of fear of the former. In either case, the bourgeoisie tended to be hostile to the imperial wars waged for purely dynastic interests and resented the cost of maintaining the standing armies required for the purpose. It is clear that this is the theoretical system that still dominated Engels' thinking in 1891 from passages like the one in *Socialism in Germany* quoted earlier to the effect that "Russian Tsarism is the enemy of all the Western nations, even of the bourgeoisie of these nations."

Engels' letters, however, make clear that he thought the Tsar, by 1892, had become the junior partner in the Franco-Russian alliance. What was the theoretical explanation of the prowar policy of the French bourgeoisie? Of course, there was the matter of Alsace-Lorraine, but Engels clearly saw this as an issue the bourgeoisie was *using* to whip up chauvinist sentiment. What was whipping *them* up? Engels' digression in his October 1 letter to Bebel was one of a number of passages in which he pointed, in the same off-handed way, to the new, aggressive, imperialism of the bourgeoisie.³⁶ In fact, as we saw in the last chapter both he and Marx were well aware of the chauvinist sentiment of the French, and German, bourgeoisie in 1870. Nevertheless, the official statements of the IWMA emphasized the dynastic ambitions of Bonaparte and Bismarck as the driving forces behind the conflict

What we have here is a theoretical lag. Engels, perhaps earlier than anyone else, realized that the state system in Europe had dramatically changed as a result of the Franco-Prussian war. In his political response he was far ahead of his contemporaries and anticipated the antiwar left of the Second International, but he never sat down to think through what this change meant theoretically. He didn't do what Lenin was to do in his *Imperialism, the Highest Stage of Capitalism*. And that meant that when he was forced to *defend* his politics, as he was in 1891, he was at a disadvantage. Bebel could use his, and Marx's earlier writings, tendentiously misquoted, of course, for his prowar political tendency.

8. Internment

Engels' article and his defense of it are in part an obsolete hangover from the pre-1870 period when Prussia could reasonably be treated as a puppet of the Tsar and Bonaparte. Prowar socialists seized on Engels' article in 1914, when it had become an even more irrelevant echo of an even more distant past. Engels, however, was clearly uncomfortable with this version of 'revolutionary defensism' even as he was propounding it in 1891. In his article, and in his reply to Bonnier, he qualified the concept out of existence.

Even in the event of a defensive war against Tsarist Russia, Engels pointed to Prussian militarism as the main enemy. He fudged his formulas in a vain attempt to prevent Bebel's prowar articles and speeches from being misunderstood—or understood. After all, he had performed the same service for Guesde and Lafargue at the height of the Boulanger crisis when *they* flirted with chauvinism. In both cases, he was doing his best to preserve the peace between French and German socialists while pressing both to remain firm in the face of growing antisocialist, patriotic, hysteria at home. It was a task requiring a good deal of diplomacy on the part of a man who was a 'foreigner' in the eyes of both French and German chauvinists.

CHAPTER 7. BURNING DOWN THE EMPEROR'S PALACE

In the last years of his life Engels was concerned to work out a political response to the impending war danger. He effectively worked out an approach that revolutionary socialists had to reinvent during the course of World War I because the leadership of the Social Democracy did their best to bury Engels' politics after he himself was cremated. What Engels came to realize was that, in an era of universal suffrage and universal conscription, the key to revolution was a military mutiny.

1. Can Europe Disarm?

In March of 1893, *Vorwärts*, the official organ of the German Party printed a series of articles by Engels under the general title *Can Europe Disarm?* and the work was later reprinted as a pamphlet. The occasion for this series was the introduction by the government parties in the Reichstag of a bill requiring an increase the military budget. There was no question at this point of the Social Democrats' supporting the bill. The liberal deputies, still rhetorically anti-militarist at this stage, proposed to limit the term of service to two years. It was pure demagogy. They didn't expect their bill to pass, but it put the Social Democrats on the defensive. If they supported the liberals their reputation as unpatriotic would be enhanced and their own supporters could not be expected to be enthusiastic about this alliance with the liberal representatives of the employing class. It also would put them in the position of implying that if this amendment were accepted they would abandon their refusal in principle to vote for a military budget. Bebel asked Engels, in his capacity of military expert, for advice.[1] He got more than he bargained for. Engels responded with a five part series of articles outlining a model Social Democratic Bill for military reform. Engels' model bill was not introduced by the Social Democratic Fraction. We will see why.

Engels tried to show the Party how the slogan of universal service in a civilian militia could be used to exploit the increasing popular fear of war and the widespread resentment of the out-of-control economic cost of the armaments race. The pamphlet/series was certainly provoked in part by the tensions engendered within the French and German movements by the Franco-Russian alliance. In effect, it was Engels' thought-out response to Bebel's waverings over the previous year and a half.

Formally, the series and pamphlet were an attempt by a well-known "military expert" to demonstrate that it was militarily feasible to base the defense of the country on civilian reserves liable to a very short term of service. In substance, it was an attack on the standing army. Engels argued that contemporary military discipline and its mindless drill was not at all required for the defense of the country. It was required in an army whose main function was aggression against foreign countries and the suppression of the civilian population at home. Only an army isolated from the civilian population by long years of service and mindless discipline, what the Germans called *kadavergehorsam* (the obedience of a zombie), could serve that function.

The specific proposal which Engels advocated was intended to be one a Social Democratic government could make to the other European powers or which the Social Democratic delegation in the *Reichstag* could propose be adopted by the current government. And it was simple. Call an international conference for the purpose of drawing up a treaty that would immediately limit the term of service in all signatory countries and phase in further reductions over a period of four or five years. The result would be a European state system dependent on armies composed of short timers and large civilian reserves. No country need fear invasion and no country would be capable of aggression.

Engels assumed in this series the mask of a sober, moderate, practical, well-versed, military expert. His model agreement was to be phased in, not issued as an ultimatum. The reduction in service was to be reached in a series of steps. And it depended on an international agreement between the great powers that the existing governments would not and could not make.* This moderate pose has, in every case I have found, completely taken in modern historians. They dismiss Engels' proposal as 'utopian.' World War I was such a brutal, bloody, mechanized, and industrialized, affair that no one could imagine a lightly armed civilian militia playing any role in it. But that was just the point.

---

* However, as explained below, Engels did raise the possibility that Germany or, presumably, some other European power would at least *take the first steps* towards replacing the standing army with a civilian militia. Once again, this underlines the fact that Engels is proposing a campaign of political warfare with his 'modest proposal.' Initiating a process of disarmament unilaterally only makes sense if you are talking over the heads of the other governments to their people.

Engels was, as we have seen, well aware of the carnage that the next war would bring. He knew what the weaponry available to late nineteenth capitalist states could do. What he was proposing was a form of *political warfare*. In the first instance, political warfare against the German government, which, if it opposed this apparently mild measure, would be forced to acknowledge its own aggressive designs on foreign and domestic enemies. In the event of a Social Democratic victory in Germany, the political target would become foreign governments which harbored similar designs against *their* enemies.

One thing is especially interesting in this pamphlet. It is French chauvinism, as a response to the Prussian empire Bismarck built, that is the target here. Here Engels explicitly repudiates the Russian threat.[2]

The value of a civilian militia lay not in its ability to defeat a professional army, foreign or domestic, militarily, but in its ability to undermine that army's will to fight. Even in the twentieth century, at a time when military technology has developed even more horrible weapons, how often have guerilla armies enjoying the support of the people proved superior to technically more powerful regular armies.

In this series of articles, however, Engels is not concerned with demonstrating or arguing for the superiority of the militia system as an abstraction. What made the proposals in these articles dangerous for the government was their 'moderation.' They could not be dismissed as impractical. Engels himself underlined this aspect in a letter to Lafargue which spells out exactly what he thought he was doing. The occasion was the introduction of a Bill on the militia by the socialist representative Edouard Vaillant in the French Assembly. It was a Bill that Engels felt could not be taken seriously:

> Therefore, if there is to be a Bill against which the bourgeois and the military cannot raise valid objections, this fact [that it will take a period of years to develop an effective militia system] must be taken into account.
> That is what I tried to do in the articles which appeared last year in *Vorwärts* and which I sent you. ...
> Vaillant's Bill has great need for revision by someone who knows what's what in military affairs, it contains

things written in haste on which we could not stand up to serious argument.³

Since neither the German nor the French socialist parties had a chance of getting their Bills through, Engels is not arguing that the Bill is impractical *as a Bill*. That was obvious. He is saying it is not practical *as propaganda*. Effective propaganda against chauvinism had to make points that could not be dismissed. If the socialists appeared to be proposing silly and ill-conceived motions in a matter like national defense, it would be the chauvinists who would benefit and it would be better to say nothing.

After World War I, the socialist movement, strongly influenced by Lenin's 'revolutionary defeatism' slogan which scouted the danger of defeat by the enemy power, tended to emphasize opposition to military service on principle as the only possible anti-imperialist stance. Engel's position was largely ignored.

2. The Army of the Revolution

In its details, the pamphlet is a pacifist's nightmare. All adolescent males physically fit for the purpose are to be trained for combat.* This is to take place as part of their school training and, at one point, Engels proposes this, clearly with tongue in cheek, as a solution to the problem of what to do with retired and unemployable drill sergeants.

What begins as a pacifist's nightmare, however, soon turns into a Prussian officer's nightmare. After a short passage describing the difficult transition the retired drill instructors would have to undergo if they were to learn how to teach military skills to rambunctious schoolboys rather than terrorized recruits, Engels devotes considerable space to the subject of military discipline in a popular militia. After describing the brutal methods used to 'break in' new recruits in the Prussian military Engels

---

* In his letter to Lafargue which was quoted above, Engels criticized Vaillant's proposed military bill because it apparently included girls in this training! Feminist attacks on Engels would, however, be misplaced here. He was not interested in integrating the military but in undermining it.

argues that discipline in a democratic militia would be different. It would be directed not against recalcitrant recruits but against brutal officers:

> ... With the smooth-bore muzzle loader it was a simple matter to drop a pebble down the barrel onto the blank cartridge during maneuvers, and it was by no means unusual then for hated officers to be accidently shot during maneuvers. ... Now, with the small-bore breech loader it is no longer possible to do this so easily and unobtrusively; for this reason, the army suicide statistics indicate to us the barometric level of soldier tormenting fairly accurately. But if the live cartridge is put to use in "serious cases" there is every reason to wonder whether the old practice is again finding its advocates, as is said to have happened here and there in recent wars; ...[4]

Apparently, the mask of objective expert had slipped a little too far for Bebel. He wrote in a letter of February 28, 1893 that he thought the passage might be misconstrued and the author suspected of *advocating* such measures. He urged Engels to strike these sentences.[5]

The replacement of the standing army with a civilian militia was, of course, a democratic demand of long standing. It went back at least to the American War of Independence. In his private correspondence Engels had been discussing the scheme for some time but this was a public statement in the official, leading, Party paper. And Engels was proposing it not as a feature of the future socialist society but as an immediate demand of the largest party in the militarily most powerful European state. The reaction of the leadership of the Social Democratic Party demonstrated how far the best of them had drifted by this time from the revolutionary politics of Marx and Engels.

In his letter of February 28,[6] Bebel not only objected to Engels' mention of what amounted to mutiny as a provocation which would leave the party liable to prosecution by the military authorities, but advanced other, contradictory, objections to Engels' proposed bill. Such a bill, he argued, would never be practical because militarism was too profitable for business and offered to many sinecures to the sons of the nobility and the bourgeoisie. The bourgeois liberals would never support a serious attempt to cut back the military despite the disastrous economic effects of the tax required to support it. If the Social Democrats did propose such a bill then they would implicitly repudiate their long standing tradition of refusing to vote for the military budget at all.

In the event, as Bebel reported to Engels on March 12, the liberals compromised with the regime and the whole affair blew over. It became an inconsequential debate over how to improve the army. Bebel told Engels:

> It is impossible for us to use your military proposal. For tactical reasons we cannot support the two-year service plan which is the basis of the position of the Progressives and the other [bourgeois opposition] parties. And we cannot in any way support the current army because of the aristocratic character of the military command and the armies internal organization—court martials, military justice, etc., etc..[7]

But, of course, Engels' article was an attack on that military system and his proposed bill was designed to take the initiative away from the liberal critics of the military by presenting them with a scheme that would undermine the existing military system. And its revolutionary anti-militarist, anti-officer tone was one of the things that put Bebel off.

Bebel's objections reveal very clearly the conservative character of the party's famed refusal to vote for the military budget. Unlike Engels' proposal which seriously challenged the liberals and might really have embarrassed them into openly opposing the government, the traditional 'principled' stand meant abstention. It meant that the party had no answer to the question of how to defend the country in the event of a general European war. It almost guaranteed that the party would collapse in the face of such a threat. And there was an increasingly influential wing on the right of the Party that for precisely that reason was just as happy to leave the matter of militarism and the Party's opposition to it in the realm of 'principle.' *Their* real views were not to come out into the open, however, until August of 1914. The failure of people like Bebel to follow up on

Engels' approach allowed them to strike a left wing pose because it *was* just a pose.

3. "... and the German Army Is Ours"

Bebel's fright at Engels' barely disguised call for mutiny was a portent of things to come. Since at least 1866, Engels had emphasized the importance, from a revolutionary point of view, of the Prussian use of general conscription. Its introduction into modern warfare by this arch-reactionary regime forced every power to "arm the people." And this at a time when the socialist party was a growing force in every European country. It was the Achilles heel of the existing order.

And it solved a problem that had been bothering Engels since the suppression of the Commune. The old tactic of barricade fighting that had characterized every revolution since 1789 seemed to Engels to be obsolete. That tactic too had depended for its success on undermining the will of the army to fight. But it also assumed that the troops actually faced the people on the barricades. Modern artillery and modern city planning (modern in Engels' terms) made that unnecessary. The barricades with their now faceless defenders could be blown apart from miles away. Engels described his predicament to Paul Lafargue:

> You will have seen the reports in the papers of the ghastly effects, in Dahomey, of the new projectiles ... It's a capital thing for maintaining peace, but also for curbing the inclinations of so-called revolutionaries on whose outbursts our governments count. The era of barricades and street fighting has gone for good; *if the military fight*, resistance becomes madness. Hence the necessity to find new revolutionary tactics. I have pondered over this for some time and am not yet settled in my mind.[8]

Increasingly, Engels came to see the solution in the growth of the socialist party through electoral activity. But the aim of this activity was not simply the winning of parliamentary seats. Engels expressed himself very simply and unmistakably in a short phrase in a letter to Laura Lafargue. Reporting on Social Democratic victories in local elections where the voters were East Prussian peasants and agricultural laborers who were the traditional source of the Prussian army's obedient cannon fodder, Bismarck's beloved 'Pomeranian grenadiers,' Engels exclaimed "... if we get the rural districts of the six eastern provinces of Prussia ... *the German army is ours.*"[9]

4. The Fight Over *The Class Struggles in France*

It is over this issue that Engels moved into increasingly sharp opposition to the leadership of the German party including—one is tempted to say especially—August Bebel. In 1895, Engels, again at the request of the party leadership, wrote an introduction to a new edition of Marx's *Class Struggles in France*. In it he outlined a program for the German Social Democracy that, as explicitly as the censors would permit, proposed to use the electoral system to subvert the army. And he did this at a point when the conservative parties in the Reichstag were considering introducing new "Anti-Subversion" legislation that would outlaw the Social-Democratic movement which had only emerged from illegality four years earlier.

Engels faced a difficult task. For one thing, he was, as we have seen, concerned about an armed rising in the face of a disciplined, heavily armed, modern army. For another, he had to avoid giving the Prussian monarchy an excuse for the coup that he, along with everybody else, expected. It was vital that the socialists be seen as defending representative government against a monarchy. Too open a statement of the party's antimonarchical aims, however, could provide a pretext for illegality and muddy the political waters. Finally, Engels had to contend with the fact that the people, especially Bebel, who had supported him in the earlier underground struggle had clearly indicated that they would not follow him this time.

After describing at length the difficulties that made barricade fighting *in the initial stages* of an uprising no longer feasible, Engels spun out an elaborate Aesopian analogy with the late Roman empire. It was in this fable that he outlined the strategy the party ought to pursue in the face of the imminent coup. As an attempt to bypass his internal critics and avoid the appearance of calling for military mutiny, Engels' ruse was, perhaps, a little too transparent.

> Now almost 1,600 years ago, there was at work in the Roman Empire a dangerous revolutionary party. ... This revolutionary party, known under the name of the Christians, also had strong representation in the army; entire legions were composed of Christians. When they were commanded to attend the sacrificial ceremonies of the Pagan established church, there to serve as a guard of honor, the revolutionary soldiers went so far in their insolence as to fasten special symbols—crosses—on their helmets. The customary disciplinary barrack measures of their officers proved fruitless. ...

In response to this challenge the emperor Diocletian initiated a ferocious persecution of Christians—the last as it turned out. Engels explicitly, almost as if he were daring the Hohenzollern Emperor to act, compared this persecution to the proposed "antisubversion" legislation of 1894.

> But this exceptional law, too, [the emperor Diocletian's edict] remained ineffective. In defiance, the Christians tore it from the walls, yea, it is said that at Nikomedia they fired the emperor's palace over his head.[10]

The Executive Committee of the German Party was not amused by this fable. Richard Fischer, the secretary of the committee wrote Engels explaining the objections the entire party leadership had to his introduction and pressuring him to cut several passages.

> You yourself will admit that an ill-disposed opponent would have no trouble in presenting as the quintessence of your argumentation: 1) the admission that if we are not at present making the revolution it is because we are still not strong enough, because the army is not yet sufficiently infected—which is an argument [quod erat demonstrandum] *in favor* of the antisubversion bill and 2) that in case of war or any other serious complication we

would, like the Commune, raise the banner of insurrection in the face of enemy attack etc..[11]

But anyone, ill-disposed or well-disposed, who had been reading what Engels had been writing since 1866 on the consequences of universal military service would have understood what he was saying. Fischer was right to argue that no one would be fooled by Engels' Aesopian fable. But, then, Engels wasn't trying to fool anyone. He was just doing the best he could to appease the censor.

A political and literary quarrel erupted out of this attempt by the Party to censor Engels which lasted long after his death and became entangled with a series of later party disputes in the German and international movements. This story is too convoluted to treat here. It is told in a separate note. But the main point can be stated succinctly. When he died, unexpectedly, Engels was embarked on a political course that was leading him into ever increasing conflict with the leadership of the German Social Democracy including Bebel. It was a conflict over the Party's attitude towards the Prussian state in the coming war. The German Party leadership was inching its way towards a policy of civil peace in such an emergency. Engels was for taking advantage of the crisis to burn down the Emperor's palace.

SPECIAL NOTE A: ROSDOLSKY VS. ROSDOLSKY

Chapter 2 of this volume attempted to make some sense out of Engels' articles on the response of the "nonhistoric" peoples to the revolution of 1848. In that chapter I referred to the misuse of this material by Marxologists to portray Marx and Engels as German chauvinists and even proto-Nazis driven by racial hatred.[1] The methodology is the same in all cases regardless of the political view of the particular Marxologist. No attempt is made to explain to the reader what is in dispute and, therefore, no attempt to explain what position Marx and Engels together or either separately is defending. Instead, the reader is subjected to excerpts taken out of context which depend for their effect on Marx and Engels' frequent resort to the kinds of racial and ethnic terminology which were common in their day *and therefore are no indication of the specific views of the writer*. The reader, shocked by what would be in today's climate unacceptable language even in conservative circles, fails to notice that the Marxologist has not explained what was going on or what Marx or Engels thought about what was going on. For that matter, the reader doesn't know what the Marxologist thinks about the issue the reader remains ignorant of.

In 1987, an English translation of a book on *Engels and the "Nonhistoric" Peoples: The National Question in the Revolution of 1848*[2] appeared which seemed to be an exception. Its author, Roman Rosdolsky, was a scholar whose field was nineteenth century agrarian and national movements. He was also the author of a widely-respected investigation into the origins of Marx's *Capital*.[3] Politically, he was a leftist and a Marxist. In Rosdolsky's case this was not merely an intellectual or academic stance. As a young man he was a member of the Ukrainian Social Democratic party and a member of that faction which in the course of the Russian civil war came to support the Bolshevik side. He became one of the theoretical leaders of the Communist Party of the Western Ukraine. According to Professor John-Paul Himka–the translator of Rosdolsky's monograph on Engels and the national question in 1848–by the late 20s Rosdolsky had been expelled from the party because of his anti-Stalinism and was trying, like so many others, to rethink Marxism by going back to Marx. His studies of agrarian reform and revolution in Eastern Europe were driven by this aim and not simply academic interest. It was history and his own political experience that assigned him his thesis topic not his professors.

Professor Himka describes Rosdolsky's decades-long struggle to bring this material to the attention of the left public. When his monograph was finally published in German in 1964 and then in English in 1987, it found its audience. Serious students of this vexed question look to Rosdolsky as a guide and his work has had a significant impact on the whole debate. And that is the problem.

Despite his seriousness and obvious good faith, despite his past and despite his political views—which are in fact quite close to those Engels actually held—Rosdolsky has produced an account which completely distorts the evidence. None of the anti-Marxist diatribes has surpassed Rosdolsky's monograph in this respect. The reason for this paradox is not obvious although an attempt at an explanation will be made at the conclusion of this note. But first the extent of the distortion has to be documented.

In the first place, despite the title of the work, it is not really about Engels' gaffe, his use of Hegel's metaphysical category "nonhistoric peoples." Instead, Rosdolsky tries to explain, or justify, Engels' blunder by attributing to him a position which he did not hold. And the only way to do this is to bowdlerize the writings of Engels (Marx is largely ignored) to such a degree that he is portrayed as holding a position which is the opposite of the one he actually defended.

Briefly put, Rosdolsky's thesis is that Engels looked to the more or less immediate transition from the bourgeois revolution to a proletarian one.[4] Given this illusory hope, Engels and Marx were not too particular about the revolutionary allies they chose. In particular, the Polish and Magyar nobility along with the German bourgeois were chosen because they were the *immediate* enemies of bureaucratic absolutism and their victory would open up the road to the proletarian revolution. Engels and Marx were ignorant of, and not concerned about, the problems of the peasantry and ethnic minorities oppressed by these "revolutionary democrats." In any case, Marx and Engels believed both the peasantry and the small ethnic groups scattered throughout Eastern and Central Europe to be medieval relics bound to disappear with the triumph of modern civilization.

As a slightly caricatured version of sections of the *Communist Manifesto* this sketch has merit. But, as volume 2 of this work went to considerable length to prove, these widely misused sections of the Manifesto were an aberration.[5] And it was Marx's aberration, not Engels'. More importantly, Rosdolsky's thesis is concerned, not with the Communist Manifesto, but with the *NRZ* and its policy toward democratic revolution and peasant revolt in eastern Europe. Here, Rosdolsky hasn't a leg to stand on. His thesis allows him to "excuse" Engels, attributing his "nonhistoric peoples" line to an excess of zeal and an "underestimation of the peasantry." In fact, however well-intentioned, Rosdolsky's thesis both distorts Engels' position on agrarian revolution in 1848 and fails to come to grips with the real deficiencies in Engels' (and Marx's) treatment of the national question.

1. Marx and Engels on 1846

Central to Rosdolsky's argument is the Polish uprising of 1846, the reaction of the Polish Democracy to it, and Marx and Engels' alleged support of the "democratic" Polish nobility in this uprising. In defense of this thesis Rosdolsky relies on a series of indirect arguments since he cannot rely on Marx and Engels' *explicit* statements on the role of agrarian revolt in Eastern Europe.

One device is to use quotes from Engels in which he *emphasizes* the antifeudal programs and proclamations of Magyar, German and Polish democrats. Rosdolsky then proceeds to argue that the democrat in question was merely paying lip service to the demands of the peasantry. There are a number of instances of the use of this device.[6] But what do they prove? That Engels, writing in the midst of a revolution, with the means of communication available to a newspaper editor in 1848, was often unaware of information available to scholars a hundred years later? It is a pretty obvious point and one that says nothing about Engels' politics. What these quotes used by Rosdolsky do prove is that Engels *was* concerned with the agrarian question and that he *did* think it vital for the revolution. Rosdolsky's thesis requires Engels to either be indifferent to, or ignorant of, the peasant movement.

But there is more to these quotes than that. Engels was writing as a propagandist. I use the term not in our contemporary sense. He was not lying "for the good of the cause." What he was trying to do was to *influence* the outcome of the revolution not just report on it. When the *NRZ* printed a commentary by a democratic member of the Polish gentry or a speech by a left wing democratic representative to the Frankfurt Assembly it was doing so in order to encourage those political tendencies. That most such democrats were half-hearted and timid in the defense of their own interest, let alone the interests of their real or potential class allies, was certainly obvious to Marx and Engels. It was obvious to any intelligent observer, including the people who were organizing the counterrevolution. All the more reason for Marx and Engels to encourage those democrats who were, timidly, moving in the right direction. Of course, Marx and Engels could be held accountable if the *NRZ* had consistently avoided any criticism of the half-hearted democrats. But no historian of the period or of socialism has accused the *NRZ* of that failing. Quite the contrary. The usual complaint is that the paper's biting attacks on the Frankfurt Assembly and the democratic movement in general "went too far." If the Marxologists have not attacked the paper for being too critical of the democratic gentry, it is because the Marxologists, not the *NRZ*, have ignored the "peasant question" in 1848.[7]

The most dubious device used by Rosdolsky is his insistence that Marx and Engels were responsible for everything their correspondents wrote. Since many of their sources were Polish and Hungarian democrats, and since many of them *were* frightened by the prospect of a repeat of the 1846 uprising by Galician peasants, and since they often did pay lip service only to the slogans of agrarian revolution, this device allows Rosdolsky to impute sentiments and slogans to Marx and Engels which they cannot be shown to have held by any other means. What is worse, Rosdolsky insists on this "guilt by association" *even when Marx, as editor, explicitly disavows the politics of the correspondent.* Rosdolsky quotes the following editorial comment by Marx introducing a report by a correspondent:

> We print below a letter we have received from a Polish noble in Lviv; we have not altered a single line of the letter. The reader will easily distinguish the purely factual account from the attempts of a nobleman to explain the relationships of various classes, which he does not understand, as plausibly as possible. [Emphasis in original]

Rosdolsky v. Rosdolsky

Rosdolsky comments:

> The reader can here object: The lines you just cited clearly show how *critically* the *Neue Rheinische Zeitung* judged its noble-Polish correspondents! Right. But, unfortunately, this is the *only passage* in which the editors express their scruples about these correspondents' conceptions. And however interesting this passage is it does not change the entire picture of the *Neue Rheinische Zeitung*'s "Polish politics."[8]

For the record, this reader does object. Marx's editorial comment does make clear how critically the *NRZ* judged the Polish nobility. And this reader also would point out that, far from being the only passage where this point is made, it is only one of many. And it does not change the *NRZ*'s "Polish politics" it reaffirms them.

At other times, Rosdolsky simply asserts what he needs to prove without any attempt to base his interpretation on anything that appeared in the *NRZ*. The following is a good example:

> Only when the revolution was defeated and in Hungary mortally wounded , only then did the *Neue Rheinische Zeitung* sporadically put forth the idea of an Austrian "*peasant war*" that might come to the aid of the revolution and Hungary.[9]

In fact the first article on the Hungarian revolution in the *NRZ*, depends for its effect on an extended comparison of the Hungarians under Kossuth with the Polish insurrectionaries of 1830.[10] The point of the comparison is to emphasize that the Hungarians began with the step the Poles would not take: emancipation of the peasantry from all remaining feudal obligations. Coincidently, this article is the same article in which Engels first states his "nonhistoric peoples" thesis. Rosdolsky could hardly have missed it.

At times, Rosdolsky just misses the point. An example is the following quote from this same article by Engels:

193

> Let us suppose that the March revolution was purely a revolution of the nobility. Does that give the Austrian *'Gesamt Monarchie'* the right to oppress the Hungarian nobility and, and thereby also the Hungarian peasants, in the way it oppressed the Galician nobility and, *through the latter* the Galician peasants as well?[11]

Rosdolsky interprets this to mean that Engels was apologizing for the Polish gentry who routinely blamed the Imperial state for the financial burdens they passed on to the peasantry. But this is a misinterpretation. Although this specific citation is somewhat unclear, everything else Marx and Engels wrote on the subject makes the meaning unmistakable. At least as early as *The German Ideology*, Marx and Engels had come to some very definite conclusions as to the role of absolute monarchy in the transition from feudalism to capitalism. In this view, the absolute monarchy maintained itself by balancing between contending social forces none of which was strong enough to remake society in its own image. In the case of the peasant vs. noble conflict, the monarchy presented itself to the peasant as its protector against the rapacious demands of the gentry, and it promised the gentry protection against the *jacquerie* of the peasant. The Imperial state oppressed the peasant by means of (through) the landlord *and vice versa*. In Marx and Engels' view of the 1848 revolution the democratic gentry like the democratic bourgeoisie were breaking out of this pattern when they attacked the monarchy. *And this meant they had to come to terms with the working class and peasantry or face ruin.* In hindsight we, and Rosdolsky, know that the democratic gentry and bourgeoisie failed to measure up to their task. In Engels' marvelous phrase also summing up the matter in hindsight, they failed "to do their damned duty."[12]

Rosdolsky emphasizes only one side of this dynamic. And Engels emphasizes the other—at least in the bowdlerized version of the *NRZ* articles presented by Rosdolsky. Rosdolsky's emphasis on the antifeudal, reforming policy of Maria Theresa and Joseph II is a theme that recurs throughout the book. Although it is never explicitly stated or counterposed to Engels' analysis here,* it is the basis of Rosdolsky other writings on the subject.[13] Ironically, Rosdolsky's portrait of the gentry mirrors that of the peasantry often mistakenly ascribed to Marx. They are *nothing but* a feudal relic incapable in any circumstances of playing a revolutionary role.[14]

But the most serious error on Rosdolsky's part is one of omission. Marx and Engels explicitly dealt with the problem of agrarian revolt in Poland and its relation to the Polish Democracy and Polish national independence on any number of occasions. One of the most extended discussions of these issues was the 1848 memorial banquet in honor of the very 1846 insurrection which plays such an important role for Rosdolsky. And Rosdolsky does not mention this incident. He cannot because his whole thesis would collapse if he did.**

Chapter 2 already contains extensive excerpts from Marx and Engels' speeches on this occasion and I will not repeat them here. It is sufficient to remind the reader that they consisted of a virulent attack on the Polish "democratic" nobility. These "democrats" could not fight for an agrarian democracy "the only democracy possible in Eastern Europe" because of their class blinders. What has to be emphasized in this note is that Marx and Engels' made this attack on the Polish "democratic nobility" *to their faces*.

Let us imagine the scene. The occasion is a memorial to a revolution violently crushed just two years before by Austrian troops who were assisted by a peasant uprising widely believed at the time to have been instigated by Metternich. And it should be noted that the extent of Metternich's involvement is still in dispute. Even Rosdolsky admits that

---

* For one example, see Rosdolsky's cryptic remark that "it was the Austrian *counter-revolution* that could reap the fruits of the "peasant emancipation" which circumstances had forced upon Austria; ..." Is Rosdolsky saying that it was the absolute monarchy that was playing a progressive role as against the rebellious gentry and bourgeoisie? It isn't explicit here but if it is made explicit it makes sense of much of his argumentation.

** The *MEW* volume containing these two speeches, volume 4, appeared in 1959—five years before Rosdolsky published his book in German. Rosdolsky references other material in this volume.

there was *some* involvement. Metternich and his officials on the spot, according to Rosdolsky, utilized this uprising even though they did not instigate it.[15] Other scholars argue that Metternich was involved in the uprising from the beginning. But to the Polish exiles, English Chartists, and German artisan-communists gathered in London in 1848 Metternich's role was an accepted fact. And the Poles were heroes while the Ukrainian peasants were bigoted reactionaries in the pay of Austria, political descendants of the French peasants of the Vendée who rallied behind the priests against the Jacobins and the first French republic. On this occasion, before this audience, Marx and Engels chose to denounce the Polish gentry. They openly attacked the nobility and, by praising democrats like Lelewel, put *them* in the awkward position of having to agree implicitly with this political attack on their countrymen. If Lelewel and his supporters did not, in effect, disown their right wing compatriots in front of this international audience they would be disowning the revolutionary movement of 1846 and its antifeudal demands.

The uprising of 1846 is now a long-forgotten incident. It is hard for us to imagine what the impact of Marx and Engels' speeches would have been. An analogy based on a conflict more familiar to us might be a speaker at a rally honoring veterans of the Abraham Lincoln Brigade who insisted on reminding the audience of the negative role Stalin's government played in the Spanish Civil War. Rosdolsky's attack on the Polish "democratic" nobility is not any harsher than the ones delivered by Marx and Engels and his was made almost fifty years after any one entertained any illusions about the revolutionary or "democratic" potential of the Polish *szlachta*. Indeed, Rosdolsky's German book appeared almost twenty-five years after this social strata disappeared forever.

Lest the reader assume that Marx and Engels' attack on the *szlachta* at this memorial was, while a strong repudiation of this class, an isolated incident and that the subject was not actually referred to in the *NRZ*, I should mention that on a number of occasions in its comments on the question of agrarian revolt the paper mentioned the Galician uprising. And, in each case, the sympathies of the writer lie with the peasant rebels. It would take us far outside the bounds of this short note to collect them all here and one will have to suffice.

Rosdolsky v. Rosdolsky

In an article on the "Decree on the Abolition of Feudal Duties without Compensation in Silesia" the *NRZ* correspondent, Wilhelm Wolff, wrote in passing:

> The Junkers wish to enjoy at least one more merry carnival and exploit the November achievements of absolutism to the utmost. They are right to make haste, dancing and celebrating with defiant arrogance. For soon these divinely favored aristocratic orgies may be mingled with scenes of Galician fury.[16]

This reference passes over the head of the average reader today but it was clear to readers of the *NRZ* in 1848 and it is hard to believe that Rosdolsky missed it.* Rosdolsky never mentions Wilhelm Wolff's lengthy series on the Silesian peasant question. Engels and the German Social Democrats thought it of sufficient importance to republish the series in 1886 in book form and Engels wrote a lengthy introduction to that edition from which the above quote is taken. Wilhelm Wolff, the child of Silesian peasants himself, was a long time collaborator of Marx and Engels, a personal and political friend before, during, and after the 1848 revolution. He was a member of Marx's Communist Correspondence Committee and joined the Communist League with Marx and Engels. He ended up in Manchester as a close friend and collaborator of Engels and when he died Marx dedicated the first volume of Capital to him. Yet, Rosdolsky chooses Müller-Tellering, a bourgeois liberal whose only association with Marx was his brief tenure as the *NRZ* correspondent from Vienna, to prove that the *NRZ* soft pedaled agrarian revolution for fear of offending the gentry. And it is easy to demonstrate the *NRZ's* lack of interest in the peasantry using

---

* Marx was, in fact, well aware of the danger especially in the Hapsburg Empire of ignoring the peasantry. See his letter to Engels of 13 September 1851 in which he criticizes Mazzini for this failing. In this letter he twice brings up the Galician experience. Rosdolsky could argue of course that this was too little too late. But he can do so only because he ignores the Wolff articles. The record indicates that Marx and Engels both treated the lessons of the Galician uprising as a fact so well known that no extended comment was necessary. You just had to point.

this example because, indeed, Müller-Tellering wrote next to nothing on the peasantry. The trick will be obvious only to those readers of Rosdolsky who have in their library either the complete text of the *NRZ* or a copy of the 1886 German edition of Wolff's articles.

Rosdolsky sums up his case against the *NRZ* as follows:

> However odd it may seem, even the extreme left of the 1848 revolution, whose intellectual leadership was provided by the *Neue Rheinische Zeitung*, could not gauge correctly the extreme importance of the peasant question in Austria, the extraordinary chances it offered the revolution or the grave dangers it posed.[17]

This claim cannot stand up against the evidence. And it is not enough to argue that Marx and Engels overestimated the revolutionary potential of the German bourgeoisie and the Polish and Magyar gentry. They obviously did. But then they overestimated the revolutionary potential of the peasantry too. They overestimated the revolutionary potential of all classes as is proved by the fact that the revolution failed. In 1848 Marx and Engels supported and made common cause with all those social forces whose struggles tended to undermine the regime of bureaucratic absolutism and fought, however half-heartedly, for representative institutions and democratic liberties. They insisted that only a thorough social and economic democratization of society could open the way for the working class. A peasant who allowed himself to be won to the side of the Hohenzollern, Hapsburg or Romanov dynasty out of hatred for his immediate oppressor became an enemy of the revolution and democracy and so did a German burgher or Polish noble who sought similar refuge out of fear of social revolution.

The main problem with Rosdolsky's book is that it doesn't help explain the "nonhistoric peoples" slogan nor the politics behind it. You can't explain it by the *NRZ*'s inattention, or hostility, to agrarian revolution because Marx and Engels were not only for that revolution but they were adamant that it was (along with Jewish emancipation) the key to the democratic revolution in Eastern Europe. It was the national question, especially in its linguistic dimension, that the *NRZ* mishandled.

Engels (and Marx) saw agrarian revolution as the *solvent* of national antagonisms in the Hapsburg empire. And to some extent it was. But, as Rosdolsky rightly points out, agrarian revolt often took the *form* of national revolt. This *form*, however, and this is what Rosdolsky ignores, all too often, especially in 1849, ended up betraying the content of the struggle. Croats, Ukrainians and Czechs ended up fighting on the side of the enemy of their enemy with the usual results. And it was this problem to which Engels had no solution.

The "Nonhistoric peoples" slogan can actually be dismissed fairly easily as a bad formulation. But behind the bad formulation is real political confusion. What is the solution when a national movement chooses to follow reactionary leaders and allow its interests to be used against equally valid claims of other nations and peoples? The case of the Irish against the English or the Poles against the Russians and Germans is relatively easy. What do you do when Croats ally themselves with the Hapsburgs against Hungarians or, later, Serbs? And what do you do when nations with equally valid claims to the land assert their right to self-determination? Engels had no answer to this question. He didn't have one in 1848 and neither did Marx. They never resolved the contradiction between their often repeated sentiment that democracy, let alone a workers' state, could not survive the suppression of a whole people and the obvious historical fact that many small nations chose to defend the old regime. This is the real problem and the absurd comparisons of Marx and Engels with the Nazis obscure rather than clarify it—always assuming that the writer is interested in clarification rather than obfuscation.

Unfortunately, Rosdolsky's proposed solution doesn't get us any further. It offers an explanation of Engels' slogan that simply ignores the bulk of what Engels wrote. It too is obfuscation although I don't think that was Rosdolsky's intent.

Let us start with Rosdolsky' own solution to "the national question." Does he have one? Rosdolsky comes pretty close on a couple of occasions to saying that all movements striving for national independence are progressive. It is easy enough to attack the extreme formulations of an Engels or a Rosa Luxemburg but is Rosdolsky claiming that an independent Czech or Croat republic is always preferable to, more "progressive" than, federation or even assimilation into a larger state? At one point, Rosdolsky brings up Engels' comment on the incorporation of medieval Provençe into France. Engels in this passage is arguing for the progressive consequences of the brutal French conquest of the southern non-French speaking section of what we know as France. Engels remarks that at the time the southern part of the country was more developed economically and more advanced culturally than the northern part. He laments the loss of its beautiful language. But he argues that the inhabitants of Provençe were more than compensated by the French Revolution which freed them from medievalism and particularism.

It is easy enough to make fun of this analogy. It is unlikely that this argument would have had much appeal for the defeated Provençal nobility and patrician burghers. Even if they had lived the requisite several hundred years to witness the revolution their compensation would likely have been the guillotine. But does that mean that today, if a revived Provençal nationalism were to demand independence from France, that would be "progressive"? Rosdolsky devotes a whole chapter titled "The Realistic Side of Engels' Prognosis" in which he concedes almost everything to Engels as far as what the *NRZ* wrote in 1848 is concerned. The Austrian Slavs did prove incapable then of revolutionary activity. They did end up fighting for reaction. In his next chapter Rosdolsky simply argues that Engels was wrong in predicting that this state of affairs would continue. But he doesn't explicitly claim that the "balkanization" of Eastern Europe that resulted from the breakup of the Romanov, Hapsburg and Hohenzollern empires in 1914 was desirable.

At one point Rosdolsky actually adopts a version of the "nonhistoric peoples" line as his own.

> Thus the *Poles* in Poznań complained about the Germanophile behaviour of the Jews, the Poles in the Kingdom of Poland—about their Russophilism; the Czechs reproached the Bohemian Jews with being pro-Austrian, while the Ukrainians charged the Galician Jews with being pro-Polish. ... But it only requires a little reflection to realize we are dealing here with behaviour

typical of every genuine national minority; in general, no oppressed nationality disdains or has disdained the opportunity of reaping benefit for itself at the cost of another oppressed nationality.[18]

Allowing for the qualifier "generally" this statement is as woodenheaded as Engels' paraphrasing of Hegel.

The most striking thing about Rosdolsky's monograph is that, from the point of view of theory, he has not got beyond Engels. Both he and Engels are arguing from a position that is pre-Lenin. Engels, of course, has an excuse. Lenin's theoretical contribution was the distinction between the *right* of self-determination and the *desirability* of self-determination. Without this distinction you are stuck on one or another of the horns of the following dilemma. If you decide that, in some case or another, that the declaration of self-determination by a given ethnic group or its self-appointed leaders is wrong headed and likely to aid the forces of reaction then you are driven to argue for the suppression of that people. That is, you are driven to this conclusion logically even if you aren't happy about it. On the other hand, if you don't want to accept this conclusion, then you are pretty much forced to argue that any struggle for self-determination is desirable and "progressive."

Lenin's theoretical contribution was to resolve this dilemma. You can recognize a right to self-determination based on the argument Engels made in his editorials on the debates over Poland in the Frankfurt Assembly. At the same time, you can argue politically with your friends and comrades and allies within the oppressed community that to press for self-determination either in general or at a given time is a mistake. What is even more important, the recognition of the right of self-determination provides a revolutionary movement with a weapon of political warfare against reactionary nationalism. Engels himself came close to recognizing this in the passage quoted in chapter 2 above in which he argues that *if* the Austrian Slavs, in particular the Czechs, *had* revolted against the Hapsburgs then the national interests of the Germans and Magyars would have had to accommodate their demands. And, in the case of the Poles, the *NRZ* had insisted on territorial concessions which would have left large numbers of German speaking people in a Polish state. The step Engels and the *NRZ* didn't take was to urge such concessions to national demands on the Hungarian revolutionaries as a way to win over Croat, Rumanian and German speaking peasants.

Rosdolsky doesn't make this point against Engels. Without explicitly saying so, he in effect argues that the struggle for national independence is "progressive" everywhere and at all times. His treatment of national movements in 1848 is, therefore, schizophrenic. On the one hand, he has to agree that Engels' "nonhistoric peoples" slogan had a "realistic" side—Croats, Czechs and others really were fighting for reaction. On the other hand, he attacks the *NRZ* for siding with Poles, Germans and Hungarians. Rosdolsky, in fact, is retrograde as compared to the *NRZ*. Engels' emphasis on the role of the agrarian revolution in dissolving national differences and winning the peasantry over to the side of the Hungarian republic is missing in Rosdolsky. To mention it would make nonsense of his treatment of the *NRZ* but there is something else. For Rosdolsky the national liberation movement is a good in itself. There is nothing in his treatment of the 1848 revolution that would indicate he would look with favor on the tendency of class struggle to dissolve national allegiance.

2. Two Diversions

Before attempting an explanation of Rosdolsky's peculiar treatment of his source materials, two minor points have to be dealt with. That is, they are minor points in this context since they are digressions from Rosdolsky's main thesis. In themselves they are worth several books and there are a couple of hundred pages concerning them in this and earlier volumes of *KMTR*.

The first of these two digressions is the one on Bakunin. There are minor problems here. For one, Rosdolsky, without citing any reference, claims that Engels, in contrast to Bakunin, insisted on "the claims of the Austrian Germans and Hungarians to the Slavic territories they held ..."[19] Now Engels' statements on "nonhistoric peoples" are abstract enough to allow many interpretations—that is one of the problems with them. But that also means you cannot just assign any interpretation you want to them. You are bound by the voluminous record of Marx and Engels' articles on the 1848 revolution. There is no evidence that Engels (or Marx) contemplated any long term occupation of the territory of a coherent Slav national group for the simple reason that they believed the Slavic groups in question were incapable of independent national existence. They could function for a short time as a center of counterrevolution to be again subjected to their Austrian and Hungarian overlords after the victory of the counterrevolution (which is what happened) or they would be assimilated in a multi-ethnic democratic republic. In particular, the Viennese revolutionaries whose revolt the *NRZ* championed aimed at the establishment of a German democratic republic which meant the breakup of the Hapsburg Empire and, in consequence, the liberation of the Slavic peoples of the empire from "German," that is Hapsburg, rule. In that eventuality only the Czechs in Bohemia, where there was a substantial German speaking population, presented any problem. And Engels position there was clear. If the Czechs side with the Germans against the Hapsburgs then the question of borders will have to be negotiated. Otherwise the Czechs will have to be fought.

In some passages, Rosdolsky himself insists that Engels was not arguing for German nationalism. But, in this chapter, he strains to contrast the Slavic nationalist Bakunin against the alleged German nationalist Engels.

Bakunin's revolutionary sentiments are taken at face value by Rosdolsky while being dismissed as overly romantic. But the problem with Bakunin's Slavic Federation with its all-powerful Slavic Council was not just that it was unrealizable except as a possible propaganda device of Tsarist imperialism. It of necessity had to counterpose itself to the real Slavic nations that existed. Czechs and Russians as well as Poles. That is the point of Engels' analogy with a "pan-German" state embracing Flanders, Denmark, Alsace and England (presumably minus Scotland and Ireland.)

Although he quotes from Bakunin's *Confession* as well as the two appeals to the Slavs, Rosdolsky nowhere mentions the most obvious fact about the first named document. It is openly, explicitly, aggressively, pro-Tsarist. The Tsar is to be the liberator of the Slavs. Rosdolsky quotes Bakunin's libertarian rhetoric about "Freedom" (what orator in 1848 could do without such phrases?) but ignores the most salient feature of Bakunin's proposal—that as a condition of Slav unity the struggle of the peasantry against their freedom-loving gentry masters be suppressed! This omission is especially striking because the example Bakunin chooses is exactly the Galician uprising on which Rosdolsky places so much stress in his attack on Engels! As far as Bakunin's pro-Tsarist *Confession* is concerned one could dismiss it as a document extorted under duress, but Rosdolsky uses this remarkable document when it suits him and then ignores its pro-Tsarism and in particular Bakunin's call on the Tsar to take over from the despised German Hapsburgs the role of protector of the freedom-loving Slavic gentry against peasant uprisings. Bakunin in these documents speaks as a pure and simple nationalist with no social program whatsoever. He is pro-peasant simply because the Slavs were overwhelmingly a peasant people. And their oppressors are German, German-Jewish and Hungarian burghers and lords but not their Slavic lords and certainly not their Little Father. Bakunin's hostility to the bourgeoisie was racial and social. It was part of his hostility to the modern world.

This is the contrast. Engels' denunciations of the democratic gentry (and bourgeoisie) are suppressed and he is condemned for ignoring the peasantry. Bakunin's support of the gentry (Slavs only of course) is likewise suppressed and he is praised for his freedom loving rhetoric. This is not the way to write history and even for a polemic it goes too far.

3. The Neue Rheinische Zeitung and the Jews

Rosdolsky's digression on the Jews follows the same pattern as his treatment of the *NRZ* on agrarian revolution. Rosdolsky begins by quoting extensively one of the *NRZ*'s Vienna correspondents, Eduard Müller-Tellering, whose denunciations of the Jewish bourgeoisie in Vienna because of their alleged betrayal of the revolution are full of the language which was typical of the period.* These quotes are conflated with Marx and Engels' articles on the role of the Jews in Prussian Poland who opposed Polish independence (out of fear of the Polish peasantry among

---

* For a longer discussion of this whole question of Marx's use of the economic stereotype of the Jew see *KMTR I*. Müller-Tellering is chosen as an example by Rosdolsky, as he has been chosen by others, because he *later* became a political antisemite; his first attempt in this field being an attack on Marx.

other reasons) and were, naturally, celebrated by the right wing press and other spokesmen for Prussian Junkertum. The latter instantly became "friends of the Jews." Rosdolsky flatly states, on this slender basis, that the NRZ shared the "illusions [of mid-nineteenth socialists] about the real content of anti-Semitic sentiments among the people and even thought it possible to use these sentiments for revolutionary purposes." Rodsolsky cites no evidence that the NRZ or Marx or Engels ever made such appeals to antisemitism. He can't because there were none. For evidence of Marx's antisemitism, he refers to the later's 1844 article "On The Jewish Question." The sophistication of Marx's approach to the question is praised and Marx and Engels are absolved of the charge of being simple antisemites like Müller-Tellering. But Rosdolsky concludes by reluctantly agreeing that Marx and Engels capitulated to the "socialist antisemitism" that was endemic (Rosdolsky claims) in the early workers' movement. "They only saw the anticapitalist source of popular antisemitism and overlooked its reactionary essence."[20]

What Rosdolsky forgets to do in this sketch is—to mention what the NRZ's position on the "Jewish Question" *was*.* It was—Jewish emancipation. Full civil rights for people who practiced the Jewish religion.

That was the only "Jewish Question" that existed in 1848. Modern racialist antisemitism was only a small cloud on the horizon. Marx died in 1883 when this modern phenomenon was in its early stages. When Engels, in1890, was asked to address himself to this new movement he denounced it as a recrudescence of the "feudal socialism" Marx had repudiated in the *Manifesto* and remarked "with that we can, of course, have nothing to do."[21]

Here again, as in the case of agrarian revolution, we are dealing with a demand which Engels especially emphasized was one of the two litmus tests that determined the seriousness of the democratic revolution in Eastern Europe. It was not just that Marx, Engels and the NRZ were on the progressive side in this matter, they insisted on making it a key demand.

---

* Except in a footnote. Here Rosdolsky says that he is "going to leave aside the tremendous *practical* distinction: that Marx and Engels, as well as all later socialists(sic?), championed the complete emancipation of the Jews." Why this point is to be left aside is not explained.

Engels mentions it time and again in his articles. Yet, Rosdolsky goes so far as to accuse the *NRZ* with failing to "dissociate itself from the antisemitic "popular opinion,..." [22]

But Rosdolsky goes further. In a sweeping generalization on a very controversial subject he indicts the *entire* movement in this short addendum to his book with almost no reference to the history involved.

> We have come to the conclusion that the deplorable position of the *Neue Rheinische Zeitung* on the Jewish question was a *children's disease of the workers' movement.* And it was, furthermore, a disorder from which the socialist movement of almost every country suffered.[23]

What evidence for this blanket condemnation does Rosdolsky mention? There are essentially three:

1) Marx and Engel's use of harsh language to describe the betrayal of the Poles by the German Jewish bourgeoisie and the similar behavior of the Jewish community in Vienna.

2) Marx and Engels, like most early socialists, indeed like most of their contemporaries, Gentile and Jew, of whatever political coloration, accepted the stereotype of the economic Jew, the money lender and financier.

3) "Revolutionaries" (unnamed) equivocated during the Dreyfus case and, in the Ukraine in 1882-1883, the *Narodnaya Volya* even encouraged pogroms.

Now the first thing to note is that only items 1) and 2) have any connection to Marx and Engels. Both were dead by the time of the Dreyfus case and Marx died without ever hearing about the Ukrainian incidents. Engels did have occasion to comment on modern, racialist antisemitism in 1890 and, as we have seen, condemned it. The *NRZ*, whose policy is presumably the matter under discussion, had ceased publication over forty years before either of these two events.

As for item 1) Rosdolsky agrees that the Jewish bourgeoisie did behave in the way the *NRZ* claimed but that other ethnic groups behaved in similar fashion for understandable historical reasons and Marx and Engels did not attack them in such abusive language. Now, Rosdolsky, when he comes to write this sentence, has already written 189 pages detailing just such intemperate attacks on Croats, Serbs, Rumanians, Transylvanian Saxons and Czechs. It is the point of his book! The fact is that Marx and Engels attacked the German Jewish bourgeoisie with no more and no less vitriol than they attacked the rest of the German bourgeoisie or the pro-Hapsburg nationalists.

Charge number 2) is the only serious one. There is one important connection between the religious antisemitism that Marx knew and modern racialist antisemitism. Both depend on the stereotype of the economic Jew. In fact, in the modern period, especially in the case of the Nazis, the concept of an all-powerful Jewish conspiracy controlling the modern world through its control of finance reached paranoid dimensions previously unknown. And there is no question that in 1844 Marx accepted this general stereotype although without the accompanying notion of an all-powerful conspiracy. Even in that essay, however, his principal argument was that this stereotype was obsolete. In the modern bourgeois world, as opposed to the medieval world it grew out of, the reduction of all human relations to the cash nexus was not something peculiar to the Jewish money-lender. And it was on the basis of this kind of argument that Marx opposed the legal restrictions against people who practiced the Jewish religion.* And that was the only antisemitism he knew. Nevertheless, it is true that this stereotype of the Jew as financier, usurer and speculator was the major ideological prop of antisemitism then and is still now. And it is true that, in 1844, Marx accepted this view of capitalism and the relationship to it of the "economic Jew." An antisemite could always argue that Marx agreed with the antisemitic picture of the Jew's economic role even if he did not

---

* We also have to remember that Marx had always seen this bourgeois world as a step forward, a step towards real human freedom, as compared to the medieval world it grew out of.

share the antisemite's preference for the "Christian-Germanic" Europe of old.

If Roman Rosdolsky had not been the author of *The Making of Marx's Capital* he might be excused for using the essay "On the Jewish Question" as evidence against the *NRZ*. But certainly Rosdolsky, of all people, had to know that Marx had, by 1847, already left behind the economic views expressed in his essay "On the Jewish Question." The Marx and Engels of the *NRZ* no longer saw huckstering and money-worship as the defining characteristic of capitalism. Capitalist exploitation of wage-labor was rooted in the process of production not in exchange. It was a mistake for socialists to concentrate their fire on those economic activities which were seen as particularly "Jewish." One of Marx's earliest works on political economy, his 1847 polemic against Proudhon's *The Poverty of Philosophy*, was an attack on precisely the kind of petty-bourgeois "socialism" that was such a fundamental part of political antisemitism.* I don't think it would be an exaggeration to say that the ideological influence Marx's economics exercised over the socialist movement, on the right as well as the left, played an important role in inoculating the labor movement against antisemitism.

Rosdolsky's sweeping attack on the *workers' movement* is simply an attempt to bolster a weak case by making an accusation so broad that it can only be answered by a several volume work. And, indeed, there is a vast literature on the subject. Unfortunately for Rosdolsky, he chose to formulate his accusation in a way that is easy to refute. Had he used the term *socialist* movement he would have been on better ground since that term, especially before Marx, was used in such a loose and broad way that any critic of the capitalist system could be called a socialist. And, in fact, the use of the term "national socialist" to describe their movement was widely used by antisemites long before Hitler. Marx and Engels very consciously chose to call themselves "communists" in the 1840s precisely to avoid being put in the same political category as those "socialist" critics of the capitalist system who did not want a class-based movement from below.

---

* Proudhon's notebooks, published only in recent times, reveal him to be one of the first modern racialist antisemites, but Marx did not know this.

Rosdolsky's formula also might have worked if had referred to antisemitism as a disease within the working *class*. There is an enormous literature on the subject of the effect of antisemitic demagogy on workers. In Germany, the most thoroughly studied case for obvious reasons, the overwhelming evidence is that the Nazis had no success in their attempt to win electoral support in the industrial working class prior to 1933.[24] After Hitler's seizure of power, the industrial working class was subjected to a measure of totalitarian control greater than that of any other stratum of the population so it is all but impossible to gauge the strength of working class support for the regime. The extreme measures they took to prevent any form of organization by this class would indicate that the Nazis themselves had no great confidence in their ability to win over this particular constituency.

The situation is more complicated in France, especially when it comes to the Dreyfus case, and in this case too there is an enormous and highly controversial literature.[25]

But as to the workers' *movement* there can be no question. Antisemitism, as a political movement not a personal prejudice, came into being as an alternative, an antidote, to the growing influence of the socialist and trade union movements in the working class. It defined itself as a "national" or "völkisch" movement as opposed to a class movement. A worker who voted for or joined such a movement was by that act repudiating the workers' *movement*.

In any case, what does all this have to do with 1848? Nothing, really. It is, in part, a reaction to the language of the *NRZ* which meant something quite different in 1948 than it did one hundred years later. In part, it is an attempt by Rosdolsky to buttress his case on another, unrelated, question by smearing Marx and Engels as antisemites.

4. Rosdolsky: 1929 and 1948

In the case of most other Marxologists, manhandling of the evidence and blatant distortion of the primary sources on the scale practiced by Rosdolsky would be a sure sign of the author's political hostility towards Marx and Engels in particular and the left in general. It is comparable to the worst excesses of cold war anticommunist pseudo-scholarship. But to make that judgement would be a mistake. Rosdolsky's own political *bona fides* cannot be questioned. I think that the book can be explained only as a gross over-reaction by Rosdolsky to his own earlier *uncritical* defense of the *NRZ*'s treatment of the national question. And both the original defense and the later attack on the position of the *NRZ* flow from Rosdolsky's response, not to the problems posed by the national movements of the 1840s, but to the problems posed by national independence movements in his own time and in particular to the Ukrainian nationalist movement before, during and after World War II.*

Ukrainian independence became a possibility only as a result of the October 1917 revolution in Russia. The left wing of the social democrats and of the socialist revolutionaries eventually ended up on the Bolshevik side during the civil war which engulfed the Ukraine as well as Russia and supported federation with the Soviet Union on the basis of the principles Lenin proposed. The advocates of Ukrainian independence tended to look for German support against both Russia and Poland. After 1920, the Ukraine was divided. The western Ukraine became a part of Poland and the eastern part a formally independent state within a federated Soviet Union. Rosdolsky became a leader of the Communist Party of the Western Ukraine.

According to J. P. Himka, in his introduction to *Non-historic Peoples,* the splits in the Ukrainian movement led to vigorous polemics over the national question. One participant, Volodymyr Levynsky, attacked the Bolsheviks as Russian imperialists. In the course of his polemic, he attacked Engels and the *NRZ* as concealed German imperialists and argued that Lenin was doing the same thing only as a Russian imperialist.

In his thesis, written in 1929, after he had been expelled from the *CPWU,* Rosdolsky wrote as a defender of the *NRZ,* although not a completely uncritical one. He emphasized the inadequacy of the formula "nonhistoric peoples," but he argued that Engels had been basically right. (There is no mention, by the way, of the agrarian question.) The most

---

* This is not a rare phenomenon. Polemicists of the left, right and center have often, without necessarily any intent to deceive, used an alleged discussion of Marx's politics as a device for commenting on contemporary problems. For this purpose it was not necessary to pay much attention to what Marx or Engels actually wrote or to the circumstance in which they wrote.

Rosdolsky v. Rosdolsky

interesting thing about this thesis is the way Rosdolsky uses Lenin. He quotes from Lenin's article "The Discussion on Self-Determination Summed Up"[26] in which *Lenin* defends the policy of the *NRZ* (but not the formula "nonhistoric peoples" which is not mentioned.) Lenin does this mainly by emphasizing, rightly, the concrete situation facing revolutionaries in 1848-9 but he also comes close at one point to using the "hierarchy of values" argument. "The several demands of democracy, including self-determination, are not an absolute, but only a *small part* of the general-democratic (now; general-socialist) *world* movement. In individual cases, the part may contradict the whole; if so, it must be rejected." Rosdolsky merely repeats this argument.

Neither Rosdolsky nor Lenin notice that Engels never used the term self-determination in this context nor that his "nonhistoric peoples" formula cannot be reconciled with the principle. Both Rosdolsky and Lenin quote at length Engels' statements in 1848 and later in which he more or less clearly enunciates the *concept* summed up in the formula "self-determination" without pointing out (or probably noticing) the logical contradiction. They repeat Engels' confusion rather than clearing it up. The pressure on both Lenin and Rosdolsky to do this is easily understood. To simply state that Engels' formula was a mistake that obscured rather than clarified his real politics would have given aid to their opponents. German Social-Democrats in World War I and Stalinists in the 1920s could have claimed Engels as a supporter of their chauvinist policies and denounced Lenin or Rosdolsky as "revisionists." Such demagogy would have helped obscure the issue. But Lenin and Rosdolsky's approach did not help matters.

As Ukrainian nationalism veered sharply to the right, like nationalism throughout Eastern and Central Europe in the 1920s, Rosdolsky could certainly see the analogies with the behavior of the "non-historic peoples" in 1848-49. But then the Second World War intervened.

By 1940, national independence was no longer a question only for colonial peoples or small ethnic groups on the fringes of Europe. The French, the Belgians, and the Dutch had become "nonhistoric peoples." It looked like any day the English might become "nonhistoric" too. By the end of the war, "national liberation" summed up the aspirations of tens of millions of Europeans and they were soon followed by hundreds of millions of people in formerly colonial countries who took the opportunity presented by Europe's prostration to make their own bid for freedom. In Eastern Europe, Russia's suppression of national rights ran sharply against the current. Even those national movements like the Ukrainian which were tainted by their collaboration with Nazism were partially protected by the aura of "national liberation."

In this social context, Engels' jaundiced view of national movements was distinctly out of fashion. In 1929, arguing against a Ukrainian nationalist like Levynsky, Rosdolsky could defend his views with ease. Lenin's Soviet Union of federated republics seemed an attractive ideal. Nationalism in Eastern Europe was strongly tinged with fascism and antisemitism; antisemitism here being defined as a movement whose aim was not only to deprive Jews of their civil rights, but to subject them to a reign of terror and drive them from the country because of their "race."

By 1948, however, when Rosdolsky sat down to rewrite his thesis, Stalin's revived Russian empire seemed to validate all Levynsky's claims and "National Liberation" was the slogan of the antifascists (real and fake.) Besides, Rosdolsky's studies of the agrarian movements in Eastern Europe and the agrarian reforms of the Hapsburgs in the late 18th century had made him extremely suspicious of the bona fides of the 19th century Polish and Hungarian gentry and their ideological spokesmen.

To Rosdolsky, the thesis that Engels had been misled by his reliance on self-styled Polish and Hungarian "revolutionary democrats" must have seemed an ideal solution. The NRZ had been completely wrong but with the best of intentions. Marx and Engels were not chauvinists or imperialists as Levynsky claimed but their politics on this question were, nevertheless, worse than useless. At this stage, Rosdolsky may even have been unaware of Engels' writings on the subject of agrarian revolution. The sources he cites in his 1929 thesis hardly mention the subject of agrarian reform and do not contain the important speeches at the memorial banquet in 1848 in honor of the Polish insurrection of 1846. Certainly, in 1948, the more complete sources Rosdolsky refers to in the 1964 and 1986 editions of his book were not available. The conclusion would seem to be that Rosdolsky rethought his position and rewrote his thesis in response to the political and ideological pressures of 1948 without being in a position to know what was really going on in 1848. Later, when he did have access to the facts of the case, he was so committed to the thesis he couldn't see the evidence before his eyes.

SPECIAL NOTE B. "CONSTITUTIONAL" OR "REVOLUTIONARY" WAR?

In the introduction I mentioned that the American Civil War was one of only two times after 1848 when Marx and Engels supported a war waged by a bourgeois government. The interesting thing is that, so far as I have been able to discover, none of the prowar socialists in World War I referred to this example. Why?

1. Lincoln and Slavery

Part of the problem for us is that the treatment of the American Civil War by the American academic establishment is as ideological and encrusted with myths as are the similar accounts of the French and Russian Revolutions. In general, historical scholarship tends to divide into two camps. One is an apology for the South that claims its fight was not in defense of slavery, which was disappearing anyway for economic reasons, but in defense of the South's genteel, cultivated, agrarian society based on Jeffersonian ideals against the new, vulgar, bourgeois order based on the worship of Mammon.

This view, which was pretty much the established one from the late nineteenth century through the 1920s, is now discredited although Shelby Foote's defense of the basic thesis still gets a respectful hearing.

The dominant view, most recently advanced in James McPherson's best selling history of the war, can best be described as Lincoln-olatry. It was Lincoln, a statesman as well as a consummate politician, who restrained the more extreme abolitionists whose ideas, while noble, were too far in advance of the general population. At the same time he kept the border states in the union. Only his untimely death prevented him from reuniting the nation without the trauma of Reconstruction.

The only voices of any note that raise questions have come, not from scholars, but from literary men. Edmund Wilson in the 1950s and, more recently, Gore Vidal have taken Lincoln's own words seriously. They believe he meant it when he claimed that he was fighting not to destroy slavery but to defend the Union. Wilson compares Lincoln to Bismarck. Both were modern nation-builders only half understood by their contemporaries. Vidal emphasizes Lincoln's role in the creation of the "imperial presidency," a Bonapartist institution which reduces the legislative branch of government to a cheering section whose only serious role is to represent their constituencies when it comes time to distribute federal patronage.

There are a few accounts of the split in the Republican Party which finally forced Lincoln into freeing the slaves and set the country on the road to Reconstruction but it would be a digression to go into that here. Special Note C gives a brief account of some of the literature on this much neglected issue.

1. The Abolitionists in Charge

The abolitionists were not simply ideologues; they were an organized political tendency with serious supporters in the press and a popular following among Midwestern immigrants and farmers who feared the spread of the slave system, and in the Northeast where republican sentiments were strong and where abolitionist sentiment had long taken the form of civil disobedience backed by state and local authorities against the Southern-dominated federal government. With the secession of the Southern States the Congress—in which the weight of Southern votes had been grossly inflated in comparison with the more populous North as a result of some of the more bizarre features of the Constitution—was suddenly in the hands of an abolitionist majority. Northern politicians who for decades had seen the Southern minority control the Presidency, the Supreme Court and the Senate because the Constitution gave each State the same voting strength in the Senate and disproportionate weight to Southern states in Presidential elections, now found themselves in control of the Senate and the Presidency. What is more, even in the House of Representatives the size of Southern delegations had been determined not simply by the number of citizens in the State but also by the number of slaves who, of course, could not vote. Every Southern delegate had represented not just the free citizens but three-fifths of the disenfranchised slaves. Now, the "slave power" was reduced to a small minority of border state representatives who, in addition, found it difficult to play the role of opposition without bringing on themselves the suspicion of treason. The abolitionists were ready for a revolution. And the growing casualty list in what was to become arguably the century's bloodiest war only embittered them and the country they represented.

2. Marx on the Secession Crisis

Marx reflected the spirit of this new abolitionist majority, which he was familiar with through his writings as a correspondent for a leading abolitionist daily, the *New York Daily Tribune*, in a long comment to Engels.

> On studying these American affairs more closely, I have come to the conclusion that the conflict between South and North—for 50 years the latter has been climbing down, making one concession after another—has been at last brought to a head (if we disregard the effrontery of °chivalry's° fresh demands) by the weight which the extraordinary development of the °North Western States° has thrown into the scales. The population there, with its rich admixture of newly-arrived Germans and Englishmen and, moreover, largely made up of °self-working farmers°, did not, of course, lend itself so readily to intimidation as the °gentlemen° of Wall Street and the Quakers of Boston. ... It was this self-same area in the North that first came out unequivocally against any recognition of the independence of a °Southern Confederacy°. They cannot, of course, allow the lower reaches and estuary of the Mississippi to pass into the hands of foreign states. Again in the Kansas affair (from which this war really dates), it was the population of these °North Western [States]° who came to blows with the °Border Ruffians°.[1]

Marx had already spelled out what this all meant in a letter to his uncle Lion Phillips:

> Here in London there is a great consternation over the course of events in America. The acts of violence which have been perpetrated not only by the °seceded states°, but also by some of the °central° or °border states°—and it is feared that all 8 °border states° ... There can be no doubt that, in the early part of the struggle the scales will be weighted in favor of the South, where the class of propertyless white adventurers provides an inexhaustible

source of martial militia. °In the long run°, of course, the North will be victorious since, if the need arise, it has a last card up its sleeve in the shape of a slave revolution.²

Marx summed it up in another letter to Engels:

The long and the short of it is, I think, that wars of this kind ought to be conducted along revolutionary lines, and the °Yankees° have so far been trying to conduct it along constitutional ones.³

3. Lincoln's Fear of Revolution

Lincoln's election provoked a Southern insurrection because the slaveocracy believed that any restriction on the expansion of slavery meant its downfall.* Lincoln, despite his genuine hatred of the slave system responded by attempting to appease those slave owners who were willing to support the Union cause.

The abolitionists seized the opportunity of the slave owners revolt to press the antislavery campaign. In particular, in Missouri, where the proslavery governor and legislature seized the Federal fort north of Saint Louis, the Saint Louis militia, largely made up of German American immigrants of the 1848 generation and led by Franz Siegel, Engels' commandant during the 1849 anti-Prussian insurrection in Baden, succeeded in retaking the fort and keeping Missouri in the union. Lincoln appointed John Charles Frémont military commandant of Missouri.

Frémont had been the first Presidential candidate of what was to become the Republican Party in 1854. He ran on an open antislavery platform and he was chosen as champion of the antislavery cause for good reason. In 1848 he had led the revolt against Mexico in California and helped write a constitution for the initially independent state that outlawed

---

* Eugene Genovese's *The Political Economy of Slavery* takes the slave owners at their word and effectively demolishes the then prevalent academic argument that the disappearance of slavery was already in process and the more enlightened slave owners knew that and were perfectly willing to accommodate themselves to the demise of the system gradually as long as they were not provoked by hot heads.

slavery and, interestingly enough, proclaimed the new state as officially bilingual.

Frémont began by issuing an Emancipation Proclamation in 1860—three years before Lincoln took that step. What is more Frémont's proclamation actually freed some real, live, slaves. In 1863 Lincoln emancipated the slaves in the rebel states not under Union control and, while this may have encouraged some slaves to emancipate themselves by fleeing to Union territory, it did nothing for the slaves held by "loyal" slave owners in states that remained in the Union. But Missouri was a slave state and Frémont's proclamation freed the slaves in the areas under Union military control. Lincoln's response was to dismiss Frémont and revoke the emancipation decree.

The usual explanation for Lincoln's behavior argues, as I have noted, that Lincoln was a practical politician trying to preserve the Union and persuade a reluctant populace to support eventual abolition. As we shall see in the following note, Lerone Bennett Jr. effectively demolishes this thesis in his book *Forced into Glory*. Bennett documents in great detail Lincoln's own segregationist politics which cannot be explained as simply a reflection of the era since the majority of Congress and leading journals supported not only abolition but full citizenship rights, including the right to bear arms, for the freedmen. Bennett emphasizes Lincoln's own explicit racist beliefs as a cause of this reaction. But was there something more going on?

It would take us to far afield to document the thesis but let me suggest that Lincoln's conservatism went further than his views on race. Lincoln was a Whig. A believer in the widespread ownership of property as the basis of the American experiment. His hostility to slavery as a system was clearly based on that proposition. But abolition meant the confiscation of a whole type of property. It meant the destruction of a whole class of property owners. And in Europe, increasingly in the United States too, the issue of capitalist property was being called into question. The revolutions of 1848 were a recent memory.

It is worth noting in this context that several leaders among Lincoln's abolitionist opponents, Wendell Phillips and Lyman Trumball are the most prominent, ended up later in the century supporters of the labor and socialist movements. Even in 1863 ex-48ers were prominent in John

Charles Frémont's third party effort of that year, among them Marx's personal and political friends Adolph Sorge and Joseph Weydemeyer.

4. Marx as commentator on the American Civil War

Marx, who was employed as a free-lance "European correspondent" for the *New York Daily Tribune* then under the editorial direction of the anti-slavery Charles A. Dana, generally supported the abolitionist criticism of Lincoln in his public writings and even more openly and strongly in his private correspondence. He not only considered support for the union and abolition the only principled position, he considered a Union victory a matter of vital importance for the working classes in Europe as well as America. A slave holders' victory would postpone indefinitely, perhaps forever, the development of the continent on bourgeois lines. The rise of an independent working class movement based on free wage labor would be postponed for a proportionate period of time. The implications for Europe were equally serious. Instead of a political and moral example and an economic base for the progressive classes in Europe, North America would become a vast pool of unfree labor. One gets the impression that most scholars treat these warnings as if they were rhetorical gestures. But then most scholars attribute to Marx a fatalistic view of historical development for which there is no evidence. He really believed that slavery could triumph and set back for the foreseeable future any hope for progress. Marx's passionate support for the Union was not based simply on a visceral reaction against slavery.

But there was a serious political obstacle that prevented Marx from being as critical of the Lincoln administration in public as he was in private. That was the state of public opinion in England. There were powerful forces pushing the country towards support for Southern secession. From below there was the economic crisis in the cotton trade which threatened the well organized section of the working class employed in the textile industry with serious economic hardship. At the other end of the social scale Whig politicians, even more than Tories, were sympathetic to the South for their own economic reasons.

The Tories were sympathetic to the South because they too exploited labor that, if not slave labor, was hardly free. This was especially true in Ireland and, in fact, many Tory families had themselves owned plantations worked by slave labor in the West Indies only a generation earlier.

But what about antislavery Whigs and Liberals who made up Palmerston's cabinet? The answer is that the base of the Union was in the rapidly industrializing states which increasingly threatened English economic preeminence. The slave holders were equally hostile to the industrializing North because of the threat it posed to their "Peculiar Way of Life." The ideological problem for the Liberal administration was that it was composed of people, most prominently William Gladstone, who had long fought the slave trade. Their anti-slavery principles were an important part of their stock in trade. As Marx described their dilemma:

> The whole of the official press in England is, of course, in favor of the °slave holders°. They are the selfsame fellows who have wearied the world with °antislave trade philanthropy°. But °cotton, cotton°.[4]

British liberals found the solution to this problem in the abolitionist attacks on Lincoln. If, as *they* loudly proclaimed, Lincoln was fighting to preserve the Union and not to abolish slavery then there was no contradiction between support for the Southern cause and antislavery principle. Indeed, support for the South could even be seen as a defense of the "principle of nationalities," the phrase then used to denote what we today would call the right to self-determination.

Marx, therefore, had to emphasize, as did the abolitionists, that Lincoln would have to turn the war into a war against slavery *since that was only way to preserve the Union.*

Marx's job was made even harder by what came to be known as the "Trent Affair." On November 8, 1861 the US Navy stopped the *Trent*, a British ship carrying two Confederate officers to England, arrested the officers, and transported them to the US. The ensuing scandal provided an opening for the proponents of British intervention on the Confederate side. The affair eventually blew over because, in the end, the Palmerston government decided against war with the Union. Nevertheless, Marx, and Engels, had to spend a good deal of time dealing with this side issue. But, taken as a whole, Marx and Engels' writing on this subject mirrored that of the American abolitionists.

5. Why?

All this background helps to answer the question we started with. Why couldn't Marx's support of the Lincoln administration be used as an argument for supporting one or another side in World War I?

The answer lies in Marx's advocacy of "revolutionary war." As in 1848, the confrontation in the American Civil War was between a bourgeois republic, more or less democratic, and a pre-bourgeois system based on the exploitation of unfree labor. In 1861, as in 1848, they saw the role of the working class as forcing a reluctant bourgeoisie to fight wholeheartedly in its own interest. To "do its damned duty." They made no secret of the fact that, in their opinion, this assault on an antiquated form of exploitation would immediately put a question mark over the bourgeoisie's own system of exploitation. Like the German liberals of the Frankfurt Assembly, Lincoln hesitated when faced with the decision to wage a revolutionary war or risk defeat.

Lincoln's reputation, like that of Jack Kennedy, probably was saved by his assassination. But, the American bourgeoisie as a whole did do "its damned duty." The abolitionist congress did force Lincoln to free and arm the slaves. And it used Lincoln's assassination to force through a radical reconstruction program which Lincoln himself would probably have opposed as vigorously as did his successor, Andrew Johnson. Lincoln might have well ended up impeached himself.

It is worth noting in this regard that one of the principal Congressional leaders of the abolitionist movement and radical Reconstruction was Thaddeus Stevens, a Pennsylvania manufacturer who was, perhaps, the last bourgeois revolutionary. As the proprietor of what was, by today's standards, a small manufacturing business, he hated not only the slave power but the financial aristocracy that was allied with it. His closest contemporary analogues would have been British liberals of the Cobden-Bright school. Within a decade his type, while not extinct, was replaced by the modern corporation as the dominant economic enterprise. Whatever revolutionary instincts the American bourgeoisie had possessed withered away.

"Constitutional" or "Revolutionary" War

By 1914 this was all ancient history. Few European socialists would have remembered what the American Civil War was all about. Pre-capitalist forms of exploitation were a curiosity in Europe, confined to the more backward regions of the continent, and American slavery was an historical curiosity like the Maya or Inca civilizations. If they had made the effort to unearth his journalistic essays and private correspondence what use could prowar socialists have made of Marx's echoing of the abolitionists' call for the arming of the slaves? In 1914, European, and American, prowar socialists were urging wage slaves, the only kind left in most developed countries, to fight for their masters.

SPECIAL NOTE C: THE LINCOLN MYTH

This digression is necessary since the general argument in the previous note runs contrary to the commonly received account of the Lincoln presidency. But, if you are to understand Marx and Engels' comments on the war, you have to understand that Lincoln's reputation today bears the same relation to his reputation among his contemporaries that a photo bears to the negative from which it was made. Marx and Engels' low opinion of Lincoln was not peculiar to them. Slave owners and abolitionists, copperheads and bitter-enders, all saw him as a buffoon, a man not big enough for the job. In fact, for reasons described in the preceding note, Marx and Engels were relatively mild in their public comments on Lincoln's performance. Marx's left-handed compliment—"a first-rate second-rate man"—was his way of acknowledging Lincoln's then almost universally acknowledged defects while still emphasizing the need to defend the Union against those Europeans who argued for supporting the Confederacy.

Lincoln's modern reputation is in large part due to his assassination. Indeed, it was his abolitionist opponents who began the process. They skillfully used the public outrage that ensued to push through a far more radical reconstruction program than Lincoln himself would ever have supported.

As one example of this process of historical transformation, take the famous second inaugural address in which Lincoln called for "malice towards none and charity towards all." Today, most historians quote this as evidence of his humanity and point to the contrast with the bloody-mindedness and demagogy that is the typical posture of modern statesmen in time of war. They are right. But, at the time, Lincoln's contemporaries of all political tendencies saw it as a declaration of war on the abolitionist majority in Congress and its program of radical reconstruction. And they were right too.

Then again, part of the hostility towards Lincoln flowed from the prejudices of educated people—in those days politicians and journalists were expected to make at least the pretense of being educated—confronted by the relatively new phenomenon of the politician as "regular guy." Today, of course, we are amused, but not particularly surprised, when we see a graduate of Groton and Yale munching on fried pork rinds while discussing the weather with rural notables, but Lincoln's simple, straightforward, to us moving, rhetorical style marked him as ignorant and common in the eyes of contemporaries who were accustomed to a much more elevated style.

And, then, there were the jokes, most of them vulgar, which seemed so out of place in a man called on to lead a nation in the middle of a civil war. It is easy to dismiss these objections as the prejudices of an "educated elite" but there was a point to them especially when the objections were to Lincoln's fondness for "darky" stories. This fondness reflected not only Lincoln's own unease with the notion of a racially integrated society they also were clearly an attempt to pander to the fears and prejudices of the white working classes as a means of countering his abolitionist opponents.

So what about the historical literature?

Well, in a peculiar way, the old view of Lincoln can still be found in the standard accounts such as James McPherson's best selling *Battle Cry of Freedom*. All, or almost all, mention the fact that the majority of the Republican party and of Congress opposed Lincoln: 1) because he refused to come out unequivocally for emancipation; 2) because he insisted on the union forces returning escaped slaves to "loyal" slave owners, thus turning Union armies into the notorious "slave catcher" federal marshals of the pre-1860 period; 3)because he clung, probably up to his death, to the ideal of a segregated society in which African Americans were denied citizenship and "encouraged" to emigrate.

How do the standard accounts deal with these charges? Well, by arguing that: 1)Lincoln's racial attitudes were those of his time and place; 2) that Lincoln had to take into account the prejudices and opinions of the white majority in the North; 3) that Lincoln, as a good Whig was a firm believer in the law and the constitution.

Well: 1) Lincoln's congressional opponents were of his "time and place" and they were *for* equal rights for the freed slaves; 2) the members of the anti-slavery congressional majority were *more* not less accountable to public opinion; 3) Lincoln's administration was notorious in its time because of its violation of constitutionally protected liberties.

On this last point consider the Lincoln administration's suspension "for the duration" of the writ of habeas corpus. We are not talking here about a civil right protected by the US Constitution. We are talking about a civil right protected in Anglo-Saxon common law since 1679. From the standard accounts you would assume that only Southern sympathizers

The Lincoln Myth

opposed these measures. How would you know that the 1863 convention of radical reconstructionists that nominated John Charles Frémont to run against Lincoln also made opposition to his repressive measures against civil liberties a major platform plank? Certainly not from reading the standard histories. As far as I know the most complete account of this incident can be found in a German dissertation. I will come to that in a moment. The point here is that the constitutional articles Lincoln did not want to touch out of respect for "the rule of law" were those protecting the private property rights of slave owners.

Lincoln has had his critics on the left but they have been marginalized. Gore Vidal and Edmund Wilson, literary men rather than professional historians, both emphasized Lincoln's "bonapartist" tendencies and neither pays much attention to his resistance to emancipation. There are two books—Frank Zornow's *A Party Divided* and John C. Waugh's more recent *Reelecting Lincoln* which describe the split in the Republican Party in 1863 and the formation by the more radical Republicans and War Democrats of a new Party—the party of Radical Democracy—in opposition to the Lincoln loyalists who buried the Republican party in a fusion Union Party. The problem with both books is that they fail to emphasize the extent of Lincoln's hostility to radical reconstruction which provoked the split. As a consequence, the split tends to be seen as an interesting footnote to the really serious histories of the Civil War which still tend to emphasize the military campaigns. There is, however, one recent book that does put the conflict over reconstruction and abolition at the center of the history of the Civil War.

Lerone Bennett Jr.'s *Forced Into Glory: Lincoln's White Dream* is unabashedly "revisionist" to use the favorite swear word in academic historiography. Its thesis is that Lincoln was as hostile to a racially integrated society as he was to slavery. Both, in Bennett's view, threatened the American dream of a democratic republic which promised "life, liberty, and the pursuit of happiness" to all men who were "created equal." Bennett documents in detail Lincoln's firm belief that white and black could not live in harmony and his persistent attempts to resolve the problem of slavery by a series of government funded colonization schemes which were repudiated by every African American spokesperson. Bennett also resurrects the real emancipationists—congressional leaders like Thaddeus Stevens and Lyman Trumbull, and journalist-agitators like Wendell Phillips. He also mentions that Trumbull and Phillips ended up supporters of the nascent labor and socialist movements. Bennett's book has been dismissed by academic historians as tendentious in its reading of the historical record. But no one so far has claimed that he has misquoted that record or, indeed, that his claims are unfounded. Bennett's tone is not that of sober, academic history. It is a polemic. Bennett is not only a "revisionist" but a revisionist with attitude. The book is also repetitious but, then, the author has the task of uncovering a largely hidden history of the defining moment in the Republic's history in a few hundred pages written in full knowledge of the hostility of most historians to what he was trying to do.

At this point a detailed discussion of the debate between Bennett and his critics would be a digression too far. One might argue that he has "bent the stick" too far in the opposite direction. He may have minimized Lincoln's real opposition to slavery as a threat to the hopes the white working classes—in Europe as well as the United States—placed in the American republic, Bennett may have "gone too far." But I do not think he would disagree with Marx's aphorism summing up the stakes involved. "Labor in a white skin will never be free as long as labor in a black skin is enslaved."

One last book deserves mention. It is sort of an accident. The book, *Frémont contra Lincoln*, by Jörg Nadler, is a German dissertation. The subject assigned its author was German-American immigrants in the American Civil War. It just so happened that the German-American immigrants were, generally speaking, abolitionists. Their leadership was dominated by refugees from the 1830 and 1848 revolutions. Adolph Sorge and Joseph Weydemeyer, political and personal friends of Marx, were prominent activists in this movement. The result is a book that tells the story of the 1863 split from the point of view of the Radical Democracy. I don't know of any book in English that does that. It is the only book I know of that makes clear how important the issue of Lincoln's suppression of civil liberties was to abolitionists. It was real to the German Americans because it threatened to revive the very practices that they had fought in Europe. The prospect of the revival of the police methods of the European monarchies on American soil was not an abstract threat for them.

But there was an even more immediate analogy that lept to mind. Prior to the 1860 election the federal government, as noted above, was under the control of the Southern slave owners. Its powers were used to suppress abolitionist publications and agitation. Since the driving force behind the split of 1863 was the fear that the Lincoln administration would move to reinstate the slave owners in their former positions of authority with no adequate safeguards for the freed slaves, a Lincoln administration exercising emergency powers represented an immediate danger in the eyes of Frémont's supporters. It is a shame that no American historian has done a serious study on this episode.

SPECIAL NOTE D: ENGELS' "LAST TESTAMENT":
A TRAGICOMEDY IN FIVE ACTS

Over one hundred years ago the leadership of the German Social Democratic party, including most of Engels' closest political collaborators, began the process of transforming Engels, and by extension Marx, into a proponent of peaceful reform as opposed to "violent revolution."

They were remarkably successful. Rosa Luxemburg was taken in although she felt something was wrong.[1] But she did not know and could not have known what had happened in detail so successful had the disinformation campaign been. Even today, over sixty years after David Riazanov documented the basic facts of the story, reputable historians repeat the old tale.[2] What is worse, even would-be defenders of Engels have usually botched the job, either misstating the facts outright or giving an account so sketchy as to mislead the reader. I have never come across a complete account of this story in English although the literature is enormous and I cannot claim to have checked it all.[3] Certainly, the most widely read material does not include such an account.

1. Richard Fischer and Other False Friends

As soon as the anti-socialist law lapsed in 1890 Engels opened up his attack on the party's right wing which sought an accommodation with the Prussian state as Ferdinand Lassalle had taught them. At first, the party leadership, including August Bebel whom Engels valued most highly, were put off by Engels' aggressive move. But the party as a whole was in a truculent mood and moving to the left. The electoral successes under the anti-socialist law and especially the triumph in 1890, which the right saw as proof of the possibility of a peaceful, constitutional transformation of the Hohenzollern empire, only whetted the appetite of the German working-class. To quote Samuel Gompers, they wanted more.

But the German ruling classes were not prepared to give more. They were too divided internally to suppress the workers' movement but they were united in their fear of it. In the eyes of all, not just the congenitally sanguine Engels, matters appeared to be coming to a head. In this political climate, the leadership of the SPD could not continue to ignore Engels and the revolutionary tradition which he and Marx represented.

For several years after the conflict of 1890, the Executive of the SPD positively courted Engels. In particular, they embarked on a joint project to publish Marx's political works.[4] Our story begins with an invitation in January of 1895 by Richard Fischer, secretary of the party, asking Engels to write an introduction for the projected publication of a German translation of the series of Marx's series of articles on *The Class Struggles in France*. Although we probably do not have the complete correspondence between Engels and the Executive Committee, there is no evidence in what we do have that the purpose of the introduction, from the Executive Committee's point of view, was to tone down the revolutionary form and substance of these articles. Quite the contrary. The immediate motive for publication was the threat represented by the introduction of new antisocialist legislation in 1894. The Executive Committee wanted to get Marx's subversive book off the press and distributed before the "antisubversion" bill made it illegal.[5] What many, practically all, accounts leave out is just this fact that the leadership of the SPD, at this point, was not looking for an accommodation with the government. The party was anticipating a new period of underground activity. That is what explains the excess of caution which met Engels' introduction. It also accounts for Engels' reluctant acquiescence in the censorship of his article. But it also presented an opportunity to those elements in the party who *did* want to come to terms with the monarchy.

Within a year Engels had unexpectedly died and the threat of illegalization had disappeared. The SPD was entering on a forty-year long period of peaceful activity and when it faced illegality again it was no longer the same party.

Still, even in the relatively militant mood of 1895, the party leadership found Engels' introduction too much. Subsequent generations took the emphasis on electoral action for the main point of the introduction. But that is not how the SPD leadership saw it. Richard Fischer, who had been the main contact with Engels on this question, put their objections in the letter dated March 6, 1895 which was quoted in chapter 7. It was Engels' thinly veiled call for military mutiny that made the Executive Committee nervous.

For tactical reasons Engels, living in London, did not feel he could insist on language that party leaders in Germany feared would provide a pretext for the suppression of the movement. He was not impressed with this threat himself but he felt he had to respect the opinions of those who were on the front line.

The main cut in his *Introduction,* which Engels agreed to, was of a long paragraph on the probability of serious barricade fighting occurring *after* the mutiny of the army. Since the warnings that *premature* barricade fighting was to be avoided were left in, the impression was given that Engels had issued a blanket condemnation of the tactic. That was not true. But Engels *did* agree to the cuts and thus became an unwilling accomplice to the misrepresentation of his views. On the other hand, the Executive Committee did agree to the publication of the introduction with what Fischer recognized was its main subversive message intact. The only alternative would have been to refuse to publish the piece at all after having solicited it in the first place.

At this stage all Engels had agreed to was a more moderate statement on the secondary issue of barricade fighting than he actually held. But it is important to realize that he had agreed to this because many well-intentioned defenders of Engels have tried to argue that the expurgated version of the text was published without Engels knowledge or consent. Since that is not true anyone who makes such a claim discredits their own argument and helps confuse the matter. The main falsification came later! And that is what has largely been ignored.

2. Enter Wilhelm Liebknecht Stage Right—Stumbling

Engels was already unhappy with the Executive Committee's caution. In his letter to Richard Fischer of March 8, 1895 he raised the question of the political drift implied in Fischer's letter:

> I have taken as much account as possible of your strong dubieties, although with the best will in the world I cannot make out by half what is considered dubious. Still, I cannot accept that you intend to subscribe body and soul to absolute legality—legality under all circumstances, legality even according to laws that are broken by those who wrote them,

in short, the policy of turning the left cheek to those who strike the right. ... *no* party in any country goes so far as to renounce the right to resist illegality with arms in hand.[6]

Engels went on to say that he was considering not the general question of force as opposed to legality but the specific situation in Germany in 1894–1895 when all parties expected an attempt by the monarchy to resort to some form of martial law and suspend the Reichstag. Engels makes the point as explicitly as possible in the next paragraph:

> I must also take into consideration the fact that foreigners—the French, English, Swiss, Austrians, Italians, etc.—read my pieces as well, and I absolutely cannot compromise myself so much in their eyes.

To Laura Lafargue he wrote on March 28:

> ... I have written an introduction which will probably first appear in the *N[eue] Zeit*. It has suffered somewhat from the, as I think, exaggerated desires of our Berlin friends not to say anything which might be used as a means to assist in the passing of the *Umsturzvorlage* [the Antisubversion Bill] in the Reichstag. Under the circumstances I had to give way.[7]

No sooner had Engels reached this precarious compromise with the Executive Committee than Wilhelm Liebknecht published a lead editorial in the leading party paper, *Vorwärts*, under the head "Wie Heute Man Revolutionen Macht."(How Revolutions are Made Today.) Carefully stitching together extracts from Engels' *Introduction*, Liebknecht made it appear that Engels believed the socialist party could overturn capitalism and the Hohenzollern monarchy through the use of the ballot box alone. Engels' emphasis on the use of universal suffrage to win over, not a majority of the electorate, but a decisive segment of the army was obscured.

Engels' "Last Testament"

Engels was furious. His letter to Lafargue on April 3 summed up the whole controversy:

> Liebknecht has just played me a fine trick. He has taken from my introduction to Marx's articles on France 1848–50 everything that could serve his purpose in support of peaceful and antiviolent tactics at any price, which he has chosen to preach for some time now, particularly at this juncture when coercive laws are being drawn up in Berlin. But I preach those tactics only for the *Germany of today* and even then *with many reservations*. For France, Belgium, Italy, Austria, such tactics could not be followed as a whole and, for Germany, they could become inapplicable tomorrow.[8]

Engels' reaction was to insist on the publication of the entire text *as agreed to by the Executive Committee* in *Neue Zeit*. Engels clearly felt that even in this state the article taken as a whole would expose Liebknecht's trick. He was overly optimistic. In his letter to Karl Kautsky of April 1, 1895, he repeated his remarks to Lafargue and promised to "tell off Liebknecht good and proper, and also those people [including Bebel and the other members of the Executive Committee?], whoever they may be, who have given him this occasion to distort my opinion, without so much as a word to me."[9]

No such letter is extant. And, for that matter, it is evident that letters dating to this period are missing from the Bebel-Engels correspondence.[10] The letters from Engels we do have come not from Engels own files which were handed over on the death of Eleanor Marx-Aveling to Bebel and Bernstein but from Kautsky and the Lafargues. Did Bernstein screen this correspondence? He certainly had the opportunity and he had a motive.

3. Enter Bernstein—Twirling a Long Black Mustache

Less than a year after Engels' death Bernstein took over from the incompetent Liebknecht the job of transforming a revolutionary SPD into one preaching legality at any price. Bernstein's political evolution is too convoluted to be summed up here. I will outline it briefly in the final volume of this work. What is important for the history of the bowdlerization of Engels' *Introduction* is the claim made in Bernstein's *Die Voraussetzungen der Sozialismus und die Aufgabe der SozialDemokratie* translated into English as *Evolutionary Socialism*. In this, the best known statement of his "revisionist" thesis Bernstein states that Engels, in the introduction to the *Class Struggles*—his "last testament"—urged the party to reject "violent revolution" and stick to the "slow propaganda of parliamentary activity." And that, claimed Bernstein, was all he had been arguing for in his series of articles in *Neue Zeit* in 1898.

Part of Bernstein's argument depended on the false equation of "violent revolution," or just "revolution," with the putschism of the Jacobin-Blanquist tradition. Bernstein argued that initially Marx and Engels had also been putschists but that they had abandoned that position and Engels' "last testament" was the definitive repudiation of the concept. Bernstein made that claim in his article which is chapter 2 of the book (the chapter omitted in the English translation by Peter Gay.)

The allegation that Marx and Engels were at one time adherents of putschism was shown to be pure fabrication in an earlier volume of this work.[11] The question here is: how much did Bernstein know about the history of the *Introduction* and Engels' real views in 1895. Even if we assume that Engels' files did not contain a copy of the letter to Laura Lafargue explicitly repudiating Liebknecht's (and in anticipation Bernstein's) distortion of his views, Bernstein knew the basic story and he deliberately concealed it.

To start with, the claim that this was Engels' "last testament" was nonsense since Engels did not know he was dying. Even after his illness was diagnosed as terminal cancer, he was not told of this. Bernstein knew that this was so because he was one of those who did know the truth about Engels' condition and kept the secret from the dying man.[12] Engels was actually preparing a number of manuscripts at the time. He certainly did not see this article as his last word on the parliamentary road to socialism—or on anything else.

Engels' "Last Testament"

Bernstein also had the original uncensored document. Kautsky knew that the original had been altered at the request of the Executive Committee because Engels had told him that. And in 1899 he challenged Bernstein, Engels' literary executor, to produce the original.[13] Bernstein did not respond to this challenge. Yet, in 1924, when he deposited material from Engels' files in the archives of the Social-Democracy, this original was included.

We know that Bernstein also had the letter from Richard Fischer to Engels of March 6, 1895 because he published an excerpt from it in 1926 in *Sozialistische Monatshefte*. And this letter makes clear that Engels objected explicitly to the claim that the Hohenzollern empire could be reformed peacefully.

Bernstein was Bebel's collaborator during the period immediately following Engels' death. Remember that, acting as Engels' literary executors, they collaborated in destroying the allegedly treasonous draft of Engels' instructions to the defenders of the French Republic in 1870. So Bernstein must have been familiar with Bebel's letter to Engels of 1895[14] in which he, Bebel, defended the Executive Committee's decision to censor the introduction to that year's edition of *The Class Struggles in France*.

And how could Bernstein have missed the excerpt from Engels' letter to Lafargue quoted above when it was printed in *Le Socialiste* in 1900 as a contribution to the debate over this document?

The conclusion is unavoidable. Bernstein consciously and deliberately abused his position as literary executor to falsify the record for polemical reasons.

4. D. Riazonov Discovers Engels' Original Draft

In 1924, an article appeared in the *Marx-Engels Archiv* by David Riazanov.[15] Riazanov summed up the 1899 dispute between Kautsky and Bernstein and announced that "a few days" after Bernstein had deposited Engels' files in the Social-Democratic archives he, Riazanov, had discovered the missing original draft of the document in dispute. The journal reprinted the original draft indicating the excised passages. Unfortunately, far from clarifying the matter this discovery led to more confusion. The main problem was that when Riazanov's article appeared in German translation in *Unter dem Banner des Marxismus* an editorial note was appended which ignored the roles of both Liebknecht and the Executive Committee in the affair. This note also ignored Riazanov's article and spun a new myth. This new myth now had *Bernstein* publishing the introduction in its censored form. And Engels was presented as complaining that the editing of his original draft was done without his knowledge or consent. This was not only as untrue as Bernstein's original myth, it was also easily refuted by Engels' letter to Kautsky which Kautsky had reprinted in his then widely known pamphlet *Der Weg zur Macht* (The Road to Power.) The Communists could thus be shown to be the falsifiers and Bernstein let off the hook.

Riazanov's article *did not* make this claim. It outlined the story more or less accurately. But the editorial note was so anxious to "get" Bernstein that it completely botched the job.

That the Communists and their supporters, unlike Bernstein, were acting from honest ignorance and incompetence rather than conscious duplicity didn't change the facts. In any case, in the super-heated polemical spirit of the time the Communists became so fiercely committed to their version of "the truth" that they ended up publishing their own bowdlerized text. The consequence is that most accounts recognize that something funny was going on but are unable to decide who did what. The problem is made worse because, as Engels pointed out to Fischer in April of 1895, the concern with barricades was misplaced. That was not really the issue. The real revolutionary import of the *Introduction* lay elsewhere as both Fischer and Engels understood.

5. The Communists vs. the Socialist Labor Party—Comic Relief

In 1922 the American sect, the Socialist Labor Party, which had already done so much to confuse and demoralize the American left, branched out into the international arena. Under a title, *The Revolutionary Act: Military Insurrection or Political and Economic Action*, unknown to Engels (or anybody else), the SLP republished the bowdlerized version of Engels' introduction to *The Class Struggles in France*.¹⁶ The purpose for this new title was made clear in the short preface.

The SLP had for a number of decades denounced as "anarchism" any political group or ideology that suggested that "physical force" might be a part of any revolution. The "revolutionary act" was the electoral victory of a socialist party which correctly understood Marxism (i.e., the SLP) backed up by "revolutionary industrial unions" (i.e., the SLP union front.) The SLP leadership was too well read to ignore the fact that neither Marx nor Engels repudiated force in all or even most circumstances. They got around this by identifying force with "economic action" by which they meant the kind of passive general strike that Engels had specifically repudiated as a Bakuninist fantasy.

The SLP had, in their own estimation, "held the field against all comers" by "advocating the civilized, the political method, backed by the physical force of an integrally organized industrial union ..."¹⁷ Then came the revolution in Russia. What a disaster for the SLP! It was almost as big a blow to them as it was to the Romanov dynasty.

> By peculiar circumstances, which it is not necessary here to enumerate, the proletarian revolution in Russia was accomplished by an easy *coup d'état*, [sic] a victory backed by the workers and peasants in arms.¹⁸

The triumph of the Russian Revolution seemed to confirm the beliefs of the "physical force" men whose "brains [were] made red hot" by this earth-shaking event.

In a display of *chutzpah* that even Wilhelm Liebknecht would have found difficult to match the SLPers drafted Engels into their tiny army. Not only did they explicitly claim him as a defender of legality in all circumstances, they tacked on to a pamphlet edition of his *Introduction* a title which counterposed to "political and economic action" the preparation for a military insurrection.

But as the two *main* antagonists in this dispute—Engels and the Executive Committee of the SPD—recognized, the premise of Engels' introduction was that the ballot box in 1895 Germany was a *means* of preparing a military insurrection. The same kind of military insurrection that in 1917–1918 drove the Romanovs, Hapsburgs and Hohenzollerns from power and embarrassed the SLP.

Engels' argument against barricade fighting was that it was suicidal if the army was not first won over. As Richard Fischer pointed out, only an exceptionally dense Prussian Junker could miss Engels' main point. But, apparently, the sophisticated Marxists of the SLP didn't get it. All they saw was the condemnation of barricade fighting.

Compare their emphasis on the "civilized" road to socialism with Engels' peroration which remained even in the censored version which the SLP published as its authorized version. In this peroration Engels, almost as if he were provoking the Prussian authorities, described the coming revolution in the transparent analogy quoted in chapter 7. That passage ended, let us recall, with mutinous soldiers burning down the emperor's palace.

Fortunately for the SLP, their opponents were equally blinded by factional prejudice. They too missed the point of Engels' introduction. The polemical target of this misappropriated article reprinted as a pamphlet with a tendentious title was the early Third International. With the prestige of the Russian Revolution behind them the new parties making up this International were a serious threat to the left-wing, or at least rhetorically left-wing, sects that had grown up on the fringes of the mass socialist parties of the Second International. In fact, the immediate targets of the SLP polemic, the "physical force anarchists," named in the pamphlet were the ex-SLPers who had gone over to the Workers' Party, as one of the American Communist groups then called itself.

All of these new left wing groups saw in the Russian Revolution—about which they knew almost nothing as Lenin complained—a vindication of their ultra-left repudiation of electoral activity, trade unionism and other "reformist nonsense." Only "physical force," by which *they* meant a Blanquist-Jacobin putsch, was worth a serious revolutionist's effort. The forty-year long struggle of the Russian revolutionaries to build a workingclass political party capable of taking power was unknown to them. So was the seven-month long electoral campaign by the Bolsheviks to win the confidence of the workers and peasants in uniform.

Engels' emphasis on electoral activity as opposed to barricade fighting seemed to be tailor made for use by the SLP and reformists in general in this debate. Especially if you didn't read the pamphlet with any more discernment than, say, a particularly dense Prussian Junker.

Riazanov's discovery of the documentary evidence that Engels' original had been tampered with naturally provoked a factional feeding frenzy. Both sides conspired to make a hash of the historical record while burying the real content of the article under this dispute over a secondary issue.

In the *Workers' Monthly* of November 1925, Alexander Trachtenberg published an article, "The Marx-Engels Institute" which reported, among other things, on Riazanov's discovery. He got it all wrong. Neither Liebknecht's role nor that of the Executive Committee is mentioned. Instead, *Bernstein* is accused of having made the excisions. Apparently, his source was the author of the introduction to the German language translation of Riazanov's article.

It was no trick for the SLP in its pamphlet *Who Are the Falsifiers?*[19] to show from Kautsky's account that Engels himself had agreed to the cuts. That Kautsky's account, printed in full in pages 12–13 of the pamphlet, also made clear that Engels repudiated the Liebknecht-SLP position, could be safely ignored because Trachtenberg had been found out in such a flagrant misreading of the evidence. Riazanov's article, which was much more accurate, was, of course, not reprinted or excerpted by the SLP.

There was more. The SLPers also discovered that, in 1921, Eden and Cedar Paul, members of the newly fledged British Communist Party, had published a translation of Engels' article in the *Plebs Magazine*.[20] This translation differed more from the original than did the version agreed to by Engels and the Executive Committee. Many, but not all, of the passages repudiating barricade fighting are cut and some passages are cut for no discernible reason. The Pauls' editing was as inconsistent as the SPD Executive Committee's. Still, this helped discredit the Communist version and allowed the SLP to get away with the claim that Engels agreed with them. The Pauls' themselves reinforced this view in their introduction to their bowdlerized translation. They *agreed* with Bernstein's interpretation that had Engels advocating peaceful electoral activity as the only road to socialism. But the Bolshevik revolution had, they claimed, shown Engels' article to be outdated.

The SLP version of this history was just as garbled and was not consistent with the new discovery by Riazanov which they paid no more attention to than the Communists did. From Kautsky's account in *Der Weg zur Macht,* the SLP somehow concluded that the SPD Executive Committee not Liebknecht was responsible for publishing a censored version and that the version Engels sent to Kautsky and that was printed in *Neue Zeit* was Engels' original. This version—on which the SLP translation was based—was supposed to be Engels' response to the imaginary bowdlerization of the Executive Committee. To make it all fit they tried to argue that what Riazanov had found was a first draft that Engels had edited himself before sending the later version off to Richard Fischer.

Neither Kautsky's account nor Riazanov's article justifies such a conclusion but contemporary interest centered on the polemic between the SLP and the Communists and the SLP clearly won on points.

The SLP reprinted the pamphlet in 1933 with yet a new title, also unknown to Engels, *Peaceful Revolution vs. Violence: Can Socialism be Achieved Peacefully?* The author was again given as Frederick Engels and a new preface summed up the debate from the SLP perspective.

In this new preface, the SLP referred to its front, the Socialist Industrial Union as the "nonviolent" force of the organized proletariat.[21] Even more than the earlier pamphlet this edition underlines the SLP's commitment to "legality at any cost." It is unlikely that the emperor Diocletian saw the burning down of his palace, with him in it, as an act of nonviolent protest.

A final comic touch is added in this version (besides the title.) Attempting to distance himself from the reformist tradition of Social Democracy as well as that of the Communists, the author of the preface, Arnold Petersen, claims that the SLP tried to warn the German Social Democracy of the dangers consequent on parliamentary "logrolling and

Engels' "Last Testament"

compromises" but that the German Party had refused to heed the advice of this small American sect. As a result they reduced to a mere appendix of the bourgeoisie the once proud party of ... Liebknecht and Bebel![22]

In 1967, the *MEW* published Engels' letter to Fischer of March 8, 1895[23] which should have settled the issue, but the story was now so thoroughly integrated into the Communist vs. anti-Communist debate that mere questions of historical fact no longer seemed particularly relevant or important.[24]

LIST OF ABBREVIATIONS

CORR Foreign Languages Publishing House. *Frederick Engels Paul and Laura Lafargue: Correspondence.* Moscow:n.d.

CW Lenin, Vladimir Ilyich. *Collected Works.* Moscow: Progress Publishers, 1964-1970.

GC Institute of Marxism-Leninism of the C.C., C.P.S.U. *The General Council of the First International 1870-1871 — Minutes.* Moscow: Progress Publishers, n.d.

KMTR Draper, Hal. *Karl Marx's Theory of Revolution: Vol. 1—4.* New York and London:Monthly Review Press, 1977-1990.

MECW Karl Marx, Frederick Engels. *Collected Works.* New York, International Publishers.

MEGA Karl Marx, Friedrich Engels. *Gesamtausgabe.* Amsterdam, Internationalen Marx-Engels-Stiftung

MEW *Marx Engels Werke.* Moscow, 1927-35

NYDT *The New York Daily Tribune*

BIBLIOGRAPHY

Bauer, Ernest. *Joseph Graf Jellachich de Buzim: Banus von Kroatien.* Vienna: Verlag Herold,1975.

Bakunin, M.A. *Sobranie Sochinenia I Pisem, Tom Tretii,* ed. I. M. Steklov. Moscow:Izd. Vsesoyuznovo Obschestva, 1935.

Bebel, August and Bernstein, Eduard. *Der briefwechsel zwischen Friedrich Engels und Karl Marx, 1844 bis 1883.* Stuttgart:J.H.W. Dietz, 1913.

Beike, Heinz. *Die Deutsche Arbeiterbewegung und der Krieg von 1870/1871.* Dietz Verlag: Berlin, 1957.

Bennett, Lerone, Jr.. *Forced into glory : Abraham Lincoln's white dream.* Chicago : Johnson Pub. Co., 2000

Berger, Martin. *Engels, Armies & Revolution.* Hamden, Connecticut: Archon Book, 1977.

Bernstein, Samuel. *Essays in Political and Intellectual History.* New York: Paine-Whitman Publishers, 1955.

Blackstock. Paul W. and Hoselitz, Bert F, .ed. *The Russian Menace:a collection of speeches, articles, letters and news dispatches by Karl Marx and Frederick Engels.* Glencoe, Ill.: Free Press, 1952.

Bloomberg, Arnold. *A Carefully Planned Accident.* Cranbury, New Jersey , London, Mississauga, Ontario: Associated University Presses, Inc.,1990.

Blumenburg, Werner, ed. *August Bebel's Briefwechsel mit Friedrich Engels; Quellen und Untersuchungen zur geschichte der Deutschen und Österichischen Arbeiterbewegung, Vol. IV.* London, The Hague, Paris: Mouton & Co., 1965.

Byrnes, Robert Francis. *Antisemitism in modern France.* New Brunswick, N.J.:Rutgers University Press, 1950.

Carr, E. H. *Michael Bakunin.* New York:Vintage Books, 1961.

Cerati, Marie. *Le club des citoyennes revolutionnaires et republicaines.* Paris: Éditions Sociales, 1966.

Childers, Thomas. *The Nazi Voter: The Social Foundations of Facsism in Germany, 1919-1933*. Chapel Hill, N.C. and London: The University of North Carolina Press, 1983.

Coppa, Frank J. *The Origins of the Italian Wars of Independence*. London and New York:Longman Group, 1992.

Deak, Istvan. *The Lawful Revolution: Louis Kossuth and the Hungarians, 1848-1849*. New York: Columbia University Press, 1979.

Dominick, Raymond, H. III. *Wilhelm Liebknecht and the Founding of the German Social Democratic Party*. Chapel Hill, North Carolina: The University of North Carolina Press, 1982.

Draper, Hal. *Karl Marx's Theory of Revolution: Vol. 1—4*. New York and London:Monthly Review Press, 1977-1990.

—*The Marx-Engels Cyclopedia: vol II*. New York:Schocken Books, 1985.

—*Socialism from Below*. Atlantic Highlands, NJ: Humanities Press, 1992.

—*Socialism from Below*. 2nd Edition. Alameda CA:Center for Socialist History, 2001.

—*War and Revolution: The Myth of Lenin's 'Revolutionary Defeatism'*. Atlantic Highlands, NJ:Humanities Press, 1996.

Fejtö, François. *The opening of an era, 1848; an historical symposium*. introd. by A. J. P. Taylor. London: A. Wingate, 1948.

Foreign Languages Publishing House. *Frederick Engels Paul and Laura Lafargue: Correspondence*. Moscow:n.d.

Guerin, Daniel. *La lutte de classes sous la première république*: Bourgeois et bras nus. Paris: Gallimard, 1946.

Henderson, W. O. *The Life of Friedrich Engels*. London:Cass, 1976.

Institute of Marxism-Leninism of the C.C., C.P.S.U. *The General Council of the First International 1870-1871 – Minutes*. Moscow: Progress Publishers, n.d.

Kissin, S. F. *War and The Marxists: Socialist Theory and Practice in Capitalist Wars*. Boulder Colorado:Westview Press, 1989.

Bibliography

Kohn, Hans, 1891-1971. *Pan-Slavism, its history and ideology.* Notre Dame, Ind.: University of Notre Dame Press, 1953.

Lassalle, Ferdinand. *Der Italienische Krieg und die Aufgabe Preussens*, Berlin:Verlag von Franz Duncker, 1859.

Lissagaray, Hippolyte Prosper Olivier, tr. Eleanor Marx-Aveling. *History of the Commune of 1871.* London: Reeves and Turner, 1886.

Lenin, Vladimir Ilyich. *Collected Works.* Moscow: Progress Publishers, 1964-1970.

Luxemburg, Rosa. *Gesammelte Werke.* Berlin:Dietz Verlag, 1964.

Marx-Aveling, Eleanor. *The Eastern Question: A Reprint of Letters written 1853-1856 dealing with the events of the Crimean War*, London, 1897. (Reprinted by Burt Franklin, New York, 1968.)

Marx, Karl and Engels, Frederick. *Collected Works (MECW).* New York: International Publishers, 1975-?

— *Secret Diplomatic History of the Eighteenth Century and The Story of the Life of Lord Palmerston*, ed., Lester Hutchinson. New York:International Publishers,1969.

— *Marx-Engels Werke (MEW). Marx Engels Werke.* Moscow, Marx-Engels Institut, 1927-35.

—*Marx-Engels Gesamtausgabe* (MEGA). Amsterdam, Internationalen Marx- Engels Stiftung, 1972-

Mayer, Gustav. *Ferdinand Lassalle – Nachgelassene Briefe und Schriften, Dritter Band.* Stuttgart-Berlin:Deutsche Verlag-Anstalt, 1922.

– *Friedrich Engels: Eine Biographie.* The Hague: Martinus Nijhoff, 1934.

McPherson, James M.. *Battle cry of freedom : the Civil War era.* New York : Oxford University Press, 1988.

Mehring, Franz. *Karl Marx: The Story of His Life.* New York: Covici-Friede, 1935.

Nagler, Jörg. *Fremont contra Lincoln : die deutsch-amerikanische Opposition in der Republikanischen Partei wäährend des amerikanischen Bürgerkrieges.* Frankfurt am Main ; New York : P. Lang, c1984.

Nesselrode, Karl Robert (Karl Vasilyevich). *Lettres et Papiers du Chancelier Comte de Nesselrode 1760-1856.* Paris:A. Lahure,n.d.

Nikolaevskii, Boris. "Prague During the Days of the Slavic Congress - A forgotten Article of Alfred Meissner," *Germanoslavica* Vol 2. Prague-Leipzig-Vienna:Verlag Rudolph M. Rohrer, 1931.

— *Karl Marx: Man and Fighter,* co-author Maenchen-Helfen, Otto. Bengay,Suffolk:Methuen, 1936.

Pech, Stanley Z.*The Czech Revolution of 1848.* Chapel Hille:University of North Carolina Press, 1969.

Petitfrere, Claude. *Blancs et Bleus d'Anjou (1789-1793).* Paris: Libraire Honore Champion, 1979.

Pottinger, E. Ann. *Napoleon III and the German Crisis 1865-1866.* Cambridge, Massachusets: Harvard University Press, 1968.

Robertson, Priscilla. *The Revolutions of 1848: A Social History.* Princeton, N.J.:Princeton University Press, 1952.

Rosdolsky, Roman. *Engels and the "Nonhistoric" Peoples: The National Question in the Revolution of 1848,* tr. Prof. John-Paul Himka. Critique Books, 1987.

— *Untertat und Staat in Galizien.* Mainz: Verlag Phillip von Zabern, 1992.

— *Zur Entstehungsgeschichte des Marxschen Kapital; der Rohentwurf des Kapital 1857-58.* Frankfurt: Europääische Verlagsanstalt, 1969. Wien: Europa Verlag, 1968.

— *Dissertation* Wien, 1929.

Slavin, Morris. *The Making of an Insurrection: Parisian Sections and the Gironde.* Cambridge: Harvard University Press, 1986.

Soboul, *Albert. Les Sans Coulottes en l'An II; Mouvement Populaire et Gouvernment Révolutionaire; 2 Juin 1793–9 Thermidor An II*, (Paris: Librairie Clavrueil, 1958.)

Socialist Labor Party, *The Revolutionary Act: Military Insurrection or Political and Economic Action?*. New York:New York Labor News Co., 1922.

Steenson, Gary P. *Karl Kautsky 1854-1938: Marxism in the Classical Years*. Pittsburgh: University of Pittsburgh Press, 1978.

Torr, Dona. *Marxism Nationality and War: A Text-Book in Two Parts*. London:Lawrence and Wishart Ltd., 1940.

Waugh, John C.. *Reelecting Lincoln : the battle for the 1864 presidency*. New York : Crown Publishers, c1997.

Wilson, Stephen. *Ideology and Experience: Antisemitism in France at the Time of the Dreyfus Affair*. London and Toronto: Associated University Presses

Živkovič, Andreja and Plavšič, Dragan. *The Balkan Socialist Tradition*. London:Porcupine Press, 2003.

Zornow, William Frank. *Lincoln & the party divided*. [1st ed.] Norman, University of Oklahoma Press, 1954.

NOTES

INTRODUCTION

1. Rosa Luxemburg, *Gesammelte Werke, Band 4,* p. 135-140.

2. Lenin, "Under a False Flag," *Collected Works,* 21:137.

3. Gary P. Steenson, *Karl Kautsky 1854-1938: Marxism in the Classical Years.* (Pittsburgh, University of Pittsburgh Press, 1978).

4. Steenson, *Karl Kautsky,* p. 179.

5. Ibid., p. 184.

6. Lenin, op. cit., p 140.

7. Ibid.

8. Ibid., p. 148.

9. Ibid.

10. Ibid., p. 221.

11. Ibid., p. 146.

12. Luxemburg quote

13. See Special Notes B and C.

CHAPTER 1

1. See Samuel Bernstein, *Essays in Political and Intellectual History,* (New York: Paine-Whitman Publishers, 1955) p. 26 ff. See also Daniel Guerin, *La lutte de classes sous la première république: Bourgeois et bras nus,* (Paris: Gallimard, 1946), for a description of the complexities of revolutionary foreign policy.

2. Frederick Engels, "The Frankfurt Assembly Debates the Polish Question," *NRZ,* August 20,1848. *MECW* 7: 350.

3. *MECW* 2:137-150.

4. See Frederick Engels, "The State of Germany," *The Northern Star,* October 15, 1845. [*MECW* 6:15-21]. By the time this article appeared Engels was already well on his way to a political position which we would recognize as Marxist. This influenced his language and his method of argument. There is no evidence, however, that this recent political development was responsible for his opinion that the French occupation of the Rhineland was a boon to the Germans.

5. *MECW* 2:139-140.

6. Frederick Engels, "Germany's Foreign Policy," NRZ, July 3, 1848. See *MECW* 7:165.

7. Ibid., p. 166.

8. Ibid., p. 166-167.

9. Karl Marx and Frederick Engels, "German Foreign Policy and the Latest Events in Prague" NRZ, July 11, 1848. *MECW* 7:212-215.

10. Ibid., p. 215.

11. Stanley Z. Pech, *The Czech Revolution of 1848,* (University of North Carolina Press, 1969) pp. 48–52, 149–150.

12. Ibid., p. 153.

13. Ibid., p. 215.

14. *MECW* 7:212.

15. *MECW* 7:351.

16. *MECW* 7: 352.

17. Frederick Engels, "The Frankfurt Assembly Debates the Polish Question," NRZ, August 20, 1848. *MECW* 7:352. This is the third installment.

18. Ibid., p. 353.

19. Frederick Engels, "Three New Constitutions," *Deutsche-Brüssler-Zeitung* No. 15, February 20, 1848. *MECW* 6:540

20. Letter of Count von Nesselrode to Baron de Meyendorf, July 24, 1848 in *Lettres et Papiers du Chancelier Comte de Nesselrode 1760-1856*. A. Lahure, Paris n.d., p. 132.

21. Frederick Engels, "Defeat of the German Troops at Sundewitt," *NRZ*, June 2, 1848. *MECW* 7:34.

22. Frederick Engels, "Hungary," *NRZ*, May 18, 1849. *MECW* 9:461-2.

23. Frederick Engels, "The Frankfurt Assembly Debates the Polish Question," *NRZ*, August 20, 1848. *MECW* 7:351.

24. Benjamin Goriely, "Poland in 1848," in *The Opening of an Era: 1848* ed. François Feito, intro. A. J. P. Taylor, Howard Fertig, (New York, 1966). See p. 362.

25. Ibid., pp. 364–367.

26. See Goriely, op. cit., p 362. For an account more skeptical of the thesis that Metternich *instigated* the uprising, see Roman Rosdolsky, *Engels and the "Nonhistoric" Peoples: The National Question in the Revolution of 1848*, tr. Prof. John-Paul Himka, Critique Books, 1987. For a more detailed discussion of the issues see Special Note A.

27. Karl Marx and Frederick Engels, "Speeches at the International Meeting Held in London on November 29,1947 to Mark the 17th Anniversary of the Polish Uprising of 1830," *MECW* 6:388-390.

28. Karl Marx and Frederick Engels, "Speeches in Brussels on February 22, 1848 On the Occasion of the Second Anniversary of the Cracow Insurrection." *MECW* 6:549.

29. Ibid., p. 550.

30. Ibid.

31. *MECW* 6:518.

32. This is based on the material in the indices to the relevant volumes of *MECW*. If there is buried material to be excavated by the editors of the *MEGA*, I don't think it will change the general picture.

33. Frederick Engels, "The Movements of 1847," *Deutsche-Brüsseler-Zeitung*, January 23, 1847. *MECW* 6:520-529.

34. Frederick Engels, "The Beginning of the End in Austria," *Deutsche-Brüsseler-Zeitung*, January 27, 1847. *MECW* 6:530-536.

35. Frederick Engels, "The Magyar Struggle," NRZ, January 8, 1849. *MECW* 8:227-238.

36. Frederick Engels, "The *Kölnische Zeitung* on the Magyar Struggle," NRZ, February 17, 1849. *MECW* 8:399.

37. "Der Ungarische Krieg," *Kölnische Zeitung*, February 17, 1849. Quoted in Frederick Engels, "The *Kölnische Zeitung* on the Magyar Struggle," NRZ, February 18,1849. *MECW* 8:398.

38. Ibid., p. 399.

39. Ibid.

40. Frederick Engels, "Croats and Slovaks in Hungary," NRZ, February 19, 1849. *MECW* 8:411.

41. Frederick Engels, NRZ May 19, 1849. *MECW* 9:463.

42. François Feitö, "Hungary: The War of Independence" in *The Opening of an Era*, pp. 317-322. Also, Istvan Deak, *The Lawful Revolution: Louis Kossuth and the Hungarians, 1848-1849*, Columbia University Press, (New York, 1979) pp. 176–177.

43. Frederick Engels, *Principles of Communism, MECW* 6:341-357.

44. *MECW* 6:345.

45. *Manifesto of the Communist Party, MECW* 6:503.

46. Karl Marx and Frederick Engels, *The Communist Manifesto* para. 57. *MECW* 6:495.

47. Karl Marx, "The Threat of the *Gervinus Zeitung*," NRZ, June 25, 1948. *MECW* 7:116.

48. "The Bourgeoisie and the Counter-Revolution," *NRZ*, December 15-29, 1848. *MECW* 8:154-178.

49. Ibid., p. 16

CHAPTER 2

1. Franz Mehring, *Karl Marx: The Story of His Life*, (New York: Covici-Friede, 1935), p. 192.

2. See Claude Petitfrere, *Blancs et Bleus d'Anjou (1789-1793)*, (Paris: Libraire Honore Champion, 1979) for a discussion of the state of historical scholarship on this question. The first section of the introduction of this doctoral thesis (pp. 21-32) summarizes the scholarly debate.

3. Daniel Guérin, *La lutte de classes*. Marie Cerati, *Le club des citoyennes revolutionnaires et republicaines*, (Paris: Éditions Sociales, 1966.) Morris Slavin, *The Making of an Insurrection: Parisian Sections and the Gironde*, (Cambridge: Harvard University Press, 1986.) Albert Soboul, *Les Sans Coulottes en l'An II; Mouvement Populaire et Gouvernment Révolutionaire; 2 Juin 1793–9 Thermidor An II*, (Paris: Librairie Clavrueil, 1958.)

4. Karl Marx, "The Crisis and the Counterrevolution," *NRZ*, September 14, 1848. *MECW* 7:432.

5. Frederick Engels, "The Magyar Struggle," *NRZ*, January 8, 1849. *MECW* 8:230.

6. Frederick Engels, *NRZ*, March 2, 1849. *MECW* 8:456.

7. Kohn, Hans, 1891-1971. Pan-Slavism, its history and ideology. Notre Dame, Ind.: University of Notre Dame Press, 1953, p. 75.

8. Ibid., p.79.

9. *MECW* 7:92-3 June 18, 1848.

10. Istvan Deak, *The Lawful Revolution: Louis Kossuth and the Hungarians, 1848-1849*, (New York: Columbia University Press, 1979), p. 131–132, 157–158. Priscilla Robertson, *The Revolutions of 1848: A Social History*, (Princeton, N.J.:Princeton University Press, 1952), p. 282.

11. Deak, *Lawful Revolution*, p. 220.

12. Ernest Bauer, *Joseph Graf Jellachich de Buzim: Banus von Kroatien*, Verlag Herold, (Wien, 1975), pp. 69–71.

13. Deak, *The Lawful Revolution*, p. 80.

14. Robertson, *Revolutions of 1848*, p. 281.

15. Bauer, *Jellachich*, p. 74.

16. Frederick Engels, "From the Theater of War," NRZ, April 27,1849. *MECW* 9:351.

17. Deak, *The Lawful Revolution*, and Feijto, *The Opening of an Era* emphasize this aspect of the war.

18. See Michael Roller, *The Opening of an Era*, p. 310 for a brief discussion of the Rumanian case. Also Robertson, *Revolutions of 1848*, p. 306. The last reference claims that Slavs registered in large numbers as Magyars in the census of 1850. Since Magyars suffered some legal disabilities as a punishment for their rebellion, Robertson interprets this as an act of sympathy and solidarity for the rebels on the part of the Slavs.

19. Frederick Engels, "Democratic Pan-Slavism," NRZ February 15-16, 1849. *MECW* 8:362-378.

20. M. A. Bakunin, Sobranie Sochinenia I Pisem, Tom Tretii, ed. I. M. Steklov. Izd. Vsesoyuznovo Obschestva (Moscow 1935). pp. 510,528.

21. Ibid., pp. 300,302.

22. Boris Nikolaevskii, "Prague During the Days of the Slavic Congress - A forgotten Article of Alfred Meissner," Germanoslavica Vol 2. 1931. Verlag Rudolph M. Rohrer, Prague-Leipzig-Vienna. p. 300-312.

23. Steklov, Sobranie, iii, p.360. As late as the insurrection of 1863, Bakunin came under suspicion from the Polish left because of his continuing political friendship with those Poles who were against raising the social question. See Carr, Bakunin, p. 285 ff., p. 296.

24. Steklov, Sobranie, iii, p. 303.

25. Carr, Bakunin, p. 171.

26. Ibid., p. 149.

27. Ibid., p.159. See also Steklov, *Sobranie,* iv, p. 129.

28. Carr, *Bakunin,* p. 185.

29. *MECW* 8:365.

30. *MECW* 11:46-50.

31. *MECW* 8:371.

32. *MECW* 8:376.

33. *MECW* 8:377.

34. *MECW* 8:378.

35. Frederick Engels to Karl Kautsky, February 7, 1882. *MEW* 35:269-273.

36. There is a similar idea expressed in an article by Engels published in *Der Volkstaat* on March 24, 1875. *MECW* 24:57. This article summarizes speeches made by Marx and himself at a January 23 meeting to commemorate the twelfth anniversary of the 1863 Polish uprising.

CHAPTER 3

1.See Hal Draper, *The Marx-Engels Cyclopedia: vol II*, New York: Schocken Books, 1985, pp. xv-xvi, and pp. 160-172 for a detailed discussion of this problem.

2. E. "What is to Become of Turkey in Europe," *NYT*, April 12, 1853. (*MECW* 12:32.)

3. Karl Marx, *Secret Diplomatic History of the Eighteenth Century and The Story of the Life of Lord Palmerston*, ed., Lester Hutchinson, International Publishers (New York,1969.)

4. Lester Hutchinson's introductory essays in the work cited in the previous note are an exception to this statement.

5. Paul W. Blackstock and Bert F. Hoselitz, ed. *The Russian Menace: a collection of speeches, articles, letters and news dispatches by Karl Marx and Frederick Engels*. Free Press, (Glencoe, Ill., 1952).

6. See *Myth of Lenin's Revolutionary Defeatism*

7. There have been three attempts to collect Marx and Engels' writings on the Crimean War in an anthology.

The first was Eleanor Marx-Aveling and Edward Aveling's, *The Eastern Question: A Reprint of Letters written 1853-1856 dealing with the events of the Crimean War*, London, 1897. (Reprinted by Burt Franklin, New York, 1968.) The second was the Blackstock and Hoselitz collection mentioned in note 5. Finally there is: Dona Torr, *Marxism Nationality and War: A Text-Book in Two Parts*, Lawrence and Wishart Ltd., London 1940. The second of these collections is pretty openly an attempt to enroll Marx and Engels as Cold-War freedom fighters. The third is designed as a study guide on the question for members and sympathizers of the Communist party. The first suffers from the lack of availability of the Marx-Engels Correspondence. Without this check it is difficult to determine what Marx wrote, what Engels wrote and what some third party wrote.

8. *MECW* 39:288.

9. *MECW* 12:3-12. The article appeared on April 7, and according to the note in *MECW* was written between March 12 and 22. The note attributes this section to Engels on the basis of the Marx-Engels correspondence.

10. *NYDT*, "Revolution and Counter-Revolution in Germany", *MECW* 11:3.

11. *MECW* 12:638. Footnote 16.

12. *MECW* 11:334.

13. "Capital Punishment," *NYDT*, February 18, 1853. *MECW* 11:499.

14. *NYDT*, April 12, 1853. *MECW* 12:13.

15. "The London Press.—Policy of Napoleon on the Turkish Question," *NYDT*, April 11, 1853. *MECW* 12:18.

16. *NYDT*, July 15, 1853. *MECW* 12:192.

17. *NYDT*, April 21, 1853. *MECW* 12:32. Again note that this is an early article. Marx and Engels apparently came to the conclusion after a few months that the great clash between England and Russia that might lead to a general European war wasn't going to happen. That did not affect their judgement on what should have been done.

18. Karl Marx, "The Western Powers and Turkey," *NYDT*, October 4, 1853

19. Frederick Engels, "The War," *People's Paper*, May 27, 1854. *MECW* 13:204. *NYDT*, June 9, 1854. *MEW* 10:243.

20. . *NYDT* June 24, 1854 *MECW* 13:228.

21. Karl Marx, "Reorganization of the British War Administration ...," *NYDT*, June 24, 1854. See *MECW* 13:227-228

22. Karl Marx, "The Eccentricities of Politics," *NYDT* July 10,1855. *MECW* 14:284.

23. *MECW* 14:286.

24. Torr, Dona. *Marxism, Nationality and War: A Text-book in Two Parts*. London: Lawrence & Wishart, 1940.

25. Karl Marx, "The Sevastopol Hoax - General News."*NYDT* October 21, 1854. *MECW* 13:491.

26. *MECW* 13:713. Footnote 364.

27. *MECW* 39:499.

28. Karl Marx, "The War Question," *NYDT* August 5, 1853. *MECW* 12:212.

29. Ibid..

30. Frederick Engels, The European War," *NYDT*, February 2, 1854. *MECW* 12:557-558.

Karl Marx's Theory of Revolution: V 5

CHAPTER 4

1. *MECW* 16:271.

2. *MECW* 16:272.

3. *MECW* 16:273.

4. *MECW* 16:163; For a modern historian's account of Napoleon III's fears and their basis see Bloomberg, Arnold. *A Carefully Planned Accident.* Cranbury, New Jersey , London, Mississauga, Ontario: Associated University Presses, Inc.,1990,18-25.

5. *MECW* 16:337. Contemporary historians also make this point. See in particular Frank J. Coppa's *The Origins of the Italian Wars of Independence.*

6. *MECW* 16:354.

7. *MECW* 16:215.

8. *MECW* 16:216.

9. *MECW* 16:217.

10. *MECW* 16:240.

11. *MECW* 16:247.

12. *MECW* 16:250.

13. See Chapter 3 and Special Note A, Volume 4 of this work.

14. *MECW* 40:382. Marx to Lassalle, 4 February 1859.

15. *MECW* 16:380.

16. *MECW* 40:405. Marx to Lassalle, 17 March 1859.

17. Lassalle, Ferdinand. *Der Italienische Krieg und die Aufgabe Preussens*, Berlin:Verlag von Franz Duncker, 1859. See p. 360.

18. Mayer, Gustav. *Ferdinand Lassalle – Nachgelassene Briefe und Schriften, Dritter Band.* Stuttgart-Berlin:Deutsche Verlag-Anstalt, 1922. See Lassalle to Marx, June 1859, p. 214 ff.

19. See E. Ann Pottinger, *Napoleon III and the German Crisis* for a detailed study of this crisis.

20. *MECW* 42:71,76,77,84,87.

21. *MECW* 42:76.

22. *MECW* 20:54.

23. Ibid..

24. *MECW* 20:65.

25. *MECW* 20:67.

26. *MECW* 20:74.

27. *MECW* 20:73,74.

28. *MECW* 20:69.

29. *MECW* 20:78.

30. *MECW* 20:74,75

31. *MECW* 20:75.

32. *MECW* 20:78.

33. *MECW* 20:76.

34. *MECW* 20:164.

35. *MECW* 20:165.

36. *MECW* 42:276

37. *MECW* 42:279, 284, 285

CHAPTER 5

1. Quoted from a resolution passed by a Chemnitz workingclass anti-war meeting in "The First Address of the General Council of the International Working Men's Association on the Franco-Prussian War", *MECW* 22:6.

2. The most extreme version of this thesis can be found in *Crippled from Birth* by Richard W. Reichard (Iowa State University Press, Ames, Iowa 1969). Reichard claims that the German socialist movement
 was never a serious opposition. The Bebel-Liebknecht vote itself received no support and was not really that antiwar to begin with. For the more standard interpretation see, S. F. Kissin, *War and The Marxists: Socialist Theory and Practice in Capitalist Wars* (Westview Press, Boulder Co., 1989) and Heinz Beike, *Die Deutsche Arbeiterbewegung und Der Krieg von 1870/1871* (Dietz Verlag, Berlin, 1957).

3. See Hal Draper, *KMTR*, vol. 4 (Monthly Review Press, New York 1990) Special Note C for a discussion of Mehring's political evolution.

4. Raymond H. Dominick III, *Wilhelm Liebknecht and the Founding of the German Social Democratic Party*, (University of North Carolina Press, Chapel Hill, 1982). pp.195-197. Dominick hasn't a clue as to what Marx and Engels' were saying. His summary of their views is idiosyncratic and he provides no evidence for his interpretation. His account of the near split in the *SDAP*, however, is well-documented. Heinz Beike also gives a similar account of this episode. See *Arbeiterbewegung* p. 34.

5. Franz Mehring, *Karl Marx: The Story of his Life*, (Covici, Friede, Inc., New York 1935), Translated by Edward Fitzgerald. p. 462 ff.

6. Ibid..

7. See *KMTR*, vol. 4, Chapter 4 for a treatment of the Lassalleans' pro-Bismarck policy.

8. Actually this was only *one* of Liebknecht's positions. Prior to the beginning of the war he did take the standard anti-Bonaparte view of the origins of the war. (See Dominick, Chapter 6.) But the *no lesser evil* line was the one he took in defending his antiwar position.

9. Mehring quotes only Marx's letter to Engels of July 20, 1870 and Engels' letter of August 15, 1870 to Marx. We will discuss both of these letters in their context later. Probably, Mehring was using the collection edited by August Bebel and Eduard Bernstein. *Der Briefwechsel zwischen Friedrich Engels und Karl Marx* published by Dietz Verlag in 1913.

10. Boris Nicolaevsky and Otto München-Helfen, *Karl Marx: Man and Fighter*, (Methuen, 1936)

11. *Karl Marx: Man and Fighter* p. 320.

12. The use of Marx quotes as a polemical weapon in World War I is worthy of a book itself. It would be a digression here. The story is documented in Hal Draper, *War and Revolution: The Myth of Lenin's "Revolutionary Defeatism,"* (Humanities Press, Atlantic N.J., 1996).

13. For this history see *KMTR*, vol. 4, Special Note A.

14. *The Myth of Lenin's 'Revolutionary Defeatism'* Part II has a long discussion of Gregory Zinoviev's tortured analysis of Marx and Engels' statements.

15. Heinz Beike, *Die Deutsche Arbeiterbewegung und der Krieg von 1870/1871* Dietz Verlag, Berlin, 1957.

16. *The General Council of the First International 1870-1871 - Minutes,* Institute of Marxism-Leninism of the C.C., C.P.S.U. Progress Publishers, Moscow, n.d.. p. 131.

17. Marx to Lassalle February 4, 1859. *MECW* 40:380.

18. Marx to Engels September 16, 1868, *MECW* 43:101.

19. Marx to Georg Eccarius and Friedrich Lessner September 10, 1868, *MECW* 43:93.

20. Lenin, *CW* 21:308.

21. *The Role of Force in History*, *MECW* 26:486-491.

22. Marx to Engels, September 14, 1870. *MECW* 44:76-77.

23. *GC Minutes,* p. 32.

24. Quoted from the resolution of the French Section of the *IWMA* in *The First Address of the General Council of the International Working Men's Association on the Franco-Prussian War, MECW* 22:4.

25. *GC Minutes,* p. 30.

26. Marx to Engels, July 20, 1870. *MECW* 44:3.

27. Marx to Laura and Paul Lafargues July 28, 1870. *MECW* 44:12.

28. Marx to Engels July 28, 1870. *MECW* 44:10.

29. Ibid.

30. Ibid.

31. Marx to Engels August 1, 1870. *MECW* 44: 22.

32. Dominick p. 194.

33. Ibid p. 195

34. Ibid..

35. See Engels to Laura Lafargue October 14, 1892. *Corr. III* p. 200.

36. *MECW* 44:36. *MEW*

37. See Chapter I p. 75.

38. Engels to Marx August 15, 1870. *MECW* 44:46.

39. Engels to Kautsky, February 7,1882. *MECW* 46:192.

40. Engels to Marx August 15, 1870. *MECW* 44:45.

41. Beike, pp. 85-94.

42. Engels to Marx, August 15, 1870. *MECW* 44:48.

43. Dominick p. 197. Beike attributes this statement to a lead article by Hasselmann, p. 44.

44. "First Address of the General Council of the International Working Men' Association on the Franco-Prussian War," *MECW* 22:5.

45. Beike (p.18) mentions the Chemnitz meeting but he does not quote the resolution which contains the declaration that is the title of this chapter nor does he include it in his appendix of documents. Marx, however, did quote it in his first address.

46. "First Address of the General Council of the International Working Men' Association on the Franco-Prussian War," *MECW* 22:6. Beike, by the way, does *not* reprint this address in his appendix containing major documents of the period.

47. *GC* p.32.

48. *MECW* 44:3.

49. *MECW* 44:10.

50. Marx to Engels, August 17, 1870. *MECW* 44:50.

51. Ibid., 51.

52. Second Address of the General Council of the International Workingmen's Association on the Franco-Prussian War, *MECW* 22:263.

53. *MECW* 22:260 ff.

54. *MECW* 22:71,74.

55. Liebknecht's biographer says "the date on the masthead of *Der Volkstaat* was always(sic?)at least three days later" than the publication date. See Dominick p. 191.

56. Ibid..

57. Ibid., p. 261.

58. Ibid.,

59. Ibid..

60. Marx to Engels, 10 September 1870. *MECW* 44:69.

61. Engels to Marx, 12 September 1870. *MECW* 44:71.

62. *MECW* 44:70.

63. *MECW* 44:71.

64. See discussion of Steamship subsidy debate in KMTR 4 pp.104-106.

65. See Marx to Engels, September 10, 1870 and again September 14 for Marx's organizational activity around the issue of recognition of the Republic. *MECW* 44:70,77.

66. Martin Berger has written a monograph on *Engels, Armies, & Revolution* which discusses this issue of Engels' military expertise. In general, he denigrates the attempts of some to exaggerate Engels' influence on military thinking. But he does recognize that Engels was well read in the subject and that, *when he published anonymously*, as in did in *Po und Rhein*, he received a hearing. See Chapter 2 of Berger's book. For the reception of *Po und Rhein* see page 52.

67. See Gustav Mayer, *Friedrich Engels: Eine Biographie*, p. 197 and footnote on p. 544.

68. *International Review of Social History*, v. 1, 1956, p. 239.

69. See *MEW* 19:351-354. History of the Commune of 1871. London, Reeves and Turner, 1886.

CHAPTER 6

1.Frederick Engels to August Bebel, December 22,1882 in *August Bebels Briefwechsel mit Friedrich Engels; Quellen und Untersuchungen zur Geschichte der Deutschen und Österreichischen Arbeiterbewegung, Vol. VI.* (Mouton & Co., The Hague, 1965.)

2. Frederick Engels, Introduction to Borkheim's pamphlet *Zur Erinnerung für die deutschen Mordspatrioten, 1806-1807*, in *MEW* 21:350f; dated by Engels Dec. 15, 1887.

3. E: to Paul Lafargue, October 25, 1886. Corr. I:391.

4. E, to Laura Lafargue, September 13, 1886. Corr. I:369.

5. E: to Lafargue, October 25, 1886. Corr. I:381.

6. Frederick Engels to Salo Färber, October 22, 1885. *MEW* 36: 374-5.

7. Ibid.

8. *MEW* 3:6.

9. E. to Laura Lafargue, May 9, 1888. Corr. II:123.

10. *MECW* 27:237-250.

11. Rosa Luxemburg, *Gesammelte Werke*, p. 145,146. This quotation begins in paragraph 28 of chapter 7 if the reader wants to check one of the too-numerous-to-mention English translations of this work.

12. Engels to P. Argyriades, July 1892. *MEW* 38:398. Also, Engels to Sorge, 24 October, 1891. *MEW* 38:184.

13. Engels to S. Faerber, October 22, 1885. *MEW* 36:374-5.

14. See KMTR 4 for a discussion of the *socialist* response to Boulanger.

15. See R. F. Byrnes, *Anti-Semitism in Modern France, vol. I*, for a comprehensive description of this chauvinist movement. While not all of Byrnes judgements can be trusted and the book suffers from a tendency to attribute to individuals and movements sentiments that are not supported by the sources referenced, it does give the reader a overall feel for the political mood that was sweeping France and aroused Engels' concern.

16. See *KMTR* 4, Chapter 8.

17. E/Lafargues: *Corr* 3:90.

18. See KMTR 4, Chapter 4, p. 104 ff.

19. *MEW* 38:159.

20. *MEW* 38:162.

21. Blumenburg, Werner, ed. *August Bebels Briefwechsel mit Friedrich Engels*. London, The Hague, Paris: Mouton & Co., 1965, p. 446.

22. Ibid. 450.

23. Ibid. 452.

24. *MECW* 27:242.

25. *MECW* 27:245.

26. Ibid..

27. *MECW* 27:246.

28. *MECW* 27:250.

29. See footnotes 12 and 13 above.

30. Engels to Laura Lafargue, August 17, 1891. *Corr.* III, p. 96.

31. See note 11, chapter 6.

32. But, see Hal Draper's *War and Revolution: Lenin and the Myth of Revolutionary Defeatism*, (Humanities Press, Atlantic Highlands, New Jersey, 1996) for a discussion of the brief revival of the "special Russian position" during the Russo-Japanese War.

33. *MEW* 38:398.

34. *MEW* 38:498-500,503.

35. Blumenberg, p. 437.

36. Engels to F. Danielson, October 29-31, *MEW* 38: is a good example.

CHAPTER 7

1. Bebel to Engels, February 11, 1893 in Blumenberg, *Briefwechsel*, p. 661-664. The actual request is in the postscript.

2. *MECW* 27:383 ff.

3. Engels to Paul Lafargue, January 3, 1894. *Corr.*III;322.

4. *MECW* 27:389.

5. *Briefwechsel*, p. 669.

6. Bebel to Engels, 28 February 1893. *Briefwechsel* p. 669-70.

7. Ibid., pp. 671-672.

8. Engels to Paul Lafargue, November 3, 1892. *Corr. III*:207.

9. Engels to Laura Lafargue, August 17, 1891. *Corr.* III:98.

10. *The Revolutionary Act*, p. 39-40. *MECW* 27:524.

11. *Sozialistische Monatshefte* October 1926 p.676

SPECIAL NOTE A: ROSDOLSKY V. ROSDOLSKY

1. "Ot redatskii," *Kontinent*, no. 9 (1976): 265.

2. Roman Rosdolsky, *Engels and the "Nonhistoric" Peoples: The National Question in the Revolution of 1848*, tr. Prof. John-Paul Himka, Critique Books, 1987.

3. Roman Rosdolsky, *Zur Entstehungsgeschichte des Marxschen Kapital; der Rohentwurf des Kapital 1857-58*. Frankfurt: Europäische Verlagsanstalt, 1969. Wien: Europa Verlag, 1968.

4. Rosdolsky, *Engels*. p. 4. This is actually a précis of Rosdolsky's thesis by the translator, Prof. Himka.

5. Hal Draper, *KMTR II*, p. 195f. See also *The Adventures of the Communist Manifesto*, p. 227f,(Center for Socialist History, Berkeley California, 1994) by the same author.

6. See especially Chapter I, on the Czechs, for this practice.

7. *KMTR II*, chapters 12 through 14.

8. Rosdolsky, *Non-historic Peoples*, p. 61.

9. Ibid., p. 67.

10. See Chapter 1, p. 45 for a discussion of this article.

11. CW, 8:399.

12. *MECW* 26:306.

13. Roman Rosdolsky, *Untertat und Staat in Galizien*. Verlag Philipp van Zabern, Mainz (1992).

14. Rosdolsky, *Non-historic Peoples*, p. 151.

15. Rosdolsky, *Non-historic Peoples*, p.72.

16. Wolff, Wilhelm. "Decree concerning the interim settlement of seignorial-peasant relations in Silesia" *Neue Rheinische Zeitung*, December 29, 1848. Quoted in "Wilhelm Wolff" by Engels in *MECW* 24:142.

17. Rosdolsky, *Non-Historic Peoples*, p. 67.

18. Ibid., p. 192.

19. Rosdolsky, *Non-Historic Peoples*, p. 163.

20. Ibid., p. 201.

21. *MEW* 22:49-51.

22. Rosdolsky, *Non-historic Peoples*, p. 201.

23. Ibid..

24. See Childers, Thomas. *The Nazi Voter: The Social Foundations of Facsism in Germany, 1919-1933*. Chapel Hill, N.C. and London: The University of North Carolina Press, for a discussion based on regression analysis of social class as a predictor of voting behavior in the period.

25. Wilson, Stephen. *Ideology and Experience: Antisemitism in France at the Time of the Dreyfus Affair*. London and Toronto: Associated University Presses, for a discussion of responses of the working classes, organized and unorganized to the Dreyfus Affair. Chapter XI, 'A Kind of Socialism' is especially relevant.

26. Lenin, *CW*,22:320. The passage Rosdolsky uses begins on page 341.

SPECIAL NOTE B: "CONSTITUTIONAL" OR "REVOLUTIONARY" WAR?

1. *MECW* 41:297.

2. *MECW* 41.276.

3. *MECW* 41:400.

4. *MECW* 41:291

SPECIAL NOTE D: ENGELS' "LAST TESTAMENT"—A TRAGICOMEDY IN FIVE ACTS

1. Luxemburg, Rosa. *Gesammelte Werke, Band 4,* Berlin:Dietz Verlag, 1974, pp. 490-496.

2. Berger, *Engels, Armies & Revolution,* to take one example, is quite confused on all this. On the one hand, he recognizes that Engels was not counting on a parliamentary path to socialism but he seems to be unaware of the deliberate falsification by Bernstein and Liebknecht and the censorship of the Berliners. Dominick, has a long discussion of Liebknecht's confused ideas on "The Road

to Power" but covers this important episode in a couple of vague sentences. Steenson fails to mention this incident in either his biography of Kautsky or his book *Not One Man Not one Penny*, which is devoted to the Social Democracy's position on the war question.

3. Riazanov and *MEW* do sketch the outlines of this story.

4. *MEW*:39;February 2, 1895, p. 403;February 12, 1895; p. 409.

5. The *MEW* notes suggest that the party printed only a small edition of the *Class Struggles* (3,000 copies as compared to 173,000 of a pamphlet by Bebel on the party's electoral tactics) because it was embarrassed by Engels' introduction. Embarrassment there certainly was but the *Class Struggles* was an historical study not a popular pamphlet. There is no reason to believe that, at this point, the leadership of the left—August Bebel, Ignaz Auer and Paul Singer—had any objections to the pamphlet in its revised form.

6. *MEW* 39:424-426.

7. E&L *Corr. III* :368.

8. E&L *Corr. III*:373.

9. *MEW* 39:42, ME:SC 486.

10. *Briefwechsel* p.798, Bebel to Engels April 20, 1895. From March 11 until Engels death there are several letters from Bebel referring to this controversy but none from Engels to Bebel although Bebel mentions letters from Engels in his replies.

11. Draper, *KMTR 3, Part III*.

12. Kapp, Yvonne. *Eleanor Marx, Vol. 2,* Pantheon:New York, 1976, p.594.

13. "Bernstein und die Dialektik," *Neue Zeit* 17:2, pp. 46-47.

14. August Bebel to Frederick Engels, 11 March, 1895. *Briefwechsel*, p. 795

15. See also the German version *Unter dem Banner des Marxismus*, and the English version in *Workers' Monthly* Nov 1925.

16. Socialist Labor Party, *The Revolutionary Act: Military Insurrection or Political and Economic Action?*. New York Labor News Co., New York City (1922). Tr. Harry Kuhn. The pamphlet claims as its author Frederick Engels but for reasons given in the text this claim cannot be accepted.

17. Ibid. p. 6.

18. Ibid.

19. *Who are the Falsifiers?*, New York Labor News Co., New York, 1926.

20. Eden and Cedar Paul, *Plebs Magazine*, London (January through April 1921).

21. Socialist Labor Party, *Peaceful Revolution vs. Violence: Can Socialism be Achieved Peacefully?*, New York Labor News, 1966. p. XI.

22. Ibid., p. X.

23. *MEW* 39:424.

24. I have found four references which give an accurate, if sketchy account of the story. There are two political biographies of Engels published by Moscow which cover this incident, (*Friedrich Engels*, Gemkow, et al., *Friederick Engels*, Ilyichov et al.) a note in the Marx-Engels Werke (*MEW* 39:605, note 455) and Gustav Meyer's biography of Engels. (*Friedrich Engels* 2:499, Gustav Mayer; p. 304 in the one volume English translation.) The first three sources, however, do not, for obvious reasons, discuss the various distortions widespread in Communist sources which have the censored version being published without Engels' consent or knowledge. Gustav Mayer wrote his biography before the Russian Revolution so he couldn't comment on this source of confusion although he clearly demonstrates the falsification contained in the reformist version of events. Popular, non-scholarly accounts regularly make a mess of the story.

To select a few needles from this haystack consider the following cases:

◆In "Italian Communism Today," *Marxist Perspectives* Fall 1978, Max Gordon thinks that "After publication of the 1895 essay, he [Engels] complained that it had been edited to make him appear in favor of peaceful tactics at any cost .. .."

◆Mukergee (*Duumviri of Revolution*) writes as if Engels tried to get his manuscript text published and failed.

275

◆ Henderson in his two volume biography (Henderson,2:677) speaks only of Liebknecht's distortions and Engels' outrage over them. He thinks that Engels asked Kautsky to print the full version and that Kautsky did the job on Engels' original (Ibid., p. 738.)

◆The American biographer of Liebknecht, Raymond H. Dominick III thinks that the Executive Committee is responsible for Liebknecht's article although his own research indicates that Liebknecht's increasingly eccentric behavior as editor of the *Vorwärts* led to its being put under Executive Committee control only in 1896. See Dominick, p. 371 for the attempts to remove Liebknecht. For his discussion of the dispute which is the subject of this note—three sentences in all—see p. 367.

INDEX

Abolitionists
    Relations with Lincoln 216
Agyriades, Paul (Panajoinis)
    Engels letter to 174, 175
Appeasement
    Real meaning of 108
Bakunin, Michael
    "Agent of the Tsar" 67
    "Confession" 203
    And "Slavic Council" 66
    And "Slavic Federation" 203
    And 1846 uprising .. 66, 202, 204
    And agrarian reform 202
    And peasant jacquerie 66
    Appeal to the Slavs 64
    As "friend" of NRZ 70
    Confession 68
    Conversation with
        Alfred Meissner 65
    George Sand's alleged libel ... 67
    His "völkisch" nationalism ... 64
    Hostility to bourgeoisie 204
    On "unatural union" 69
    Relation to Ludwig Shtur 64
    The Tsar as protector
        of Poland 69
    Three resolutions at Prague .. 65
Barbés, Armand
    Marx's attack on 93
Bebel, August
    And "treason" of Engels 155
    Conservative side
        of abstention 184
    Dispute with Engels 169
    Let off the hook by liberals .. 184
    On Franco-Prussian War 135
    Prowar position in 1891 166
    Prowar position of 169
    Reichstag vote in 1870 9
    Relations with Engels 186
    Seeks Engels' advice
        on conscription 179
    Urges moderation on Engels   183
Becker, J. P.
    Marx's advice to 126

Beike, Heinz
    On Franco-Prussian War 124
Bennett, Lerone Jr.
    Forced Into Glory 227
    On Lincoln as segregationist . 219
Benson, Camillo Count Cavour
    Dismissed after great victory . 101
Bernstein, Eduard
    And "treason" of Engels 155
    And Engels' correspondence   235
    Conceals Engels' draft 237
    On M&E's "putschism" 236
Bismarck, Prince Otto von
    "Agent of the Tsar" 161
    "Universal suffrage"
        as plebiscite 111
    As instigator of
        Franco-Prussian War 125
    As pupil of Lassalle 109
    Conservative Junker or radical...109
    On universal suffrage 113
Blind, Karl
    Prowar activities in
        Crimean War............. 95
Bonaparte, Louis
    "The principle of
        nationalities" 110
    As "Liberator" 101
    As product of stalemate 100
    Engel's opinion of 141
    In Crimean War 81
    Italian Campaign of 1859 11
Bonnier, Charles
    Engels letter to 175
Brunswick Committee
    On Franco-Prussian War 136
Camphausen, Ludolph
    Ridiculed by Marx 53
Carr, E. H.
    On NRZ and Bakunin 69
Chemnitz Congress
    Marx's comments on 143
Congress of Vienna 19
    Louis Bonaparte as defende . 125

Cossacks
    And Croats and Hungarians .. 42
Cracow Uprising 35
Croatian Nationalism in 1848 60
Croats
    And Italian revolution 59
    As Habsburg policeman 59
Czechs
    As "non-historic" people 56
    As enemies of revolution 58
Dana, Charles
    As editor of the NYDT .. 80, 220
Delescuze, Charles
    As French patriot 130
    As martyr of Commune 130
DeutscherBrüsseler Zeitung
    On Hungarian Revolution 39
Diocletian, Emperor
    Burning the palace of 242
Draper, Hal
    Crimean War .... -iii-
    Franco-Prussian War .... -iii-
    On "Non-Historic Peoples" . -iii-
    Responsibility for V 5 ...... -iii-
Eccarius, Johann George
    Marx's advice to 126
Engels
    "Counterrevolutionary peoples 54
    "Last Testament" 236
    "Peace at any price" 161
    "Prowar" aberration 164
    "Underestimation of peasantry 191
    1891 letter to Laura Lafargue . 174
    A "christian" army 187
    A pacifist's nightmare 182
    Agrees to censorship 233
    And agrarian reform 191
    And French chauvinism 167
    And Hegel's schema 55
    And military insurrection 240
    And Pan-Slavism 85, 176
    And Prussian rural workers .. 117

And Russian revolution 167
Appeasement of Bebel 166
Articles in Pall Mall Gazette . 141
As "defensist" 166, 176
As "utopian" 180
As "Young German" 21
As advocate of
    "peaceful reform" 231
As anti-Prussian 119
As French patriot 154
As pacifist 160, 161, 174
Correspondence with Fisher . 187
Courted by SDP leadership .. 231
Criticizes Marx on L-B vote . 137
Dispute with Bebel 169
Electoral activity and
    revolution 185
Germans as mercenaries 23
In defense of 3rd Republic ... 16
In Pall Mall Gazette 16
Introduction to
    "Class Struggles" 232
Lett to Nadejde 163
Letter to Bonnier 175
Letters to Sorge and
    Argyriades 174, 175
Nat. Lib. & Soc. Revolution .. 32
On "fragging" officers 183
On "How to fight
    the Prussians" 153
On "kadavergehorsam" 180
On "Non-Historic
    Peoples" 63, 73, 189
On "Pan-Germanism" 203
On "Progress" and the
    Nation State 70
On "progressive" nationalism . 75
On "specialness" of Russia .. 175
On "The Russian Menace" .. 159
On "the Sixth Power" 82, 96
On Albigensian crusade 200
On barricade fighting ... 185, 233

278

Index

On capitalist imperialism 176, 177
On Czech revolt 201
On female conscription . 181, 182
On Holy Alliance and Poland . 20
On Hungarian Revolution 32
On Jewish emancipation 38
On Liebknecht's
  antiwar vot 129,152
On Liebknecht-Bebel vote .. 137
On Louis Bonaparte's
  incompetewnce 141
On Magyar "nobility" 41
On Mexico and US 71
On Palacky 57
On Polish agrarian revolution . 38
On Polish Nationalism 38
On Prussian Army 30
On universal
  conscription ... 113, 179, 185
On universal suffrage .. 117, 185
On Vaillant's conscription bill 181
On völkisch nationalism 73
Principles of Communism ... 47
Prowar position of 1891 166
Relations with Bebel ... 186, 188
Revolution in Russia 162
Slav nationalism as anti-Tsar .. 85
Subversion of military 187
The "MIlitary Expert"
  dodge 103, 113, 118, 147
Treason of 157
Tsarism as dependent
  on Western Powers 162
Turkey as "living sore" 84
War against Russia 25
Fischer, Richard
  And military insurrection ... 240
  Invitation to Engels 232
  Secretary of SDP 232
  Correspondence with Engels 187
  On Commune 187

France 1793-94
  Importance as precedent 52
Frémont, John Charles
  And civil liberties 227
  In American civil war 218
  Third Party candidate
    in 1864 .... 220, 227
Garasanin, Iliya
  As opponent of Tsarism 85
Garibaldi, Giuseppe
  Marx's opinion of 106
Genovese, Eugene
  And slavery 218
  On "Political Economy
    of Slavery 218
German Liberalism
  Congress of Vienna to 1848 .. 20
German Unity
  "In a Prussian Barracks" 110
Gironde
  As war party 19
Gladstone, William Ewart
  Pro-Confederacy position ... 221
Gompers, Samuel
  "More!" 231
Guillaume, James
  As French chauvinist 123
  On M&E as Prussian patriots 123
Haberkern, E
  Responsibility for KMTR V .. -iii-
Hapsburgs
  And Holy Alliance 20
  As revolutionaries 40
Himka, Professor John-Paul
  Introduction to Rosdolsky .. 210
  Translator of Rosdolsky 189
Hohenzollerns And Holy Alliance . 20
Hungarian Revolution
  And agrarian reform 44
  Sympathy for among Slavs ... 62
Hungarians
  As "non-historic people" 56

279

Hungarians and Slavs 42
Italian "War of Liberation"
    And agrarian reform 102
Jacobins
    As peace party 19
Jellachich, Joseph Graf zu B
    And Italian revolution 59
    As Habsburg
        policeman 53, 60, 61, 76
Johnson, Andrew
    And Reconstruction 222
Kautsky, Karl
    Der Weg Zur Macht 238
    On World War I 10
    Publishes Engels' expurgated
        "Class Struggles" 235
Kölnische Zeitung
    German Democrats &
        Magyar nationalism 43
Kossuth, Louis
    And agrarian reform 46
    And Croat nationalism 59
    Marx's attack on 106
    On Crimean War 91
Lafargue, Laura Marx
    Engels' 1891 letter to 174
Lassalle, Ferdinand
    As partisan of
        Louis Bonaparte 107
    As partisan of Prussia 102, 105,107
    Demagogic attack on M&E . . 108
    On Bonaparte in Italy 11
Lelewel, Joachim
    And 1846 uprising 196
    In Polish
        Democratic Association. 34
    On Jewish emancipation . . 38, 46
    On Polish agrarian
        revolution 38, 46
Lenin
    Anticipated by Marx on War . . 94
    In role of Dr. Watson 15

On Bonaparte in Italy 12
On capitalist imperialism 178
On Marx, Engels and war . 10, 80
On self-determination 201
On Tsarism 10
On World War I 12
Lessner, Friedrich
    Marx's advice to 126
Levynsky, Volodymyr
    Influence on Rosdolsky 210
Liebknecht, Wilhelm
    As investigative reporter 123
    Hatchet job on Engels'
        Introduction 234
    On Franco-Prussian War 121, 135
    Reichstag vote in 1870 9
Lincoln, Abraham
    And abolitionists 216, 228
    And civil liberties 226, 228
    And Reconstruction 215, 228
    And slavery . . . 215, 218, 221, 227
    As "regular guy" 225
    Contemporary attitudes re . . . 215
    Marx and Engels' opinion of . 225
    Modern interpretations 215
Luxemburg, Rosa
    On Engels "prowar" position 175
    On Marx, Engels and war 10
    Taken in by Bernstein et al. . . 231
Mänchen-Helfen, Otto
    On Franco-Prussian War 122
Manchesterism
    And "appeasement" 86
    Dependent on Tsarism 88
Marx
    1847 polemic against
        Proudhon 208
    And "Trent Affair" 221
    Answer to Engels' criticism . . 142
    Anticipation of Lenin 94
    As advocate of
        "peaceful reform" 231

Index

As agent of Bismarck 123
As antiwar activist in Crimea . . 95
As diplomat 127
As pacifist 106
as pan-German nationalist 49
Attack on Armand Barbès 93
Attack on Blind's
   prowar position 95
Attitude towards "democrats" 192
Condemnation of
   prowar "revolutionaries" . . . 93
Foreign policy
   of the workingclas 96
Indifference to fate
   of Turkish Empire 83
On Allied War Aims in CW . . 95
On American civil war 220
On Bismarck as provocateur . 125
On Brunswick Committee . . 144
On causes of Italian Campaign 100
On Chemnitz Congress 143
On David Urquhart 90
On England in Crimean War . 95
On English sympathy
   for Confederacy 220
On Franco-Prussian War 123
On French chauvinism 130
On Garibaldi in Italian war . . 106
On Kossuth in Crimean War . 91
On Kossuth in Italian war . . . 106
On Mazzini 197
On Palmerston 81
On Polish agrarian revolution . 37
On roots of World War I . . . 100
On war aims in Crimean War . 92
Rosa Luxemburg imitation . . . 37
Supports "even reactionary
   governments" 122
Marx and Engels
   "In a Prussian Barracks" 150
   "Workers' Party" 115
   1793-94 as precedent 52

And agrarian reform . . . 190, 194
And the NYDT 80
As pacifists 160, 163
As Prussian patriots 121
Attitude towards "democrats" 192
Letter to the Brunswick
   Committee 147
On "bourgeois freedoms" . . . 116
On "Non-Historic Peoples" . 190
On "The Eastern Question" . . 79
On "The Russian Menace" . . . 81
On "Two reactionary powers" 80
On 1846 Polish uprising 191, 195
On Alsace-Lorraine 147
On American civil war 215
On Bonaparte in Italy 11
On England in Crimean War . 81
On Franco-Prussian War 121, 124
On French chauvinism 148
On German Nationalism 29
On Hungarian Revolution 32
On Jewish emancipation 198
On Joachim Lelewel 196
On Liebknecht's antiwar vot . 129
On Louis Bonaparte in CW . . 81
On Polish agrarian revolution 195
On Polish Nationalism 33
On results of Franco-Prussia 149
On Tsarism 9
On universal suffrage 112
Opinion of Lincoln 225
Pacifism in 1848 19
Prowar position in 1848 21
Retreat from "prowar" policy 100
Vendée 52
Marx-Aveling, Eleanor
   On "The Eastern Question" . . 79
McPherson, James
   Lincoln biography 226
Mehring, Franz
   As Prussian patriot 122
   Biography of Marx 121

281

Karl Marx's Theory of Revolution: V5

Metternich
    As fomentor of revolution . 33, 35
Mieroslawski, Ludwig 35
Müller-Tellering, Eduard von
    Attack on Marx 204
    Correspondent of NRZ 197
Nadler, Jörg
    Frémont contra Lincoln 228
Nationalism
    Ands anti-Semitism 212
Neue Zeit
    Publishes Engels' expurgate . . 235
Nicolaevsky, Boris
    On Franco-Prussian War 122
NRZ
    "Anti-semitism" of 205
    "the main enemy" in 1848 21
    And "the Jews" 204
    George Sand's alleged libel . . . 67
    Nat. Lib. & Soc. Revolution . . 32
    On Hungarian Revolution 32
    On Jewish emacipation 206
    On Poland 26
    On Prague uprising 24
    Sea-Girt Schleswig-Holstein . . 28
Palacky, Frantisek
    Pro-Hapsburg position 57
Palmerston, Henry John Templeton
    Pro-Confederacy position . . . 221
Paul, Eden and Cedar
    Bowdlerization of Engels 241
Phillips, Wendell 228
    Abolitionist and
        proto-socialists 219
Plebs Magazine
    Bowdlerization of Engels 241
Poland
    As lynch-pin of Holy Alliance . 20
Polish Democrats
    George Sand's alleged libel . . . 67
Potreson, Alexander N.
    On Marx, Engels and war . 10, 80

Proudhon, Pierre Joseph
    As antisemite 208
Prussia
    And Italian "War of Liberation 102
Riazanov, David
    Discovers Engels' first draft . 237
    Discovers origninal of
        "Class Struggles" 231
Robespierre
    As pacifist 19
Romanovs
    And Holy Alliance 20
Rosdolsky, Roman
    And national liberation 199
    And Ukrainian nationalism . . 210
    Historian of Capital 208
    On "Non-Historic Peoples" . 189
    On role of Metternich
        in 1846 195
    Political history of 189
Schleswig-Holstein
    As stalking horse for Prussia . 107
Schweitzer, Johann Baptist
    As Prussian patriots 121
    As pupil of Lassalle 111
    On Franco-Prussian War 135
SDAP
    On Franco-Prussian War 121
Siegal, Franz
    In American civil war 218
Slav Nationalism
    As progressive force 90
Social Democratic Party
    Misuse of Marx and Engels 9
    World War I 9
Socialist Labor Party
    "Who are the Falsifiers" 241
    And Russian Revolution 239
    As defenders
        of "non-violent reform" . . . 238
    Peaceful Revolution v.
        Violence 242

Index

Sorge, Adolph
    And Frémont campaign 220
    Engels letter to 174
Stevens, Thaddeus 228
    And Reconstruction 222
Temple, HerLord Palmerston
    "Agent of the Tsar" 81
The Communist Manifesto
    "the workers have no country" 46
    Nationalism and
        Internationalism 48
    On "Vaterland" 48
    On Polish Nationalism ... 33, 39
Trachtenberg, Alexander
    Botches Riazonov's article ... 241
Trumball, Lyman 228
    Abolitionist and proto-socialist 219
Tsar
    As French revolutionary 167
Tsarism
    And Pan-Slavism 56, 79
    As protector of
        English Liberalism 88
Unter dem Banner des Marxismus
    Botches Riazonov's article ... 238
Urquhart, David
    On Crimean War 90

Vendée
    Dissident views—
        Right and Left 52
        significance in 1848 52
    Ukrainian uprising of 1846
        compared 196Victor Emmanuel II
    Swindled at Villafranca 101
Vidal, Gore
    On Lincoln 215
Villafranca di Verona
    Peace Treaty of 101
Waugh, John C.
    Reelecting Lincoln 227
Weydemeyer, Joseph
    And Frémont campaign 220
Wilson, Edmund
    On Lincoln 215
Windischgrätz, Prince Alfred
    As defender of Magyr nobility 45
Windschgratz, ... 45
Wolf, Wilhelm
    And 1846 uprising 197
Zornow, Frank
    A Party Divided 227